"A superb study at the dynamic intersection of imperial, Hawaiian, cultural, and childhood histories. Joy Schulz is a passionate writer, and her work is filled with surprising implications for the history of nineteenth-century Hawai'i."
—David Igler, author of *The Great Ocean: Pacific Worlds from Captain Cook to the Gold Rush*

"Compelling and thought-provoking. . . . While the political story has been told, Joy Schulz adds considerably to our understanding of the social and cultural milieu of settler children who came to see the islands of their birth as their birthright. *Hawaiian by Birth* underscores the importance of family relations and generational difference to understanding the complexities of American empire. Clearly and concisely written, the book is well suited for classroom use."
—Seth Archer, *Western Historical Quarterly*

"Schulz's child-centric approach is methodologically invigorating, and her interweaving of social and political events and trends with interpersonal emotions and tensions is a valuable contribution. . . . Hers is an engaging and persuasive reminder to take the history of children and childhood seriously. . . . Strong primary-source research and an engaging writing style make this book a valuable contribution to scholars of American relations with Hawai'i."
—Emily J. Manktelow, *Journal of Pacific History*

"We understand that the normative, heterosexual family constitutes the nation-state. This remarkable, innovative study reveals the centrality of that family in 'birthing empire' through a history of childhood. Race, gender, sexuality, class, and religion intersect to advance U.S. imperialism in the Pacific and settler colonialism in Hawai'i."
—Gary Y. Okihiro, author of *Island World: Hawai'i and the United States*

"Both general reader and scholar will benefit from reading Schulz's excellent contribution to the study of nineteenth-century Hawaiian history and the role the children of white missionaries played in shaping it."
—*Reading Religion: A Publication of the American Academy of Religion*

T0385682

"Joy Schulz sheds new light on a remarkable group of individuals: the children of the first Christian missionaries in the Hawaiian Islands. Much has been written about the missionaries (who radically transformed the islands in the early to mid-1800s), but less has been written about their children."
—Clifford Putney, *Journal of the History of Childhood and Youth*

*Hawaiian by Birth*

# HAWAIIAN BY BIRTH

*Missionary Children, Bicultural Identity, and U.S. Colonialism in the Pacific*

JOY SCHULZ

UNIVERSITY OF NEBRASKA PRESS | LINCOLN

Portions of chapter 1 previously appeared in
"Birthing Empire: Economies of Childrearing and
the Formation of American Colonialism in Hawai'i,"
*Diplomatic History* 38, no. 5 (November 2014):
895–925. Published by Oxford University Press.

Portions of chapter 5 previously appeared in "Crossing
the *Pali*: White Missionary Children, Bicultural Identity,
and the Racial Divide in Hawai'i, 1820–1898," *Journal of
the History of Childhood and Youth* 6, no. 2 (Spring 2013):
209–35. Published by Johns Hopkins University Press.

Library of Congress Control Number: 2017944083

Set in New Baskerville by John Klopping.
Designed by N. Putens.

*For Jaden, Jett, Ava, and Alea*

CONTENTS

# ILLUSTRATIONS

## ACKNOWLEDGMENTS

This project would not have been possible without the full encouragement and support of the University of Nebraska–Lincoln Department of History. Research and travel grants provided by the department allowed me to travel to Honolulu and New England to conduct extensive archival research. I would like to especially thank James LeSueur, Margaret Jacobs, Lloyd Ambrosius, and Loukia Sarroub for their commitment to this project. Most importantly, I thank Tim Borstelmann, my graduate adviser and friend, whose teaching made me a better student, scholar, and writer.

Additional research was made possible by the National Endowment for the Humanities and American Historical Association's "Bridging Cultures at Community Colleges Initiative: American History, Atlantic and Pacific Project." I would like to thank Jim Grossman, Philip Morgan, Bill Deverell, Tom Osborne, Dana Schaffer, and Cheryll Ann Cody for their personal efforts in support of the Bridging Cultures project.

Numerous institutions and archival specialists also helped me prepare this manuscript. I would like to thank those at the Hawaiian Mission Children's Society, Cooke Library, Harvard University, Williams College, Mt. Holyoke College, Huntington Library, and Library of Congress for their kind and thoughtful aid. Special thanks I give to Carole White, John C. Barker, Kylee Omo, Sara Lloyd, Patricia Albright, Linda Hall, Carrie Hintz, Ben Brick, and Kathy Walter. I also thank Anne Foster, Ted Melillo, the late Jennifer Fish Kashay, Gary Okihiro, Hugh Morrison, Mary Clare Martin, Karen Sanchez-Eppler, Geri Shomo, Andrew Graybill, and Cari Costanzo Kapur, as well as the anonymous peer reviewers, who gave the generous gift of their time in reading various drafts of the project or answering specific research questions.

Early encouragers of this project also included the Society for the Historians of American Foreign Relations and the Society for the History of Childhood and Youth. I thank their journals for allowing me to reprint portions of published work within this book.

I am extremely grateful to the University of Nebraska Press and my editor, Bridget Barry. Bridget's enthusiasm for the book and efforts on my behalf have made the lengthy process of editing and publication more than worth it. I also thank Jane Curran for providing her wonderful copyediting skills.

Finally I acknowledge my husband, Marc, and daughters, Sophia and Penelope, for their unwavering support. I am always grateful for you.

*Hawaiian by Birth*

**1.** Travel from New England to the Hawaiian Islands in 1819 required a six-month journey by sea around South America. Contemporary travel accounts, such as this 1806 map of the Western Hemisphere by English cartographer John Cary (1754–1835), would have demonstrated to the American missionaries the enormity of their decision. Missionary children, unlike their parents, centered their world in the Pacific Ocean. From John Cary, *Cary's New Universal Atlas, containing distinct maps of all the principal states and kingdoms throughout the World. From the latest and best authorities extant* (London: Printed for J. Cary, Engraver and Map-seller, No. 181, near Norfolk Street, Strand, 1808). Wikimedia Commons.

# Introduction

*Imperial Children and Empire Formation*
*in the Nineteenth Century*

*Kauhua Ku, ka Lani, i-loli ka moku; Hookohi ke kua-koko o ka Lani; He kua-koko, pu-koko i ka honua; He kua-koko kapu no ka Lani.* (Big with child is the Princess Ku; the whole island suffers her whimsies; the pangs of labor are on her; labor that stains the land with blood.)

Ancient Hawaiian *mele*[1]

In 1819, when passenger travel across the Pacific Ocean was unfathomable to most Americans, seven couples and five children left New England and made the nearly six-month sea voyage around Cape Horn to the Hawaiian Islands, arriving in 1820. The young missionaries left behind their worldly possessions but took with them the prayers and financial support of the newly established American Board of Commissioners for Foreign Missions (ABCFM). The missionaries were soon joined by others. Between 1819 and 1848 the ABCFM launched roughly 150 missionaries across the Pacific Ocean to the Hawaiian Islands. As the first U.S. missionary organization with an international agenda, the ABCFM hoped to evangelize the small, independent island kingdom according to Congregational and Presbyterian theology.[2]

American missionaries embarked upon their voyages to the Hawaiian Islands with hopes of transforming the kingdom into a Christian nation. Believing they could refrain from political interference and economic pursuits, missionaries eschewed personal possessions and money, placing their material well-being in the hands of Hawaiian *ali'i* (the chiefly class), as well as donors in the United States. American missionaries did not embark upon a program of territorial acquisition in the Hawaiian Islands, yet their decision to have children altered their course. As one missionary revealed, "Most of us came from home without even thinking whether we should ever have a child to provide for, and asked no questions about such a matter."[3] By the 1850s missionary parents were reevaluating their economic choices as they sought to protect the futures of their children, who together numbered over 250.[4] Domestic concerns became political ones, and the American missionaries began to rationalize policies transferring land and political power to their control.

In fact, the number of white children born in the Hawaiian Islands influenced more than missionary policy. Children did not retain their missionary parents' qualms about using the Hawaiian land for material benefit or shaping the islands into what they termed an "Anglo-Hawaiian" society.[5] In reality the essence of their childhoods had groomed them for little else. Through parental neglect, as well as their parents' imperfect attempts to racially segregate them, the children developed an aggressive independence that tended to question both parental and native authority. In the process the children cultivated a deep possessiveness over Hawaiian lands, which culminated in their revolt against the Hawaiian monarchy at the end of the nineteenth century.

American missionary parents could not have anticipated in 1820 the critical role their children would play in the overthrow of the Hawaiian monarchy in 1893 and U.S. acquisition of the Hawaiian Islands in 1898. With the birth of the first white child in the islands, the missionaries began to view childhood in the islands as a critical and contested battlefield upon which they were to wage war for American cultural values and Protestant Christianity. As historian Emily Conroy-Krutz notes, "Their goal was to export an evangelical Protestantism that was Anglo-American in its roots and its culture, and in so doing they made claims about the

**2.** In 1820 American missionaries entered a world unlike any they had ever known. For their Hawaiian-born children, the islands were their only home. Image of male native standing on shore, Puna, Hawai'i, ca. 1910. Library of Congress, Prints and Photographs Division, LC-USZ62-61291.

proper role of the United States in the world."[6] Not only did the children of American missionaries propel the Hawaiian and U.S. governments toward their 1898 conflagration, but the children themselves became subjects of a colonial project, their American parents constructing and transmitting a religious and cultural agenda for them, as well as for the indigenous Hawaiian population.

American missionaries initially did not seek government positions or financial reward, but they did demand economic security for their children, arguing to the ABCFM that they needed family stipends, subsidized private education, and the right to pass on to their children profits derived from the land. In the Hawaiian Islands, American missionaries became hostage to the most fundamental of concerns: household economics.[7]

In the process missionaries found acceptance among Hawaiian elites, including Kauikeaouli (Kamehameha III), who reigned from 1825 to 1854, promulgated a constitution, opened ancestral lands to private ownership, and created a legislature limiting monarchal power. Kamehameha's government—which included former missionaries—sold land to the missionary families at cheap prices, in part to reward their efforts at teaching Hawaiians to read and write a missionary-transcribed Hawaiian language, but, more importantly, to keep their children in the islands. Missionary children, the beneficiaries of such changes, disregarded the enormity of Kamehameha's changes and aggressively pursued additional political and economic gifts. Native Hawaiians, noting the missionary families' increasingly secular agenda, tried to stem the tide, arguing to the Hawaiian king in 1845 that white settler power had grown too strong. Hawaiian monarchs Kalākaua (r. 1874–91) and Liliʻuokalani (r. 1891–93), who retrenched against American missionary influence, found that the missionary children—now adults—were willing to use violence and U.S. Marines to maintain their privileged positions in the islands.

## The ABCFM in the Pacific

The Hawaiian Islands, made up of eight main islands and hundreds of tiny islands, are the northernmost islands considered part of Polynesia, a triangle of over a thousand islands in the Southern and mid-Pacific Ocean. The people of Polynesia shared a common ancestry and similarities of language and cultural beliefs. A sea people, Polynesians navigated by the stars at night and fanned out across the Pacific Ocean. For nineteenth-century Europeans and Americans, the Hawaiian Islands represented the center station along major shipping routes from the Americas to Canton.[8]

The Hawaiian Islands had only been known to the United States since their "discovery" by British Captain James Cook in 1778, and Americans had little information except what had been given them by Hawaiian "converts" to Christianity, a handful of Hawaiian youth who had made it to New England shores aboard merchant ships and had embraced the religion and language of its residents. Their strange stories of human sacrifice, infanticide, polygamy, idolatry, and sexual promiscuity enthralled the American populace, as did descriptions of the "dancing ground" upon which "drums pounded, gourds rattled, singers chanted and hundreds of dancers garlanded with green leaves and flowers and adorned with dog-tooth anklets moved endlessly to and fro in serried ranks, their bare brown flesh glistening with sweat." Honoring Laka, goddess of hula, chanters and dancers, who had undergone years of rigorous training, celebrated birth, mourned death, and praised the uniting of the Hawaiian nation under King Kamehameha I in 1795.[9]

Despite the peace and conformity that Kamehameha brought to a political system ruled by hereditary chiefs and religious taboos, the increased arrivals of foreign traders not bound to such beliefs had already caused internal fissures. No Hawaiian gods murdered the white men who trampled Hawaiian practice by eating and sleeping in the same quarters with women or partaking of chiefly foods such as bananas, coconuts, and pork. Hawaiian women, too, began to use foreigners to defy these *kapu* (taboos). When Kamehameha died in 1819, his successor Liholiho allowed—not uncontested—the state religion to expire.

Such was the turmoil into which the first American missionaries arrived ready to establish one God and a new set of *kapu* for the Hawaiian people. Determined to stay out of politics, the missionaries sought to influence the chiefs and chiefesses, assuming that the infusion of Christian principles into all Hawaiian society would follow. Thinking the American missionaries politically disinterested, the Hawaiian monarchs increasingly called upon their advice in trade negotiations with France, Great Britain, and Russia. "Rarely," wrote American missionary Hiram Bingham (1789–1869), "has a missionary a more favorable opportunity to exert an influence on a whole nation, than was here afforded in the circle of the highest chiefs of these islands."[10] Within five years of the missionaries' arrival, a dozen chiefs had sought Christian baptism and church membership, including the king's regent Kaahumanu. The Hawaiian people followed their native leaders, accepting the missionaries as their new priestly class. They accepted the missionary children, born on Hawaiian soil, as members of their society. The process culminated in Kamehameha III's adoption of a constitution in 1840 that proclaimed that no Hawaiian law was to be contrary to the Bible.[11]

As the first American missionary organization, the ABCFM commanded resources and attention. Formed in 1810 in the midst of New England revival and influenced by similar British evangelical societies, the ABCFM led the nineteenth-century American impetus to develop private benevolent and reform organizations capable of commanding the public sphere. These voluntary organizations were, in part, a backlash to the post-Revolutionary disestablishment of state-supported churches, yet by 1830 they shared evangelical goals, memberships, and financial contributors and had become a "benevolent empire."[12]

Missionary efforts in the Hawaiian Islands would have been impossible without the donations of the American public. Conversely, the ABCFM's efforts in the Hawaiian Islands played a crucial role in building support for American influence abroad. "We know of no Mission . . . that has hitherto left this country, which has excited such general interest and prompted so many prayers as that to the [Hawaiian] Islands," the *Boston Recorder* stated at the departure of the first company of ABCFM missionaries to the islands.[13] Contributions to the ABCFM jumped with news that the missionaries had reached the islands, and by the 1840s the ABCFM had raised for the Hawaiian mission over $700,000, roughly $15 million today.[14]

The success of the Hawaiian mission was critical to the ABCFM. Although earlier ABCFM missions had embarked to India in 1812 and Ceylon in 1815, they had yielded few converts. As an organ of the Congregationalist and Presbyterian denominations, the ABCFM hoped to counteract the continuing decline of Congregationalist influence in the United States. The ABCFM was also in the midst of reevaluating its domestic efforts among Native Americans. Working in concert with the Foreign Mission School in Cornwall, Connecticut, the ABCFM had hoped to Christianize and educate Native American, Hawaiian, and other foreign youth, in order to return them as missionaries to their own cultures. The results were not as hoped. In 1825, eight years after the school's founding, Cherokee student Elias Boudinot caused near rioting in Cornwall by marrying Harriet Gold, a white woman. The following year the school closed its doors, stating that "inquisitive curiosity" and "established prejudices" had made the students feel as "*mere shows.*"[15]

The Hawaiian Islands' strategic location in the Pacific was just what the ABCFM needed to revitalize the American evangelical missionary spirit, as well as provide future prospects for its work among Native Americans. As early as 1822 the ABCFM's *Missionary Herald* argued that from Hawai'i "salvation may go to the tribes and nations in the north-western and western parts of America, in the north-eastern and eastern parts of Asia, and on the numerous islands of the Pacific."[16] Not long after the establishment of the mission in Hawai'i, the ABCFM sent Marcus and Narcissa Whitman to Oregon Country.[17]

The diplomatic and fundraising successes of the ABCFM also grabbed the attention of the U.S. government. In 1829 President John Quincy Adams instructed Secretary of the Navy Samuel Southard to write Kamehameha III and encourage the Hawaiian monarch to support the ABCFM missionaries living among his people.[18] In 1841 the ABCFM sought and received U.S. diplomatic intervention for its Syria mission after the Ottoman Empire ordered it to leave.[19] With competing British, French, Dutch, and Russian interests in the Pacific region, a few American statesmen flirted with the idea of Hawaiian annexation as early as the 1850s. "The Pacific Ocean, its shores, its islands, and the vast regions beyond, will become the chief theatre of events in the world's great hereafter," stated U.S. senator William Henry Seward in 1851. His pronouncement became the masthead of the ABCFM's Hawaiian newspaper the *Friend*.[20] As secretary of state during the 1860s, Seward advocated the acquisition of Hawai'i and directed U.S. annexation of the Midway Islands, the halfway point between Hawai'i and Japan.

### Americans Abroad

The American missionary project in Hawai'i was part of a much larger market movement. Kamehameha I had already granted U.S. merchants a near monopoly in the Hawaiian sandalwood trade during the first two decades of the nineteenth century. Prized for its long-lasting scent and red hue, sandalwood could be made into expensive furniture, perfume, and incense, providing U.S. merchants with a product to exchange for Chinese luxury goods. By the 1830s, the king's laborers had stripped the islands of its native bark, just as U.S. whalers were joining other maritime nations in utilizing Honolulu and Lahaina as trading ports.

These U.S. industries were not small. American ships carrying furs from the Pacific Northwest stopped in the Hawaiian Islands for sandalwood and garnered as much as one million dollars annually in Canton. Pacific whaling earned ten times as much by 1850.[21] The Japanese imprisonment of U.S. whalers shipwrecked off its coast influenced the United States to forcibly open Japanese ports in 1854. On the heels of Britain's first Opium War with China, the United States negotiated the 1844 Treaty of Wanghia, allowing U.S. naval access to China for the protection of its growing economic interests in the region.

With the U.S. acquisition of California in 1848, San Francisco supplanted Honolulu as the most important Pacific port for American traders. As its nearest trading partner, Hawai'i became California's principal supplier of agricultural and manufactured goods. With the discovery of California gold and the concurrent decline in whaling, the Hawaiian monarchy shifted its focus to export agriculture, opening lands to private purchase, even by foreigners. Some in the United States saw the eventual U.S. domination of the islands. "The native population [is] fast fading away, the foreign fast increasing," declared the San Francisco *Alta California* in 1851. "The inevitable destiny of the islands is to pass into the possession of another power. That power is just as inevitably our own."[22]

Tragically, the newspaper was right. Between 1832 and 1853, over half of the native Hawaiian population perished, a shocking decline caused by the introduction of foreign diseases, such as smallpox, measles, syphilis, and tuberculosis. Some in Washington now argued that the annexation of the islands was necessary for protecting California and the Northwest Territory from encroaching French, British, and German interests in the Pacific.[23]

Missionary children in Hawai'i entered adulthood in the midst of these geopolitical changes. The U.S. acquisition of California, the Civil War, and industrial expansion brought new avenues for international trade and increasing political demands for international competitiveness. Steam power required ports, and urbanization and immigration required commercial markets to fuel continued economic growth. European states rushed to divide Africa in search of raw materials for factories back home, while the United States vied for influence in Asia. Everywhere, indigenous governments and populations suffered invasion, exploitation, and displacement. New racialist ideas appropriating Darwin allowed Europeans and Americans to justify conquest. Hawai'i, the "crossroads of the Pacific," as one missionary son called the islands, represented an American opportunity for merchant and military fueling on the way to opening Asian markets.[24]

Unlike their British missionary counterparts in the Pacific, American missionaries to Hawai'i only reluctantly drew in tandem with U.S. interests in the region. Their children, however, presided over many of these historic transformations. Sanford Ballard Dole (1844–1926), for example, led the revolution overthrowing the Hawaiian monarchy. John Thomas Gulick (1832–1923) helped U.S. and British powers open China and Japan to foreign influence. Samuel Chapman Armstrong (1839–93) founded Hampton Institute, the Virginia manual arts college for former slaves and Native Americans, which influenced American colonial education policies toward nonwhites in Puerto Rico, Hawai'i, and the Philippines.[25]

### Childhood and Empire

Throughout the nineteenth century, white missionary children in the Hawaiian Islands were avid chroniclers of the demographic, cultural, and political changes occurring around them. Through letters to parents and siblings, personal diaries, and school essays the children recorded their childhoods while capturing their own interpretation of U.S.-Hawaiian relations. At Punahou School—the Honolulu boarding school missionary parents founded for their children in 1841—students published a weekly student newspaper, laboriously hand-copied for peer consumption. As adults, white missionary descendants continued to detail their own roles in Hawaiian history through published and unpublished memoirs, newspaper editorials, speeches, and letters to each other. What is consistent throughout these sources is the missionary descendants' abiding attachment to the Hawaiian 'āina (land). Missionary sons and daughters, whether remaining in the islands or moving abroad, considered Hawai'i their home.[26]

Their prolific written record from both childhood and adulthood also reveals an astounding generational and longitudinal history of American colonialism in the Hawaiian Islands. This work attempts to correct the absence of children's voices in history by following the white children born to American missionaries in the Hawaiian Islands between 1820 and 1850 as they traveled toward political revolution in the 1890s. Students of childhood, Christian missions, or U.S. involvement in the Pacific will find within the children's written record a stunning yet tainted view of Hawaiian history. In researching this story, I made use of archival sources at Punahou School and the Hawaiian Mission Children's Society, both in Honolulu, as well as at the Houghton Library, Library of Congress, and Huntington Library. The archives at Williams College and Mt. Holyoke College provided additional records regarding the children from Hawai'i who attended these institutions as college students.

What I also have found is that placing the missionary children within Hawaiian history is fraught with complications. Although the children revered Hawai'i as the land of their birth, were considered subjects by the Hawaiian monarchy, and often called themselves "Hawaiians," this nomenclature today is highly problematic. That missionary children organized the "Hawaiian" League in 1887 to illegally force King Kalākaua to sign a new constitution and led the 1893 revolution to overthrow Queen Lili'uokalani provides a glimpse as to why the nature of their Hawaiian citizenship remains contested.[27] In this project I respect the work of Hawaiian scholars who have argued strenuously against the legacy of missionary descendants in the Hawaiian Islands.[28] As Haunani-Kay Trask writes, "Despite American political and territorial control of Hawaii since 1898, Hawaiians are not American." For Hawaiian scholars like Trask, the story of missionary childhood is irrelevant compared to the damages caused by missionary families. "We were orphaned in our own land," Trask explains. "Such brutal changes in a people's identity—their legal status, their government, their sense of belonging to a nation—are considered among the most serious human rights violations by the international community today." Trask's familial terms remind readers of an earlier Hawaiian genealogy in which the earth mother (Papa) and sky father (Wākea) created the Hawaiian Islands, out of which came the taro plant and Hawaiian people.[29]

Hawaiian scholars also point to the importance of reading Hawaiian language texts when looking at Hawaiian history. Throughout this project I have relied upon nineteenth-century native authors, such as John Papa Ii, Henry Obookiah, Samuel Kamakau, David Malo, and Liliʻuokalani. Yet native Hawaiian sources—even in their original Hawaiian language—are also problematic, for American missionaries transcribed the original Hawaiian language into a written language and translated the written language into English. Missionary-directed transitions between oral and written languages or indigenous and English translations were never seamless.[30] Sadly, as John Papa Ii (1800–1870) noted, the art of maintaining Hawaiian history through the memorization of genealogical *meles* (chants) had largely disappeared by the 1860s, many of the original chants forgotten.[31]

The efforts of Hawaiian historians to restore traditional genealogies and return Hawaiian studies to indigenous sources are complicated by the Christianity of nineteenth-century Hawaiian authors. Educated by Christian missionaries, these authors adopted the Christian faith and wrote Hawaiian history from the moral perspective of Christian converts. Even Liliʻuokalani believed her white cabinet members would not abandon her due to their shared faith.[32] The legacy of American missionary activity in Hawaiʻi continues to be a highly politicized minefield into which even Hollywood and the White House have entered.[33]

Nevertheless, I believe missionary children in the Hawaiian Islands provide a lens through which to understand American imperialism in the Pacific. Despite the efforts of Hawaiian historians, terms like *empire* and *colonialism* remain contested within the broader field of U.S. foreign relations.[34] Instead scholars more easily *describe* the impact of nineteenth-century Americans traveling abroad.[35] Emily Conroy-Krutz argues, "If empire is about states and their power, imperialism is a more flexible term that allows us to think about unequal power dynamics between groups."[36]

Ultimately children became key to the American colonization of Hawai'i. Not only was the demographic size of white missionary families significant to the development of American colonialism, but children *as* children became participants in American expansion. The process began when white children became an imperial space upon which parents and missionary teachers attempted to transplant their goals and aspirations. Hawaiian history demonstrates a crucial yet neglected aspect of historical colonialism: generational and familial transition. U.S. imperialism in particular has often, and in the case of the Hawaiian Islands most decidedly, taken nongovernmental forms and required multiple forces working together. Examining the lives of nineteenth-century white children born in Hawai'i provides a telling glimpse of why adults conquer nations and eradicate cultures, and do so believing they act righteously.[37]

### The Language of Family

Children were often utilized as symbols of cultural power by nineteenth-century proponents of colonialism, the domestic sphere serving as political discourse. American missionaries in Hawai'i, for example, fixated on the natives' "uncouth and disgusting manners," their "modes of dress and living," and lack of "taste, refinement and comfort." Missionaries wrote to their American supporters about Hawaiian defecating habits, calling native parents filthier than swine and their children as wild as goats. American missionary mothers believed demonstrating proper parenting and homemaking was essential to the Christianization of Hawaiian women, and used their growing number of children as tools to display proper obedience and respect to God.[38]

The discourse of family was already a useful tool in the continental United States, often justifying white intervention, settlement, or subjugation. New England Puritans had long argued that the "childish" ways of North American Indians should give way to Christian civilization. Timothy Dwight, Congregationalist minister, Yale University president, and founder of the ABCFM, went further, justifying the killing of Indian babies in war: "Should then these infants to dread manhood rise, /

What unheard crimes would smoke thro' earth and skies!" he opined in his 1785 epic poem, *The Conquest of Canaan.*[39]

Likewise Southern American slaveholders argued their race-based system rested on benevolent paternalism. "It is true that the slave is driven to labor by stripes," one slave owner argued in 1837. "It is not degrading to a slave, nor is it felt to be so. Is it degrading to a child?"[40] In the Hawaiian Islands American missionaries constructed their own racial hierarchy based on the analogy of a child. As one missionary argued to his U.S. supporters in 1857: "The Hawaiian people have not arrived at full manhood. They are yet in their teens."[41]

Even those noting the negative impact of white settlement in the Hawaiian Islands reverted to analogies of family hierarchy: "[Now] the children have become adults," the Hawaiian-language newspaper *Ka Hoku* proclaimed in the 1860s. "Living under parents, that is the Teachers [missionaries], is over, we have matured, our minds are made up."[42] After decades of missionary political influence, the newspaper called for the removal of foreign influence from government.

Such was the tension existing in the Hawaiian Islands as the early American missionaries reached the end of their lives and their numerous children began to raise families of their own. This project attempts to add to the body of literature utilizing domestic discourses of imperialism by allowing nineteenth-century children to appropriate and modify such discourses. White children living in the Hawaiian Islands internalized the numerous inconsistencies found between their cloistered upbringing at home, segregated preparatory education at Punahou School in Honolulu, and indigenous Hawaiian culture surrounding them. Missionary children heard their New England parents decry U.S. slavery but watched them rely on unpaid native labor for the most intimate tasks, including childcare. Children saw their parents bow in deference to Hawaiian *ali'i* but listened to them degrade the Hawaiian way of life. Children saw their parents teach in schools considered too inferior for white children to attend. "It will raise fire!" wrote one missionary son about the idea that American missionary parents should coeducate their children with "dissipated" native Hawaiians.[43]

Missionary children observed parents worry about money while preaching against earthly possessions. Taught Calvinist orthodoxy, missionary children developed distaste for the version their parents attempted to transplant in the islands. Hearing their parents extol the blessings of their homeland, the children were unimpressed with the United States when introduced to it firsthand. Missionary families decried the deaths of native Hawaiians but increasingly relied upon bonded Chinese labor to take their place. Missionary children loved their birthplace yet explored the world as if its entitled citizens. Considering themselves "Hawaiians," missionary children felt born to lead the Hawaiian race. Above all, missionary children both worshipped and despised their parents as living martyrs while searching for a cause to which they, too, could give their lives.

Hawaiian by birth, white by race, and American by parental and educational design, the children of nineteenth-century American missionaries in Hawai'i occupied an ambiguous place in Hawaiian culture. More tenuous was the relationship between these children and the United States, where many attended college before returning to the Hawaiian Islands. The supposed American acculturation of white missionary children from Hawai'i was never complete, nor was their membership in Hawaiian society uncontested, yet the roles these children played in both societies influenced the trajectories of each nation in surprising ways. Similarly, the children's cultural experiences shaped their views of religion, race, and international affairs. This complicated, bicultural childhood inspired the missionary children to participate in revolution in Hawai'i and accept U.S. annexation of the islands, even while attempting to keep the Hawaiian nation free from outside influence.

This study explores white childhood in the Hawaiian kingdom within six sections. Chapter 1 uncovers the economies of childrearing in the nineteenth-century Hawaiian Islands, demonstrating that the transition from politically disinterested ABCFM missionaries to supporters of U.S. imperialism exclusively revolved around parental concerns for their children.

Chapter 2 portrays the environmental and political impact of white childhood in the islands, the result of missionary children left isolated and unsupervised yet also forbidden to interact with indigenous Hawaiians. Missionary son John Gulick and his scientific and socialist endeavors as an adult are highlighted for their contrast to missionary ideology yet natural relationship to his childhood.

Chapter 3 examines the role Punahou School played in the construction of a white colonial agenda for the Hawaiian kingdom, as well as the development of a peer culture among missionary children who attended the school during the 1840s and 1850s. Initially a whites-only boarding school, Punahou teachers sought to raise a generation of white leaders for the islands. Punahou student newspapers, hand-copied during this period, display the level to which teachers succeeded in their mission, yielding a racially conscious student body whose geographic distance from parental influence ultimately bound the students together in a way that differed from parental hopes for their children's future in the islands. Samuel Chapman Armstrong, for example, took his Punahou experiences and racial ideology to the United States and implemented many of his own childhood lessons at Hampton Institute in Hampton, Virginia.

Chapter 4 describes the incomplete acculturation process missionary children from the Hawaiian Islands endured during their schooling in the United States. For those entering the United States during the 1850s and 1860s, Williams College, Mount Holyoke Seminary, and the American Civil War yielded defining experiences that influenced missionary children for the remainder of their lives. Yet Williams College and Mount Holyoke had changed in important ways since missionary parents had first attended them. These cultural and religious realignments further distanced missionary children from their parents but also created in the children a deep desire to return to the islands. The American Civil War became an outlet for many students to express this confusion and frustration. Sanford Ballard Dole was one son who ultimately returned to the islands to help enact a new era of American imperialism in the islands, including political revolution.

Chapter 5 dissects the complex identities of missionary children, including their ambiguous citizenship status in the United States and Hawaiian kingdom, as well as their lingering resentments and insecurities toward their parents, affecting their occupational choices and political activism. The conclusion of this study attempts to refine our understanding of nineteenth-century white children as both colonized subjects and agents of imperial change.

The path toward nineteenth-century revolution in the Hawaiian Islands began in childhood, and the following pages are, above all, a children's history. It is a tale that spans the globe and covers an important period in the history of globalization. Strong-willed, restless, and often ambivalent, missionary daughters and sons crossed boundaries and transformed nations. The children of American missionaries to Hawai'i experienced what children of immigrant parents today readily understand—religion, race, and culture are powerful yet fragile markers of personal, familial, and national identities. For the children of American missionaries in Hawai'i, it was a process that began at birth and took a lifetime.

CHAPTER 1

# Birthing Empire

*Economies of Childrearing and the Establishment*
*of American Colonialism in Hawai'i*

There was an old woman who lived in a shoe. She had so many children she didn't know what to do.

English nursery rhyme[1]

We multiply like the Jews in Egypt. . . . Perhaps we are to inherit the land.

Missionary son Amos Cooke[2]

## Domestic Economics in the Islands

Most among the ABCFM missionaries who stepped aboard New England ships traveling to the Hawaiian Islands between 1819 and 1848 believed they would never see the United States again. As part of the revivalist fervor sweeping the United States during the first two decades of the nineteenth century, young Americans—almost all college and seminary graduates—eagerly gave away their earthly possessions in order to qualify for Christian missionary service. Levi Chamberlain, for example, was a successful Boston businessman who sold his dry goods business and donated all his money and property to the ABCFM after joining the second company of missionaries to Hawai'i in 1822. Sybil Bingham gave away her small but entire fortune before leaving with her husband for the islands. Other hopeful missionaries worked off their debts before the ABCFM would commission them for service.[3]

To ensure that missionaries devoted their entire energies to developing a written language for the Hawaiian people and translating the Bible into the Hawaiian language, the ABCFM took command of the missionaries' economic resources by supplying the missionaries' domestic needs through a common-stock system administered by appointed agents who were also commissioned as missionaries by the ABCFM. The ABCFM hoped to preserve the missionaries' spiritual focus, as well as their reputations. "The kingdom to which you belong is not of this world," ABCFM secretary Rufus Anderson instructed the missionaries. "Your mission is to the native race." With supplies taking six months to reach the islands, missionaries in the Hawaiian Islands practiced rigid economy partly out of necessity, and partly out of a desire to appear trustworthy to the American churches upon whom they depended for total support.[4]

Within fifteen months of the fist missionaries' arrival in 1820, each of the seven American wives gave birth. The arrival of these infants propelled the missionaries to begin the first of many renegotiations with the ABCFM over the common-stock system. For all but one family, parenthood was new. Exhausted missionary mothers demanded private food quotas rather than sharing all meals at the "good old long table."[5] The new mothers no longer wanted to rotate cooking responsibilities, required three times a day for as many as fifty missionaries and Hawaiian guests. A few mothers flatly refused to continue their communal duties, and the remaining couples soon reverted to operating as nuclear families.[6]

The economy of childrearing was a distracting and familiar topic for the ABCFM board in Boston. By 1822 the seven-year-old Ceylon mission was pressuring the ABCFM to establish a seminary in the United States to which it could send its children, some as young as eight years old. The board stayed silent during eight years of continual agitation from the Ceylon mission until 1830 when, according to the board, "the case of [the missionary] children was concisely and ably stated" by their parents for the first time.[7]

The Ceylon missionary parents presented to the board an economic argument, arguing their own inability to provide for the futures of their children. The American parents did not believe they could educate, employ, settle, and marry their children in Ceylon. As missionaries who earned no income, and who were not allowed to individually profit in any way from their work, they had no resources to offer their children to return to the United States. Lumping their children together with native children in rudimentary missionary schools, they argued, would be woefully inadequate, as well as morally dangerous. This fear of raising white missionary children in a non-Christian environment, and the corresponding impetus to racially segregate the white children, would be echoed by missionaries in the Hawaiian Islands.[8]

Within six years of the Hawaiian mission's founding, the Hawaiian missionaries were also debating the "condition and prospects of [their] children."[9] In personal correspondence American missionaries in the islands were consumed with fear for the future of their children. "Of all the trials incident to missionary life, the responsibility of training up children, and of making provision for their virtue and usefulness . . . is comparatively speaking, the only one worthy of being named," wrote missionary mother Lucy Thurston.[10] "When my thoughts turn to their future prospects in life, a darkness visible seems to brood over their path," Abigail Smith declared. A "thorough education" for her children, the missionary mother stated, was the "only *personal* luxury I crave."[11]

The Hawaiian missionaries wrote letters to the board: "The education and future prospects of our children constitute a subject of increasing solicitude with us," the missionaries wrote to Boston.[12] "Children over eight or ten years of age . . . ought to be sent or carried to the United States," missionary Hiram Bingham wrote, "in order that they might escape the dangers of a heathen country . . . and at the same time allow the parents more time and strength for missionary work." Bingham rationalized that while parents could give very young children the "rudiments of education," there was "no employment into which the parent could with propriety thoroughly initiate them as a business for life." Bingham and his fellow missionary parents in Hawai'i conflated worries regarding future employment opportunities for their children with their views of Hawaiian culture, which they believed had nothing to offer their children but dissipation, paganism, and intellectual malaise.[13]

The ABCFM missionaries also regarded the lack of New England–style preparatory schools and colleges in the islands as a severe hindrance to their children's upbringing. Although they attempted to replicate the New England model for Hawaiian elites—such as at the Royal School in Honolulu—the majority of missionaries focused their attention on teaching native Hawaiians a written Hawaiian language, the same language they forbid their own children to learn. Missionary parents wanted their children to learn English, Greek, and Latin, a task, the parents argued, for which they had no time. The Congregationalist requirement that a male missionary be seminary ordained guaranteed that ABCFM missionaries to Hawai'i were well educated, but missionary parents also desired the same advantages for their children.[14] Our children "have a right to an education by inheritance," the Hawaiian mission appealed in a joint letter to American churches.[15] "We could more easily do with only half a loaf of bread than without the means of educating our children," missionary Ephraim Clark stated.[16]

Missionary parents were hindered in their parental goals by Hawaiian cultural differences. The nineteenth-century American practice of apprenticing one's son into his eventual occupation proved difficult for missionary parents in the islands. "There is not a mechanic in all the islands with whom any missionary would suffer his son to live in order to learn a trade—there is not a merchant with whom he would allow him to become a clerk—not a farmer to whom he could entrust him," missionary Dwight Baldwin emphatically wrote. The "low character of the native population" and the "almost universally irreligious and immoral character of foreigners with whom the islands abound" make us "afraid to settle our children here," Baldwin concluded.[17]

Despite the missionaries' arguments that there were no educational or employment opportunities for their children in the islands, the official position of the ABCFM was that "as a *general* rule . . . children should be educated under the inspection of their parents." ABCFM secretary Jeremiah Evarts reminded the missionaries that "impurity and profaneness of language" also existed in U.S. schools. Missionaries who exchanged their own parental guardianship for the perceived benefits of an American education were simply exchanging "*one degree of danger with another,*" Evarts cautioned. He encouraged the missionaries to have faith that God would bless their parenting efforts in the islands.[18]

Not least on the ABCFM's mind was the financial impact of providing for the education of missionary children, an expense bound to increase with the size of missionary families. "Should the Board make it a part of their plan to defray the expense of sending your children [to the United States] for education, this item of expenditure would in time become very great . . . *the public mind would not probably bear the expenditures to which such a system would give rise,*" Evarts wrote.[19] Considering that the eventual number of children born to American missionaries in Hawai'i numbered over 250 by the 1850s, Evarts's worries proved prescient.

The ABCFM secretary attempted to blunt these practical considerations by sympathizing with the missionaries. "Parents find trying difficulties everywhere," Evarts wrote. For those missionaries who persisted in their demands to send missionary children to the United States, Evarts suggested they see the benefit behind the increasing importance of the Hawaiian Islands to American commerce: "opportunities of obtaining a gratuitous passage," Evarts argued, "would be to those enjoyed by your brethren [in Ceylon], probably, as ten or twenty to one." Missionary parents in the islands remained unconvinced. Begging a ship captain to grant free passage to the United States for a six-year-old was the easy part. Parents still had to arrange U.S. guardianship and provide tuition for their children.[20]

Such was the standoff in 1830 when the Ceylon missionaries finally convinced the ABCFM to alter its policy. Rather than establish a seminary for missionary children in the United States, which the board found prohibitively expensive and unnecessary, the ABCFM agreed to provide one-way passages for missionary children to the United States to attend existing American schools. In 1833 the board extended its policy to missionary children in the Hawaiian Islands, and in 1834 it granted annual stipends to missionary children studying in the United States. By 1846 ABCFM missionaries had sent more than one hundred missionary children to the

**3.** The whale ship *Averick* brought the fifth company of ABCFM missionaries to the Hawaiian Islands in 1832. At least thirty missionary children rode similar vessels on the six-month voyage back to the United States for schooling. The children were usually between the ages of six and ten, and over half traveled unaccompanied by an adult. Mission Houses Museum Library.

United States. Over thirty Hawaiian-born missionary children made the six-month voyage around Cape Horn, nineteen unaccompanied by an adult. Most of the children sent to the United States to live apart from their parents were between the ages of six and ten.[21]

### The Missionaries Rebel

Placing a dollar amount upon the cost of raising one's child, while a fairly routine occurrence for parents in the United States today, was disastrous to the nineteenth-century "disinterested benevolence" of ABCFM missionaries in Hawai'i.[22] While scholars have noted the impact of the Panic of 1837 upon decreasing American financial contributions to ABCFM missions, the demands of childrearing and the expectation that "God will not suffer children to be *losers*, by the sacrifices of their parents in his cause" played the more important role in transitioning the missionaries in the Hawaiian Islands toward new thinking regarding the accumulation of wealth.[23] Through their role as parents, missionaries developed a settler mindset toward the Hawaiian Islands, a colonial mentality having permanent impact upon the nation's domestic culture and political sovereignty.

By 1832 the Hawaiian missionaries were discussing a move from the common-stock system to fixed salaries. Realizing the increased expense the ABCFM board would incur from such a measure, the missionaries resolved that each family should estimate not only their current expenses but what their expenses were "likely to be in [the] future."[24] Clearly some missionaries had begun contemplating a kingdom of this world. Nevertheless, the missionaries continued to eschew private property. In 1836 the mission collectively wrote, "No man can point to private property to the value of a single dollar, which any member of the mission has acquired at the [Hawaiian] Islands."[25] Dwight Baldwin noted, "Every member, I think, to a man, has been engrossed in labors for the benefit of the people. And it is certainly true of nearly every one, that he has turned his attention to no provision whatever which his children might need in America."[26]

Assailing many parental minds was the difficult process of shipping young children back to the United States to be thrown upon the goodwill of relatives or other guardians whom the board could procure. By the 1830s missionary feeling had decidedly cooled to the idea. For some parents it was due to the lack of relatives to whom they could send their children. Reports of missionary children who had been tossed around families did not ease their minds regarding the capacity of the board to adequately place their children. Others did not trust their own relatives—"Unitarians," as one missionary called his—to safeguard their children's moral upbringing.[27] Some parents, unwilling to allow their children to travel alone, simply did not want to leave the islands for the yearlong journey required to personally place their children in American homes and schools.[28]

Parents were also obligated to obtain permission both from fellow mission members and the ABCFM board to leave the islands. This could prove challenging, as Abner Wilcox discovered when trying to take his young son Albert to the United States to receive surgery on a club foot. Their trip was almost stopped by the arrival of a doctor in Honolulu, who the mission depository agent thought might be able to provide cheaper medical services. From Boston, board secretary Rufus Anderson requested reconnaissance from other members of the mission regarding the medical necessity of Albert's trip.[29]

More subtle influences shifted missionary parents away from sending their children to the United States, including cultural and economic changes occurring both in North America and the Hawaiian Islands. In the United States the market revolution of the early nineteenth century drove rural residents to the cities for wage employment, and the consequent rise of the urban middle class changed the nature of domestic relationships. No longer business partners, husbands and wives now divided their duties between public and private spheres. Women commanded the domestic front, in part, by developing complex theories of motherhood to justify the amount of time spent at home in their non-wage-earning capacities.[30] Theories exalting the nurturing role of motherhood and the need for constant companionship with one's children in order to oversee their moral upbringing culminated in the 1847 publication of Horace Bushnell's immensely popular *Christian Nurture*: "It requires less piety . . . to be a martyr for Christ than it does to . . . maintain a perfect and guileless integrity in the common transactions of life," Bushnell admonished parents.[31]

American missionary mothers in the Hawaiian Islands actively pursued subscriptions to American publications and were familiar with the new parenting theories.[32] While not all of them embraced the popularized attitudes, they eventually admitted that "with adequate facilities [and] increased paternal faithfulness the children of missionaries may be trained up here." With contributions to missionaries dipping in the United States by the end of the 1830s, parents worried that "placing their children so far out of their own influence" to be influenced instead by a country "where the missionary spirit is low" might adversely cause their children to "be lost to the mission."[33]

A more important reason behind the missionaries' reversal regarding the proper location for the education of their children was the economic changes occurring in the islands. As the missionaries explained, "The increase of foreigners of a good character . . . leads to the hope that were there no other employment for our children they might at least some of them, find employment as clerks, overseers, or laborers on the plantations."[34] More to the point, one missionary noted, "Natives are rapidly dying off. . . . Foreigners are multiplying—lands are now put as it were into the market to be leased out to the highest bidder for 25 years."[35]

With comfort found in the increasing number of white immigrants to the Hawaiian Islands, missionary parents could also look to the 1840 Hawaiian constitution as a model of good governance, surpassing even their own American political system. No law, the constitution specified, was to be contrary to the Bible, meaning the moral landscape upon which missionary children played had dramatically shifted in favor of long-term Protestant influence and success.[36] No greater example of this astounding transformation existed than in King Kamehameha III's voluntary revolution in ancient landholding patterns. In the 1830s all Hawaiian lands were partitioned by the Hawaiian king, and according to the 1840 constitution, no one could "convey away the smallest portion of land" without his consent.[37] With the decline of the Hawaiian sandalwood trade by the 1830s, however, the development of agriculture became increasingly important to the continued economic viability of the islands. The rise of the Pacific whaling industry meant as many as three or four hundred ships stopping each year to buy supplies from the islands. King Kamehameha III's leasing of land to foreigners knowledgeable in agriculture meant potential trade opportunities for the kingdom, as well as avenues for missionary children to earn wages and acquire land.[38]

Consequently, almost as soon as the ABCFM had granted yearly stipends to missionary children sent to the United States, missionary parents in Hawai'i adjusted their family budgets to include keeping their children in the islands and educating them in a yet-to-be-created New England style preparatory school. In 1838 the missionaries resolved that the adoption of salaries was necessary to the "missionary cause," but they made it clear that any accumulation of wealth was for their children, "not . . . for ourselves."[39] In 1840 the missionaries hastened the Boston board to settle the amount of their salaries "as soon as possible" and complained that the board's proposed $540 per year was "sufficiently low" for sustaining a family.[40] At least one missionary also threatened to take his family back to the United States unless the board established a boarding school for missionary children in the islands.[41]

In the end missionary families took matters into their own hands. Utilizing whatever mission resources they could muster, the parents in 1841 built a school at Punahou (fresh spring), two miles outside Honolulu. Native Oahu governor Boki had gifted the land to Hiram Bingham, who, eschewing property as required by the ABCFM board, transferred the gift to the Hawaiian mission. The missionaries then determined that the use of mission property for the purpose of educating their children would free missionary labors for the native people, a "most economical expenditure." The missionaries also notified the Boston board that they had convinced Daniel and Emily Dole, ABCFM missionaries who had arrived that year, to change their plans from missionary work among the native Hawaiians to teaching the white missionary children. "The Lord has graciously sent us instructors to take charge of the school just at the time they were needed," the mission informed Boston.[42]

Punahou School, and the consequent retainer of scores of missionary children in the islands, might not have been possible without the aid of Kamehameha III. By 1840 the American missionaries were educating fifteen thousand indigenous Hawaiian children in schools across the islands. The mission had also established boarding schools at Hilo and Wailuku and the Royal School, a Honolulu academy for the children of Hawaiian chiefs. That same year the king established the first Hawaiian legislature and took financial responsibility for the support of all native elementary schools, a propitious act that eased the financial strain on the mission as it began to focus on retaining and educating its own children in the islands.[43] Emily Dole noted that Kamehameha's investment came as "a great relief to the mission, especially at this juncture of establishing a boarding school for the children of the Mission."[44]

Faced with the realization that continued foreign encroachment was inevitable, the first Hawaiian legislature made primary education compulsory in 1840. So important did the Hawaiian government consider missionary schools to the ability of the indigenous population to maintain its national independence that the legislature soon enacted a law requiring a man to demonstrate his ability to read and write before being allowed to marry. Hawaiian royalty additionally looked to the missionaries to teach their own children the English language, in order to prepare the monarchs to operate within a region increasingly crowded by American and European diplomats and naval vessels.[45]

Two years after Kamehameha created the first public education system, the ABCFM transitioned to a salary system. The board allotted each couple $450 per year and granted children under ten $30 and children over ten $70 annually. The board abolished the common-stock system but retained the depository at which missionaries could purchase goods. Missionary parents could now give their children a New England education in the islands and save their personal incomes for their children's futures.[46]

Still, missionaries worried about their children. Although Punahou School did not charge tuition to the missionary families, parents hoped the board would provide financial aid for the school's operational costs. Some argued that the allowance for children under ten precluded parents' abilities to pay for their children's board at the school, around $25 per year. "You doubtless anticipate that *money* is again to be the subject of discussion. And you are right," one missionary wrote the board in 1842.[47] "Is it a small matter for a feeble mother to lie on her couch and see her children growing up and running wild without education?" asked another. Missionary parents retained the ever-present fear that without formal schooling their children would fall into ruin.[48]

More seriously, missionaries had begun to leave the mission because of their children. "My father has left the Board so we haf to work for our living," explained ten-year old Sarah Andrews (1832–99).[49] Sarah's father justified his 1842 departure from the ABCFM as necessary for the support of his family. "It is my duty to look forward a little and see how I can accomplish my own designs to do the missionary work," Lorrin Andrews stated. "What I call my own designs is the education of my children." Andrews had made the momentous conclusion that the earthly success of his children would signal the spiritual acquiescence of the Hawaiian Islands to Protestant Christianity. Some missionaries wanted Andrews to leave the islands, but Andrews refused. Instead he taught school to Sarah and her four siblings before joining the Hawaiian government as a member of the Privy Council and, later, as a Supreme Court justice. Andrews was among the first American missionaries to reverse their economic challenges by offering their political services to the Hawaiian monarchy. Others, such as Reuben and Mary Tinker, resigned from the ABCFM and returned with their five children to the United States.[50] After Elizabeth Judd's parents severed their relationship with the board in 1842, Judd (1831–1918) wrote "a new and happier life opened to us all." In 1843 the Hawaiian government appointed her father, Dr. Gerrit Judd, secretary of state for foreign affairs.[51]

In Boston, the ABCFM held its ground. Salaries were one thing, but the accumulation of private property and the acceptance of government appointments were quite another. Sereno Bishop (1827–1909) thought his parents' salary "comparative opulence" to the family's previous way of living, but Sereno's father was incensed the board still required the family to send all supplemental income to the mission depository. Sereno's stepmother annually earned between $400 and $500 making and selling butter, all of which she dutifully sent to Honolulu.[52] "The only course that is safe for the minister and missionary . . . is, *in holding on in his spiritual course*," board secretary Rufus Anderson reminded the mission in 1846. "We all most earnestly deprecate having any other one from the mission coming into any sort of official connection with the government," Anderson added in reference to former missionaries like Andrews and Judd.[53]

Missionary parents continued to agitate. "The existing regulations of the mission in regard to herds . . . are offensive to some of our members, and are regarded by them as *absurd*," mission depository agent Levi

Chamberlain wrote the board in 1847. At least one missionary thought it was time for the missionaries to "have the right of making and using property as clergymen do at home," Chamberlain noted. "Thus they may be able in due time to make provision for their families."[54] With Punahou School's opening as a preparatory school, parents now argued that it was "inadequate." Parents also wanted a college. As one English-language Hawaiian newspaper declared, "Every civilized, educated and Christian nation must have an elevated institution of learning, well officered and well endowed."[55] With greater opportunities for keeping their children in the islands, parents now worried about "capital" for funding advanced education for their children. Less than eight years before, the Hawaiian mission adamantly had declared that it was "very undesirable that any brother should turn aside from his work to engage in labor or [trade]." Missionary parents now argued for permission to privately invest in the indigenous economy, create institutions solely for the benefit of their white children, and establish white settlements outside ABCFM control, certainly impressive goals for a minority American population living outside formal U.S. power.[56]

Missionary parents knew they held the upper hand and, according to the board, were growing "impossible to guide." At the 1848 general meeting in Honolulu, the mission counted 130 mission children, not including the ones who had been sent to the United States. Missionaries demanded the board grant them permission to acquire private property for their children. Chamberlain summarized parental feeling at the meeting: "They recommend that every obstacle [to acquiring private property] be removed . . . that we may have it in our power to obtain means to provide for our children either by settling them in the islands or doing something to educate them in the United States. . . . [I]s it not the duty of parents to provide for their children? Our sons must have employment, and, if they remain in the islands, they must have land, horses and cattle, and who shall provide all these things for them?"[57]

Chamberlain further advised: "Colonization by means of missionaries might well receive the attention of the wise men who have connected themselves with the missionary enterprise." Although couched in house-hold concerns, Chamberlain and his fellow missionaries were advocating total colonization, the impact of which would be nothing less than the transformation of the islands in accordance with their Protestant religion, liberal political values, and private property laws: a bequest to their numerous offspring.[58]

### The ABCFM Reacts

In 1848 missionary parents prevailed. In fact, the ABCFM board had received enough personal correspondence from individual missionaries in Hawai'i for Rufus Anderson to estimate that as many as twenty-six of the forty missionary families in the islands would return to the United States for the sake of their children. Anderson estimated the cost of returning these families to the United States would be $26,000, "not to speak of the missionary labor and influence at the islands." To lose over half of its missionary presence in the islands, after spending "about seven hundred thousand dollars on the Sandwich Islands people since the year 1819," was untenable to Anderson and the board. Thus, he wrote, "nothing short of the certainty of far greater evils would have induced the Committee to such a risk" as the one the board took that year.[59]

"I know not whether the communication I am about to make will take you by surprise," Anderson wrote the Hawaiian mission on July 19, 1848. Such was the beginning of a momentous announcement from Boston. No longer would the ABCFM stand in the way of its missionaries pursuing the ownership of private property in Hawai'i. Additionally the board would transfer all mission lands and property to individual missionary families. In order to encourage the colonization of American missionary families in the islands, the ABCFM would concede control over Protestant Hawaiian churches and allow American missionaries to obtain their own financial support from their native Hawaiian congregations.[60]

"O Brethren," Anderson wrote, "you have only come to a *new epoch* in your labors at the islands. You will need to gird yourselves up anew, that you may become the fathers and founders of the Christian community that is to exist in that North Pacific." The goal, Anderson explained, "is to keep the greater part of your children with you at the Islands, and to give them such an education and setting up, as you can *there*—as our fathers did in the first settlements of this country." After decades of arguing, Anderson now agreed that white colonization in the Pacific could accomplish the long-term goals of the ABCFM: namely, to establish a Protestant Christian outpost in the Pacific region.[61]

At this critical juncture the Hawaiian government again assisted the missionaries. Kamehameha III had already established his preference for foreign advisers, and the newly established Hawaiian legislature had agreed with him that it was necessary to "select persons skilful like those from other lands to transact business with foreigners." Beginning in 1845 these advisers, including former missionary Gerrit Judd, presided over what became known as the Great *Māhele*, one of the most astounding volitional acts of a national sovereign in history. The king divided all Hawaiian land among the crown, chiefs, and common people, and again divided crown lands between him and the Hawaiian government. Private individuals, "whether native or foreigners," could for the first time seek permanent title to their land grants and claims. Individuals could sell their titles, and by 1850 even alien residents could buy and sell property to anyone.[62]

Native Hawaiian John Papa Ii, who served Kamehameha III and later sat in the House of Representatives and on the Hawaiian Supreme Court, described the Hawaiian response to Kamehameha's act: "It was said that he was the greatest of the kings, a royal parent who loved his Hawaiian people more than any other chief before him."[63] Later Hawaiians would remember Kamehameha III differently. "The real loss of Hawaiian sovereignty began with the 1848 *Māhele*," Lilikalā Kameʻeleihiwa writes.[64]

The ABCFM missionaries in Hawaiʻi were forthright in their efforts to take advantage of the *Māhele*. The ABCFM mission pursued land titles for its homes and churches, property that at one time had been granted to the mission by the king and chiefs. The ABCFM then sold the titles to individual missionaries. Transactions between the ABCFM and individual missionaries often were written for "$1.00 and services rendered." For example, former missionary Richard Armstrong bought 1,382 acres of land from the government in Haʻikū, Maui, for $2.00 and services rendered.[65] As nineteenth-century native historian Samuel Kamakau noted, "The missionaries were given land by the chiefs without any payment. They left these to the American Board when they moved away from the land, and those missionaries who wished to own the lands given by the chiefs bought them of the American Board. . . . They were clever people!"[66]

Missionaries also acquired property from the Hawaiian government through gifts, gifts for service, and outright purchase. All sales of government lands were crucial to the government's revenue stream, yet astoundingly the Hawaiian government justified transactions with missionaries as being necessary for the care of missionary *children*. In a joint statement the Foreign and Interior Ministries argued in 1850: "Much has been said against sales of land to individuals of the American missionaries at low prices. But nothing can be more unreasonable and unjust. It is well known that these parties are severing their connection with the Board in Boston with a determination to seek support for themselves and families on the Islands, that they return poor and in most cases with numerous children all born in the Islands."[67]

The ABCFM plan appeared to work. By 1850 the missionaries owned close to eight thousand acres of former government lands. The mission reported to Boston that "all" at the 1849 general meeting agreed that the board's changes allowing private property and income "would be likely to diminish the number of [missionary] returns" to the United States. Although some missionaries worried about the ability of their native congregations to support them, the board assured missionaries who left the formal care of the ABCFM that they could still receive grants-in-aid and provision in old age as needed. Their children would still attend Punahou School free from tuition.[68]

### The Hawaiian Evangelical Association Is Born

Within the first few years of the ABCFM announcement, at least six families took advantage of the plan and left the support of the mission, yet new conflicts soon arose. Rumors reached Boston that these former missionaries were engaged in government surveying and were serving in the Hawaiian national legislature. The "Resolution relaxes no man's responsibilities and leaves him no more at liberty than he was before to become a legislator, mechanic, surveyor, landbroker or speculator, trader, banker, or money broker," Anderson wrote missionaries in 1851; "grasping after worldly gain, is no part of the object of this act." Although missionaries released from the ABCFM were to raise their own financial support, the ABCFM limited the ways in which they were allowed to do so.[69]

Income raised from secular occupations jeopardized one's relationship with the ABCFM. In a private letter to his son, Richard Armstrong predicted, "The native churches will never support the missionaries; they can help, but the burden must rest somewhere else. The missionaries will of necessity in this way be more or less engaged in secular pursuits." Armstrong had already left the mission to serve the king as minister of public instruction, a position looked upon very skeptically by the ABCFM. Meanwhile the California gold rush, a boon to Hawaiian farmers and merchants supplying San Francisco, caused prices of goods in the islands to rise. Missionary families sent another flurry of letters to Boston arguing against the board's expansive definition of ill-gotten gain.[70]

Clearly the ABCFM hoped the missionaries would earn full financial support as pastors in the islands, while training their own children and a native pastorate to carry on after their retirement. The board also hoped to end its financial support of the missionaries without sacrificing any of the missionary spirit. The board had no desire "to change this mission into a mere secular community, into a *colony*," Rufus Anderson complained. "It was a far different proposal that was commended to your attention." Financing changes were "forced upon us," Anderson reminded the missionaries, because "the parental feelings of not a few of you seemed likely to overpower your missionary self-consecration, and bring you home."[71]

The Boston board now realized that missionary practice had intractably shifted to include secular pursuits, demonstrating an agenda that in later decades the U.S. government would formally undertake in the development of its colonial possessions. Missionary families easily justified their land purchases. As Kameʻeleihiwa notes, "It was not surprising that these influential foreigners used the new system to their advantage. . . . They firmly believed that by acquiring and developing Hawaiian *ʻĀina* they were teaching the ignorant Natives how to improve the economy and become a 'civilized' capitalist nation."[72]

Not all the missionaries were ready to end the communal property and salary system. Abigail Smith wrote that the family's purchase of land in 1854 "was the first direct effort we had made to increase our possessions, and we should not have done this, had it not seemed very necessary in the new arrangements for our support." Smith rationalized her acquiescence to the new ABCFM policies regarding private property: "Land here costs a great deal—but it will never probably cost less than now and perhaps our Heavenly Father designs this to be a comfort to us and our dear children in future years."[73]

The majority of missionaries, however, had shifted away from such sentimentality toward communal life. In 1854 the ABCFM transferred formal governing power over Congregational activities in the islands to the newly created Hawaiian Evangelical Association (HEA). With this action the ABCFM gave the missionaries "home rule" status, and the board considered its missionary work in the Hawaiian Islands essentially finished. Still the economic concerns of the missionaries stalled efforts to train a native pastorate. Some missionaries argued that they could find few viable candidates, but other missionaries blamed fellow missionaries. "But why have the missionaries been so tardy in bringing forward a native ministry?" one missionary wrote the board. "A pastor can get a larger salary from a larger flock than from a small one. . . . To carve up their mammoth churches and form distant parishes with distant pastors would so reduce the number who contribute to their support that the amount would not meet the wants of their families."[74]

The U.S. Civil War in 1861 devastated American contributions to ABCFM missions just as it devastated American churches. The Presbyterian, Methodist, and Baptist denominations each split, in part, over the issue of slavery, and the ABCFM, made up of Presbyterians and Congregationalists, was not exempt from the controversy. The board lost donations from Southerners, who were convinced the ABCFM was a Boston abolitionist group. It also lost the support of Northerners for accepting donations from slave owners. To hasten the end of ABCFM financial support to missionaries in the Hawaiian Islands, Rufus Anderson traveled to the kingdom in 1863 to conduct meetings with the HEA. The HEA finally agreed to divide most large churches, giving

**4.** Missionaries Amos and Juliette Cooke and their seven children, ca. 1860. Missionary families, on average, were quite large. Amos Cooke left the ABCFM to begin the successful mercantile business Castle & Cooke with partner and former missionary Samuel Castle. Many of their children remained in the islands, and the two partners would later finance the business ventures of several missionary children. Mission Houses Museum Library.

new churches to native pastors, and allowed native pastors and laymen to join all religious governing bodies in the islands. From this point forward the ABCFM considered itself an "auxiliary" to the HEA. While some missionaries retained partial support from the ABCFM until their deaths, others were told to depend upon their children, now landowners, merchants, lawyers, surveyors, government workers, pastors, and teachers in the islands.[75]

### Missionary Descendants Come of Age

The American missionaries to Hawai'i arrived with idealistic notions of preaching a message of spiritual conversion to the Hawaiian people without entangling themselves in political and economic concerns.

With the birth of the first missionary child in 1820, missionary *practice* changed. Not only were white missionary children aware of these changes, but they actively participated in completing their parents' revolution. The children's understanding of these events, however, almost totally differed from that of their parents. Missionary children felt both a tremendous pride in and responsibility toward their parents' work. "Should they not be considered among the greatest men on earth?" young Levi T. Chamberlain II (1837–1917) asked in a school essay.[76] "Perhaps there is no other missionary station whose success has equaled that of the mission," a student writer in the *Punahou Gazette* argued to peers, at the same time missionary parents debated returning to the United States in the 1840s. "Can ye who have spent the best portion of your lives and strength in laboring for these inhabitants give them up now in their present critical circumstances?" the writer admonished missionary parents.[77]

Missionary children knew their parents felt great trepidation regarding the future, yet the children seemed to possess a better grasp on the domestic economy than either the missionaries or Boston board. Seventeen-year-old James Chamberlain (1835–1911), who worked in the mission depository, ridiculed the board for shipping fully assembled rocking chairs, "while if they had been packed in boxes ten times the amount of freight would have been saved." Chamberlain also noticed when friends Curtis Lyons and Henry Lyman earned "more than $100 per month" as government surveyors, compared to his $100 per year at the missionary depository. "Curtis sent down $1000 the other day to be put at interest for him," Chamberlain wrote his sisters Martha and Maria.[78]

In a particularly resourceful move, Henry Lyman (1835–1904) asked the Hawaiian minister of the interior to appoint his father as land agent for the southern half of Hawai'i. Lyman was too young to hold the position himself but asked his father to use his new position to make the younger Lyman a government surveyor. "This arrangement was perfectly satisfactory to me," Henry wrote, "to the no small discontent of my father, who was not at all pleased with the idea of becoming, even nominally, a government official." Lyman's tale reminds us that parental guilt is a powerful weapon in the hands of a child. "On second thought," Henry noted, "[my father] concluded for my sake to accept the situation, though it involved a compulsory sacrifice of inclination on his part."[79]

Missionary children understood the financial hardships their parents experienced. At the depository Chamberlain observed that there was "hardly a missionary that is not in debt," with "some of them having taken twice their salary in goods and other things." Even though former missionaries Samuel Castle and Amos Cooke charged the missionaries lower prices than native Hawaiians and other foreigners who shopped at the former ABCFM depository, the burgeoning market for Hawaiian goods placed even the Chamberlain family in debt to the store.[80] Missionary children worried about their "duty and privilege" to help aging parents. "I feel that you have a claim upon me. I am your oldest son," Warren Chamberlain (1829–1914) told his father. "Perhaps the King might favor me in some way." Chamberlain was not the only missionary son who hoped for government patronage in establishing a financial future in the islands.[81]

The U.S. Civil War also boosted the Hawaiian economy at a time when many missionary children were entering adulthood. With the Union embargo on Confederate sugar, northern states increased their importation of Hawaiian sugar. In 1860 the Hawaiian Islands contained twelve plantations exporting one and a half million pounds of sugar annually. By 1866 the kingdom possessed thirty-two plantations who together exported nearly eighteen million pounds that year. Missionary children benefited. Former missionaries and successful Honolulu mercantilists Castle and Cooke financed missionary sons Samuel Alexander and Henry Baldwin in the sugar industry. Baldwin's brother Dwight joined former missionary Elias Bond at the Kohala Sugar Plantation. Alexander's brother James began a plantation with their father. Joseph Emerson became plantation manager at Kaneohe, Oahu. Emerson's brother Oliver worked as a plantation overseer before entering college.[82]

Encouraging his parents to begin planting sugar on their land, missionary son Albert Wilcox (1844–1919) became one of the most successful planters in the islands. "Albert has quite a mind to go to cane planting," his mother, Lucy Wilcox, wrote in 1862. Wilcox's brother Edward

(1841–1934) also spent time working on a sugar plantation. "We usually worked till midnight four days in the week. I got $1 a day and board, and $1.00 extra for the night work, making $10.00 a week," Edward Wilcox remembered. "This seemed like *affluence beyond the dreams of avarice*."[83] Their brother George Wilcox attended Yale University in order to study engineering and returned to the islands to build water irrigation systems for sugar plantations.[84] Rufus Anderson proved prophetic in his encouragement to missionary parents in 1849: "As for your *children*, the great field of enterprise now is certainly in the part of the world where you are."[85]

Missionary daughters also entered the changing Hawaiian economy, particularly as teachers. As Maria Whitney (1820–1900) explained in 1878, "While we were connected with the Seminary at Lahainaluna, we received a larger salary from Government than we needed for our support. [We] invested $1,000.00 in the stock of the Sugar Plantation at Kohala, Hawaii, which after more than 12 years of patient waiting, is now paying dividends."[86] In 1870 Anderson noted over thirty missionary daughters employed in the islands.[87]

Missionary daughters also owned land. Although Jean Hobbs concluded in her study of missionary land deeds that "comparatively small areas were left by will to descendants," many children inherited or bought land nonetheless. Jonathan Osorio writes that all but two of the missionaries who remained in Hawai'i after the *Māhele* possessed land. Helen, Elizabeth, and Laura Judd each received lots in Honolulu after their father's death.[88] "Honolulu is becoming a large place. Houses are all the time going up," James Chamberlain wrote his sisters. "There has probably been two hundred or more wood houses put up since you left." At least one peer, Chamberlain noted, had bought one.[89] Sanford Dole (1844–1926) observed that missionary lands "became in later years of great value and enriched their owners."[90]

As Hawaiian-born subjects, missionary children also took political appointments from the Hawaiian government. Joseph Emerson accepted a position with the Hawaiian Government Survey, and Nathaniel Emerson became president of the Hawaiian Board of Health. William Richards Castle and William Neville Armstrong served as attorney generals and

Samuel Mills Damon as minister of finance. Albert Judd and Sanford Dole accepted appointments to the Hawaiian Supreme Court. At least fifteen missionary sons were elected to the national legislature. In 1887 nine of the forty-nine members of the legislature were missionary sons.[91]

At a time when native Hawaiians were watching foreign diseases destroy the indigenous population, it certainly appeared as if the white missionary children had, in the words of Amos Cooke (1851–1931), "multipl[ied] like the Jews in Egypt" and "inherit[ed] the land."[92] English travel writer Isabella Bird noticed the growing discrepancy during her visit to the Hawaiian Islands in 1873. "At Honolulu and Hilo a large proportion of the residents of the upper class are missionaries' children," Bird wrote. "Most of the respectable foreigners on Kauai are either belonging to, or intimately connected with, the Mission families; and they are profusely scattered through Maui and Hawaii in various capacities."[93]

Missionary children ferociously protected their familial legacy— "our inheritance," Sanford Dole called it.[94] With the ascension to the throne of Lot Kamehameha in 1863, the children correctly sensed that native emotions had shifted against American missionary influence. Lot immediately distanced himself from the former American missionaries by refusing to support the constitution they had helped to write and by reinstituting native priests, such as medical *kāhuna*. The missionary children rose to his challenge. "We are the children of the missionary enterprise," Anderson Forbes (1833–88) declared.[95] "It is to us that the Hawaiian nation must look for . . . its advocates, its protectors and defenders," Asa Thurston (1827–59) argued.[96]

Missionary children—now adults—were concerned that the institutions their mothers and fathers had created in partnership with earlier Hawaiian sovereigns were in jeopardy. In 1865, for the first time, no one associated with the ABCFM or HEA served on the Hawaiian Board of Education. The new inspector general of schools, Abraham Fornander, was openly critical of the missionaries.[97] Soon adult missionary children were also calling the Hawaiian legislature "one of the weakest and most corrupt that ever sat in Honolulu."[98]

By the reigns of King Kalākaua in 1874 and Queen Liliʻuokalani in 1891, fortune tellers and mediums, not missionaries, played frequent advisory roles to the Hawaiian monarchy.[99] By the 1880s the term *missionary* had become an epithet. In the words of one missionary son, anyone who "would not bow the knee" to such changes "received the honorable sobriquet of 'missionaries.'"[100] Even more distressing to missionary descendants was King Kalākaua's 1886 revival of the ancient Hawaiian religion. "This was done in order to promote sorcery and bring the nation into political subjection to the king himself as the chief sorcerer," Sereno Bishop protested.[101]

Just as important as defending their parents' religious legacy in the islands were the missionary children's attempts to protect the material inheritance bequeathed by them. Bribery scandals erupting under Kalākaua, and Liliʻuokalani's final attempt to dilute the political weight of white landowners went too far in threatening the missionary descendants' interests in the islands.[102] "In order to safeguard the stability of the Government and its commercial interests," Oliver Emerson (1845–1938) concluded, "a closer relation with the United States was more and more favored."[103] Bishop was blunter: "On account of the commercial necessities of the Islands, nothing can be more certain than that some strong and efficient government must and will be maintained here."[104]

Missionary descendants in Hawaiʻi might not have been as eager to accept the formal power of the United States had it not been for their belief that Americans had abandoned their parents and left the Hawaiian missionary project incomplete. Missionary children's growing calls for U.S. annexation stemmed, in part, from their tenuous relationship with the ABCFM. "The old missionaries were not reinforced by outside aid, and on the shoulders of a native ministry was laid a burden which we can now see was too heavy for it to bear," Samuel Damon (1845–1924) assessed in 1886. "I think there are few who are truly conversant with the real state of affairs on our Islands but will acknowledge the inexpediency of this action."[105]

Missionary children interpreted the ABCFM's move to end its financial support of missionaries in Hawaiʻi very differently from their parents. To their parents, the ability to own private property and pursue individual income allowed better provision for their children. To the children, this

**5.** Sanford B. Dole (1844–1926) and George H. Dole (1842–1912). The Dole brothers were born in the Hawaiian Islands to missionary parents Daniel and Emily Dole. Sanford Dole became the first president of the Hawaiian Republic after leading the revolution against the Hawaiian monarchy. Mission Houses Museum Library.

difficult transition represented an American desertion of their parents and the islands, the effects of which they were left alone to rectify. "These men and women love the fair land of their birth and are not willing to let it return to barbarism," Emerson said of fellow missionary sons and daughters. "Their pride in the institutions which their fathers were enabled to build, spur them on to a studied and careful support of humane and worthy causes which may save their loved native land."[106] American aid, in the form of U.S. trade reciprocity, military protection, and, ultimately, annexation signaled for missionary descendants the rectification of decades of familial pressures.

Missionary children couched their pro-annexation arguments in terms of rescuing the islands from their moral decline and argued that the American churches had not fully done their part. While the ABCFM officially "favored the independence of the Islands," missionary children were not as deferential to the ABCFM position as their parents had been. White missionary children living in the islands were, in the words of one missionary son, "practically unanimous for the overthrow of the monarchy and for annexation to the United States."[107]

### Familial Colonialism and Hawaiian Sovereignty

What missionary parents and their children held in common was an inability to see their struggle as an economic one. "To us they left no heritage of gold, or jewels or land," Albert Lyons (1841–1926) addressed fellow missionary descendants in 1890. "A richer bequest they left us; we inherit the fruits of their work in the material prosperity which the Christian civilization they established here has made possible." Missionary descendants conflated their religious ideals and economic agendas, as had their parents, who argued for more wealth even while denying they sought it. "And how can I better aid the work of the Master than by earning money thus to devote to missionary enterprises which must be maintained by the contributions of Christians?" Lyons asked. After nearly a century of American missionary activity in the Pacific, the question seemed perfectly natural.[108]

While such a distant American frontier implied physical hardship and danger, the health and survival of American missionary children in

Hawai'i were never in question. The average family size of missionary families living in the islands was between 6 and 7 children. Of the 282 mission children born by 1853, only 36 had died in the islands. In fact, Rufus Anderson postulated that the sizeable number of missionary children was due to "the extraordinary healthfulness of the Islands."[109] By contrast, British children born in nineteenth-century India had twice the mortality rate as their peers back home, often succumbing to tropical diseases during their first five years of life. British colonial administrators worried that a permanent white population in India could not survive past the third generation.[110]

American missionary parents instead fixated on the moral education and economic independence of their children.[111] Missionary parents pursued both goals with inordinate fearfulness. "It has always seemed to me," Anderson complained, "that the great enemy of missions directs his chief assaults on the *parental* side of our missionary brethren, as their most assailable point."[112] Missionary children in Hawai'i derived security not only from their parents but also from the *ways* in which their parents addressed the children's needs and the *environments* in which missionary parents told the children they were secure. Missionary children learned to accept Hawaiian lands and political appointments as necessary to securing their own "civilized" place in Hawaiian society. In the case of their economic well-being, missionary children in Hawai'i pursued U.S. annexation as a form of parental protection over the institutions and property their parents had fought long and hard to secure.

The complicated familial relationships of American missionaries and their Hawaiian-born children contextualize the process by which the United States acquired the Hawaiian Islands in 1898. The political and cultural successes of the ABCFM missionaries in the first two decades of their arrival to the islands became monuments to American Protestant influence in the Pacific, which missionary children later sought to protect. The economic gains made by missionary families, the children believed, were made possible by native Hawaiian acceptance of their parents' instruction. The revolution ending the Hawaiian monarchy in 1893 demonstrates the complicated mixture of political, economic, and cultural considerations, not least of which religion played a role.

White missionary children born in the islands viewed their parents as martyrs worthy of continued recognition both in Hawai'i and the United States. In many cases the children conflated their parents' concerns about economic security with their own desires for material success. This sense of entitlement, the missionary descendants argued, was never about them. It was about protecting the legacy of their parents. Missionary children had accepted the normalcy of their parents' spiritual influence among the early Hawaiian monarchs and continued to live in their parents' shadows. In the process missionary children expected land ownership, government offices, and economic opportunity in the islands as their birthright.

American missionaries did not begin their residencies in the islands with an economic agenda, but in their role as parents, with the pressures of parenting clouding their missionary zeal, they taught their children to become colonizers. To their children the missionaries bequeathed the rationale and means to participate in one of the most dramatic periods of U.S. global expansion. The missionary experience in the Hawaiian Islands displays international affairs at the most intimate level. That the first president of the Hawaiian Republic was missionary son Sanford Dole reveals the codependence of religious and economic ideals by which nineteenth-century American missionary families in the Hawaiian Islands determined their support for and participation in the birth of an American empire in the Pacific.

# CHAPTER 2

# Playing with Fire

*White Childhood and Environmental Legacies*
*in Nineteenth-Century Hawai'i*

Come with a whoop, come with a call, come with a good will or not at all. Up the ladder and down the wall, a half-penny roll will serve us all.

English nursery rhyme[1]

In our country, children play "keep house"; and in the same high-sounding but miniature way the grown folk here, with the poor little material of slender territory and meager population, play "empire."

Mark Twain in the Hawaiian Islands (1866)[2]

Missionary children born in the Hawaiian Islands were, like all children, influenced by their environment. But more than just shape the space upon which they played, the Hawaiian Islands formed the missionary children's understanding of natural space. The white children became adults who believed their childhoods had afforded them intimate knowledge of the islands, as well as the authority to enact their environmental agenda on the islands. Their activities had become what Mark Twain called "play[ing] 'empire.'" This chapter explores the relationship between children and the environment in the context of nineteenth-century

American missionary involvement in the Hawaiian Islands, including how early connections to the land influenced adult interactions with the environment. By the twentieth century, missionary children had secured their environmental legacy of colonialism in the Hawaiian Islands.[3]

### Kāma'āina (Land Child)

As scholars of childhood have noted, the material objects a child possesses for play are not as significant as *where* and *with whom* the child plays.[4] For white children in the Hawaiian Islands, isolation from peers and even family members nurtured early and strong attachments to nature. From their earliest memories, missionary children recorded loneliness. Their childhoods of intense separation from social interaction were born out of parental fears as well as geographic realities. Outside of Honolulu on Oahu, where the largest population of ABCFM missionaries resided, missionary families were divided across five islands and seventeen stations. As one missionary son noted, most missionary families "occupied the lonely outstations, where from one year's end to another no white people except themselves . . . were ever seen."[5]

While parents had little control over where they were stationed, missionary fathers and mothers did exert enormous efforts to keep their children from interacting with the indigenous population. The two things that missionary parents most feared were the sexual freedom of indigenous practice and the explicitness of Hawaiian history. The Hawaiian creation story itself began with incest, as sky-father Wākea instituted a religious *kapu* (taboo) that separated him from his wife and half-sister, the earth-mother Papa, in order to have sexual relations with his daughter Ho'ohōkūkalani. Their father-daughter union brought forth the *kalo* plant (the Hawaiian name for the taro plant) and the first Hawaiian high chief, ancestor of the Hawaiian people.[6]

Hawaiians orally recorded and celebrated this genealogical heritage with *meles* (chants) and rituals that allowed married men and women free sexual expression. As Christian convert Samuel Kamakau explained, "The taking of many women as wives was a cause of trouble in old days. Women too took many husbands."[7] Hawaiian children followed suit. As one stunned missionary mother exclaimed, "In all social acts, [children] were taught to be alike skilled with those of adult years."[8]

American missionary families also entered a well-established environmental system based on early Polynesian settlement patterns that favored the clearing of lowland forests in order to cultivate taro, sweet potatoes, yams, and sugarcane. Farmers communally relied upon the natural flow of waters from the heavily forested mountain regions. Volcanic soils abounded in nutrients, and early Polynesian settlers learned to maintain the viability of the soil through terracing. Large mammals, potentially detrimental to maintaining sloping island soil composition, were nonexistent, as was the widespread use of money.[9]

Put off by a social system containing such casual views of sex and industriousness, missionary parents created their own elaborate systems to segregate their children from the Hawaiians, including forbidding their children to learn the language that the missionaries themselves were laboring to transcribe. The parents of Persis and Lucy Thurston, for example, required their children to leave the room whenever a Hawaiian visitor entered the house. "My memory of the house at Waialua is of adobe walls," George Wilcox (1839–1933) wrote, "being shut in by walls that seemed fifteen feet high, but I suppose they were about five feet really."[10] Similarly unable to participate in village life at Kailua, Sereno Bishop grew to dread the "dismal resonance of the tapa-mallets all around the village," an indigenous practice he was forbidden to watch, despite the fact, as native historian David Malo recorded, "tapa was a thing of value," and the women who beat the bark into clothing and rugs "were held to be well off, and were praised for their skill."[11]

Indigenous Hawaiians were familiar with such restrictions. Religious *kapu*, such as men and women eating in separate quarters and abstaining from certain foods retained for the *ali'i*, had dominated the lives of the *maka'āinana* (people) until the death of King Kamehameha I in 1819. Kamehameha's favorite wife Ka'ahumanu and his son and successor Liholiho allowed the restrictions to expire, and U.S. missionaries worked to replace the traditional Hawaiian *kapu* with biblical commandments, as well as New England prescriptions regarding time management, literacy, and agricultural development, such as planting corn and herding goats for milk.[12]

Like their British counterparts in India, U.S. missionaries in the Hawaiian Islands taught their children to denigrate unclean dwellings and unclad natives who slept on mats next to their animals.[13] They also invented new taboos for their own children for fear Hawaiian cultural habits could influence young minds. With numerous native servants and visitors entering missionary homes each day, the pressures upon both parents and children to maintain such restrictions was, according to missionary daughter Ann Eliza Clark (1833–1938), "simply immense if not crushing." Missionary children saw the great lengths their parents undertook to separate them from the indigenous Hawaiians and, in their isolation, grew to despise the natives and their culture.[14]

Part of the missionary children's disdain for indigenous culture stemmed from their frustration over the amount of time their parents spent with Hawaiians. Elizabeth Judd wrote in her journal that her parents' Honolulu kitchen and parlor "always seemed filled with natives."[15] Sophia and Elizabeth Bingham's mother taught two to three hundred native children in a school the Bingham girls were forbidden to attend.[16] Missionary children learned from an early age that their own mothers were not like Hawaiian mothers, who carried their children to work with them and, in the words of David Malo, "nursed their children with the milk of their own breasts."[17] Fathers, too, were noticeably absent. Often traveling around the islands to preach, missionary men left their sons behind. One missionary son pointed out, "It is glorious to die for one's country, but what becomes of the solemn obligation to cherish the wife and educate the children?"[18]

The irony of the missionary *kapu* against their children's interactions with natives is that the missionaries themselves could not maintain them. As in other nineteenth-century colonial contexts, almost all missionary families employed native domestic help. The Thurston family, for example, utilized one man to cultivate *kalo*, their primary food source, and another man to do the washing and bring fresh water

**6.** Mothers and daughters at a Luau-Native Feast, ca. 1900–1910. Library of Congress, Prints and Photographs Division, LC-USZ62-69814.

from ten miles away. They also used a native cook and female natives for sewing and infant care. Some missionary families also relied on native wet nurses.[19]

Missionaries in Hawai'i argued that native labor freed their own time to educate the natives. It was the same argument missionary parents used for eventually sending their children away to attend schools in New England or Punahou boarding school in Honolulu after it opened in 1841. "The missionary mother who is qualified to give her own offspring a thorough education on missionary ground, without calling in the aid of others," missionary Hiram Bingham wrote, "is, or ought to be, qualified to teach a multitude of those whose mothers cannot teach them well at all."[20] The message was clear from the beginning: the most important roles for missionary parents were ones that did not include their children. In response to such "abnormal" childhoods, as one son put it, missionary children turned to the environment, exploring the land and cultivating their fascination with adventure, danger, self-reliance, and independence.[21]

## Playing Empire

For American children born in the Hawaiian Islands, their early tropical environment became, in the words of historian Elliott West, the "original measure for the rest of their lives." In his study of nineteenth-century children growing up on the American frontier, West notes that the environment often divided families as it shaped "ideas of what was possible" among children differently than their parents' own reality.[22]

Nowhere was this more obvious than in parent-child interactions regarding the ocean. Stationed at Hilo, Henry Lyman considered the beach his "principal playground."[23] Although missionary parents generally did not know how to swim and feared the water, missionary children's earliest memories included watching through the groves of coconut trees "the active gambols of the crowd of natives sliding on the great rollers of the surf."[24] Missionary children dove off sixty-foot cliffs into the sea, descended into rat holes to find pools of water thirty-feet deep, and taught themselves to swim by tying gourds around their arms as flotation devices.[25] Part of parental anxieties included the belief that ocean sports encouraged licentious behavior, as Hawaiians tended to swim naked, but some parents adapted to their children's reality. "[Father] could not swim himself, but was very eager to have us learn," George Wilcox remembered.[26]

Missionary daughters, too, fell in love with water. Lucy Thurston and her siblings often traveled half a mile to the seashore to bathe "in the waters of the ocean, with a high sea, and a spring tide."[27] In Honolulu, "few days went by" when Kapena pool "was not visited by at least one member of the family," Elizabeth Judd wrote. "Hidden in the midst of trees . . . we bathed and picnicked to our hearts' content."[28]

Horseback riding also exemplified the independence, rebellion, and blurred gender lines of white children living in the Hawaiian Islands during the nineteenth century. Horses were initially the provenance of Hawaiian royalty, brought aboard successive waves of foreign ships after Captain Cook's arrival to the islands in 1778. Initially designed as gifts to facilitate trade, large mammals altered Hawaiian landscapes. Along with imported cattle, these ungulates scavenged unfenced lands and destroyed crops. By the 1820s, herds of wild cattle had become, in the words of one observer, "immense," and horses became necessary for ranching and herding. These large mammals eventually contributed to island soil erosion and deforestation, as delicate native vegetation in Hawaiian uplands gave way to sturdier, nonnative grasses, and naked soils washed away.[29]

For island children, however, horseback riding became one of the most popular island activities. Henry Whitney (1824–1904) loved Saturday afternoons in Honolulu when everything would shut down early so that as many as a thousand "reckless riders" took free reign of the streets.[30] The seven Gulick brothers, whose father raised colts, "all became expert horsemen."[31] Girls rode alone across the *pali* to visit friends, and those living in Honolulu rode three miles on horseback to attend Punahou. Twice Elizabeth Judd caught her horse in quicksand. "Ah! What is there to compare to our horseback excursions," she exclaimed, "when a party would dash along the road, the very horses dancing in the joy of their existence, while the sun glowed and ocean sparkled, and the mountains in the distance raised their blue heights against the bluer sky!"[32] At Punahou, girls and boys would sneak out together at night to take "tropical moonlight" horseback rides, "galloping eight or ten abreast" through the coconut grove at Waikiki and around Diamond Head, as many as forty students riding together.[33] In this regard, white children in the islands differed from their peers in the United States, who tended to self-segregate their play according to gender upon reaching school age.[34]

Given such excessive independence, missionary sons and daughters in the islands—not unlike other nineteenth-century American children—utilized play as "simple disobedience of society's rules and prescriptions." Whether shedding shoes whenever possible, to the chagrin of their white elders, or simply getting wet and dirty in their outdoor exploits, missionary children knew they were choosing something different than what their parents desired. Within this process of informal play, children "began to realize that theirs was a different world that only they

7. Hawaiian women surfing (late 1860s woodcut). Fear of their children seeing naked Hawaiian swimmers kept many missionary parents away from the water, despite their children's fascination with the native sport. Mission Houses Museum Library.

appreciated."[35] White children in the islands increasingly believed that the natural world around them belonged to them in a way their parents would never understand nor possess. In attempting to explain their feelings to their parents, the children often failed. When John Gulick (1832–1923) begged his father to allow him to become a naturalist, arguing that his love for nature was "undoubtedly implanted by the Creator," Peter Gulick refused, telling his son that all professions were "subordinate" to preaching the gospel.[36]

Instead, missionary children thwarted their parents, who were busy with the natives, in the words of one child, "from daylight to dark," by fully enjoying their years of childhood.[37] Gulick collected thousands of land shells, categorizing 185 different species and writing letters to Charles Darwin about his evolutionary findings. Missionary children living near the ocean fished, carved sailboats, and searched for seashells. In the hills they explored caves and hunted with rifles and lassoes for wild goats, pigs, and cattle. In Hawaiian jungles with trees over one

**8.** Hanapepe Falls, Kauai, ca. 1906–16. Almost all missionary children learned to swim and dive at a young age. Image by R. J. Baker, Library of Congress, Prints and Photographs Division, LC-USZ62-107033.

hundred feet tall, they used swords to hack their way or walked on the tops of tightly woven branches, their feet not even touching the ground.[38]

The children also engaged in cruelty. Unbeknownst to parents, missionary children climbed trees to drop fruits and nuts on Hawaiian heads and even turned to more violent pastimes, beating dogs and torturing cats. Missionary boys hunted for stray cats to kill, writing about their exploits in the school newspaper, the *Punahou Gazette*. "These animals are uncommonly tenacious of life," one Punahou student wrote. "It was hard work I tell you. . . . [I]t seemed as though it would never die."[39] The islands, missionary son Oliver Emerson wrote, were to us "'the call of the wild.'"[40]

Aggressiveness was not unusual in nineteenth-century play. American naturalist John Muir recalled dropping a cat from a roof and visiting the slaughterhouses as a boy. In such independent play, Howard Chudacoff notes, "the feelings of guilt that pervaded transgressions of earlier eras were more absent."[41] In their writings, white children in Hawai'i displayed notions that the islands required aggressive containment. The children also revealed possessiveness for their birth land. Parents and teachers often allowed aggressive jealousies to remain unfettered in isolated island environments, and childish play frequently centered around conquest of land, animals, and natives.

Of all the exploits missionary children undertook, one surpassed them all. Every missionary child wanted to descend into Hawai'i's Kilauea to see the "huge lake, full of bubbling, boiling red lava."[42] Dedicated to Pele, goddess of the volcano, Kilauea held spiritual significance for indigenous Hawaiians, as well for the missionaries. Attributed both with creative and destructive powers, Pele and her volcano had been shrouded in mystery until 1824 when the Hawaiian chiefess Kapi'olani "dramatically and publicly" defied Pele at Kilauea. Declaring her newfound faith in the missionaries' Christian god, Kapi'olani refused to participate in customary Hawaiian prayers and ate the sacred berries growing near the volcano's molten lava, breaking a longstanding religious *kapu*.[43]

Missionary children were aware of Kilauea's significance, and their obsession with it signified a desire to confront their Hawaiian

**9.** Haleakala Crater, Island of Maui, ca. 1930s. Library of Congress, Prints and Photographs Division, LC-USZ62-46889.

environment, as well as the cultural history of the Hawaiian people. Their desire to visit Kilauea also may have signified a self-reliant craving to create a space between themselves and their parents' religion. Just one year before Punahou School opened, the volcano erupted. Lava flowed five miles wide and two hundred feet deep. At night the light from its fire was visible one hundred miles away. Upon visiting the islands in 1866, Mark Twain named Vesuvius "a child's volcano" compared to Kilauea, whose crater was nine miles in circumference and fifteen hundred feet deep.[44] Henry Lyman visited the active volcano at least twelve times as a boy. George Wilcox descended the crater without shoes at age five.[45] Sixteen-year-old Lucy Thurston (1823–41) called Kilauea "awful" yet slept one night just two feet from its active crater.[46] Samuel Chapman Armstrong (1839–93) wrote that Hawaiian volcanoes made "all the art galleries in the world seem trifling."[47]

Missionary children grew to love the diversity and grandeur of their natural surroundings, as well as the difficulty of their conquest. In the midst of conflicting social restrictions and geographic isolation, what Elizabeth Judd called "the contrast of the dark tropical night and the adventuresome times," missionary children found identity in the land of their childhood.[48] "Children of Hawaii," Ellen Armstrong (1844–1924) called herself and her white peers.[49]

### We Are the Anglo-Hawaiians

Punahou School's opening in 1841 coincided with other important changes occurring in the islands. The decline of the Hawaiian sandalwood (*Santalum*) trade by the 1830s—the result of its over extraction and virtual extinction in the islands—meant the kingdom needed new export crops to continue its trade relationships with the United States and Europe, as well as to demonstrate its viable status as an independent nation. Increasing numbers of whaling ships were stopping in the islands, eager to purchase supplies from the kingdom. With the discovery of gold in California in the late 1840s, Hawai'i became California's nearest trading partner and principal supplier of agricultural and manufactured goods. Under the advisement of former missionaries and other foreigners, Kauikeaouli (King Kamehameha III) determined that selling private property to foreign investors and encouraging agricultural development among the Hawaiian people were vital to maintaining an independent economy.[50] "The prosperity of the Islands and their altered position relatively to Oregon and California, require a greatly increased cultivation of the soil, which will not be possible without the aid of foreign capital and labor," the king told the legislature in 1850.[51] "It is proper to sell small farms to natives and also to foreign subjects, and let them cultivate alike, that the skilful may instruct the ignorant in the work," the legislature decreed.[52]

With the constant influx of foreigners arriving to take advantage of these changes, many white children believed the Hawaiian people to be outmatched. They saw the devastation that imported smallpox, measles, and whooping cough had caused the indigenous population.[53]

Native Hawaiians referred to such illnesses as becoming "shippy," in reference to the importation of diseases.[54] One Punahou student noted, "As civilization increases, civilized custom and habits are introduced, and with these blessings, sickness and disease."[55] Historian David Igler has argued that infectious diseases in the islands were exceptionally damaging because they occurred in "wave after wave," the result of increasing commercial trade.[56]

Missionary children believed that as "Anglo-Hawaiians" they could work together for the betterment of their nation.[57] By midcentury school-age missionary children were discussing in Punahou essays and student newspapers the material and political benefits of remaining in the islands. "The Hawaiians as a *nation* are doomed," missionary son Samuel Alexander (1836–1904) declared.[58] "Whatever may be the destiny of the *native* race," Hiram Bingham Jr. (1831–1908) argued, "the very strength of this nation, mental, moral and physical, shall, for many ages, lie in the descendants of the American Protestant Missionaries."[59] By their teenage years, missionary descendants clearly had formed what sociologists have termed a "mini society." Their status as white, Hawaiian-born minorities defined their membership in a Hawaiian subculture in which the "boundaries of play territory" were the entire Hawaiian Islands.[60]

### Nā Hānai (The Foster Children)

We are "Hawaiians," Samuel Alexander stated in 1864, after living nearly thirty years in the islands.[61] Yet the aloofness with which missionary children judged humanity can be seen in their relentless drive for control.[62] By the time they reached adulthood, this ambition had merged with great opportunity. Nowhere was this more evident than in the burgeoning sugar industry. Although the sugar boom temporarily subsided after the Civil War, and some plantations even failed, Hawaiian sugar planters secured their sugar market through trade reciprocity with the United States in 1876 and brought vast new lands under cultivation through the development of sophisticated irrigation systems. Between 1867 and 1920, Hawaiian lands under sugar cultivation increased from 10,000 acres to 236,000 acres.[63]

Former missionaries Samuel Castle and Amos Cooke financed the most successful sugar ventures. Samuel Alexander and Henry Baldwin learned how to plant sugar with their missionary fathers, and together organized the Haleakala Sugar Company in 1860.[64] With financing from Castle & Cooke, Alexander and Baldwin started additional sugar plantations and engineered the first irrigation ditch to move water from wet to dry lands. With a government license the Hamakua Ditch took water from six streams on government lands to Alexander and Baldwin's private plantation.[65] One hundred years later their descendants remained among the largest landowners in the islands. Charles Cooke joined his father's investment firm and acquired the Bank of Hawaii, large shares in numerous plantations, and Moloka'i Ranch. Organizing Charles M. Cooke, Ltd. in 1899, Cooke hoped to keep these assets together after his death. As late as the mid-twentieth century, family members continued to represent the only shareholders in the holding company.[66]

Missionary sons also explored economic opportunities on nearby guano islands, as the Hawaiian sugar boom coincided with the expansion of nitrate fertilizers. Charles Judd and his father were the earliest to get involved in the nitrate trade, advising the American Guano Company on guano deposits in the central Pacific Ocean. The Judds organized Hawaiian labor gangs to work on Baker and Jarvis Islands, and Judd recruited peers Levi Chamberlain, George Wilcox, and members of the Alexander and Emerson families to manage native labor. Hawaiian laborers plotted to murder George Wilcox for his abusive management, but Wilcox survived to later organize the Pacific Guano and Fertilizer Company.[67]

Most importantly, missionary descendants utilized their extensive peer network to wrest control from the Hawaiian monarchy in 1893 and pursue U.S. annexation. Determined to maintain the gains they and their parents had made in the islands since the 1820s, missionary children reacted swiftly to Queen Lili'uokalani's efforts to dilute their political influence by issuing a new constitution. In overthrowing the queen and turning to the United States, missionary descendants rooted their arguments for annexation in the environment.

As American men began to fear their loss of masculinity amid developed, urban landscapes and to turn to bodybuilding and football as

**10.** A sugar cane plantation, Oahu, ca. 1906–16. Library of Congress, Prints and Photographs Division, LC-USZ62-98701.

mechanisms to revitalize their manhood, missionary descendants in the islands bolstered their pro-annexation arguments by arguing they represented evolution at its best.[68] "As a rule, European colonies in the tropics have hitherto been failures in this vital point of maintaining manhood and virtue," Sereno Bishop stated in 1872. "So far as I know, [our] group presents the only exception to this rule among all white communities in the tropics." Hawaiian-born whites believed their island childhoods fitted them for leadership both within the islands and American society.[69]

With the overthrow of the Hawaiian monarchy and establishment of a constitutional republic, descendants of the ABCFM pointed to their own successes in the islands as testament to the continued vitality of Anglo-Saxon civilization, as well as to the ease with which the islands might be absorbed by the United States. The Darwinian struggle in the Hawaiian Islands had been won, the missionary descendants argued, by the Anglo-Hawaiian community. In the midst of the "splendid" 1898 Spanish-American War—as American emotions flew high—the U.S. Congress finally agreed.[70]

## John Thomas Gulick (1832-1923)

John Thomas Gulick exemplified the sense of exploration, adventure, and fearlessness that characterized the childhoods of white missionary children in Hawai'i. Gulick was born on the island of Hawai'i, and his first memory was of his fascination with the sea creatures washing on shore outside his home. Gulick's freedom to explore the beaches did not last long. From age three to five, Gulick remained isolated from nearly all physical contact, kept in a dark room during daylight by his parents in their attempt to cure him of his constant eye infections.[71]

Gulick suffered his entire life from poor eyesight and endured numerous bouts of near blindness that required long periods of rest. Much later Gulick would be diagnosed with kidney problems. When Peter and Fanny Gulick finally released their son from his prison, Gulick was "nearly blind from the growth of a white film over each eye." He would later write that he saw the world as if for the first time: "The trees, the birds, the insects, were all strange interests for me."[72] Gulick's tendency toward solitude and his love for nature remained constants the rest of his life.

Gulick's missionary parents forbade their eight children any communication with native Hawaiians until the siblings were forced to ride an interisland schooner with Hawaiians in 1841. Gulick and his brothers were returning home from Punahou. "They went with none but native company, a thing which we never before permitted, and may never repeat," Fanny Gulick wrote, "but there seemed no alternative."[73]

Gulick sporadically attended Punahou School due to his poor health. Punahou students shared with Gulick an attraction to the outdoors, but Gulick infused an intellectual component into their understanding of the natural world. Gulick devoured Darwin's *Voyage of the Beagle* and researched natural philosophy, a topic his brother introduced to him after returning home from college in the United States. "A vast field of thought and study has within a few days been rapidly opening to my view," John wrote in his journal in 1852. "It is the study of God's character, as displayed in his stupendous works . . . and in connection with this, the study of the relations that I sustain to my fellow creatures on earth."[74]

Gulick's health did not deter him from seeking adventure. In May 1848, during one absence from school, Gulick convinced his parents to allow him to travel to Oregon to visit the Congregationalist mission, still recovering from the deaths of Marcus and Narcissa Whitman the previous winter. Hearing rumors of gold, Gulick soon made his way from Oregon to California, becoming a "forty-niner." Gulick struck gold. When he finally returned to the islands, Gulick gave the money he had saved to his father, who promptly invested it in ranchland. The investment helped pay college tuition for John and several brothers. Years later Gulick discovered his father had put the ranch in the younger Gulick's name. John Gulick immediately rented the land for sugar production and retired.[75]

As a child Gulick had long been fascinated with the indigenous land snails—*Achatinellae*—that covered the Hawaiian trees and hills. After returning from California Gulick traveled the islands collecting shells. "I asked myself whether I was not acting foolishly in letting shells and other natural objects defer my researches," Gulick wrote. Fellow Punahou students helped Gulick, roaming Oahu and bringing him thousands of shells.[76]

Soon after graduating from Williams College in 1859, Gulick read Darwin's *Origin of Species*. "Many good people of that day were startled and dumbfounded at his ideas of the growth of the living world, but my mind was ripe for his illuminating interpretation of nature," Gulick recalled.[77] Unfortunately, Peter Gulick did not share his son's respect for science. Throughout his stay in the United States, Gulick attempted to obtain his father's blessing in pursuing a scientific career. His father would not give it. All professions were "subordinate" to preaching and publishing the gospel. At his father's insistence, Gulick attended a seminary and decided to pursue missionary activity in Japan.[78]

Gulick had been amazed at Japanese ambassador Shimmi Masaoki's parade up Broadway in 1860 to sign a treaty opening the island nation to U.S. trade. Gulick was one of a half million New York spectators who turned out to watch the ambassador's entourage. Only several years before, in 1854, Commodore Perry had forced the Tokugawa regime to acknowledge the realities of nineteenth-century U.S. power. Japan had been closed to most outside influences for centuries. Gulick was fascinated by the thought of "opening communication with that interesting people." He decided to wait in California for the opportunity to visit the island nation. Because few ships yet traveled to Japan, Gulick waited six months. Eventually he heard that the newly appointed U.S. minister to Japan, Robert Pruyn, had chartered a ship. Gulick secured passage with the minister's party and arrived in Japan in 1862.[79]

The Japan Gulick met was engulfed in forced transformation and violent reaction. Only a handful of Christian missionaries lived in Japan, and they were strictly forbidden to proselytize. Instead they subverted the nation's customs and laws by introducing secular, Western-style education and infusing it with Christian symbols and meanings. Gulick recorded that the Japanese people were receptive to the new learning. However, the strong, negative reaction of the daimyos (provincial rulers) and samurai (warriors) to the Tokugawa shogun's (military ruler) weakness toward foreigners had caused internal upheaval.[80]

Gulick lived in Japan during much of the violence, recording the cultural abuses and racial prejudices of fellow Westerners. On September 14, 1862, one high-level daimyo and his samurai traveling from Edo (Tokyo) to Kagoshima met with an English riding party coming in the opposite direction. "These English people probably did not know that they were expected either to go off on some branch road, or to dismount and uncover their heads when the prince passed," Gulick wrote. "They remained on their horses riding on one side of the road." Samurai immediately killed one man and wounded two others. They knocked the hat off a woman in the party, trying to decapitate her with their swords. Gulick recorded: "The English government demanded $500,000 indemnity which was not granted, until in August 1863 Kagoshima was bombarded and destroyed by British warships. The *daimyo* and other leaders . . . from that day became advocates of the policy of studying the European methods of war, and of organizing the defense of Japan on that line."[81]

Despite the periodic attacks on American and British legations, Gulick stayed. He also took photographs, including some of the earliest pictures ever taken in Japan's capital city, Edo. Gulick photographed streets and temples and several officials, including a *yakunin* (two-sword samurai). Entrance into Edo was by Japanese invitation only, and Gulick's photographs translated Japanese culture for Western foreigners, just as his parents had translated the Hawaiian language for American missionaries. By the 1860s the ABCFM did not have the financial resources to begin a mission in Japan. The Civil War had ravaged its ability to unite donors in an international cause. Without the board's permission to stay in Japan, Gulick headed to China instead.[82]

In China Gulick followed his parents' missionary example. With ABCFM support Gulick learned Mandarin and traveled to Kalgan, 140 miles northwest of Beijing. For ten years Gulick and his English wife, Emily De La Cour, whom he had met in Hong Kong, visited Mongolian villages and taught children to read Chinese. "It will be of no use to send out men who shrink from a rough and somewhat lonely life," Gulick wrote the ABCFM board.[83] When Emily Gulick and their baby died in childbirth while seeking medical care in Japan, John Gulick decided to remain in the island nation for the next twenty-four years. By then the ABCFM had established a presence in Japan. Gulick married fellow Congregationalist missionary Frances Stevens and taught biology in a Congregationalist missionary school.[84]

Throughout his missionary endeavors Gulick retained his deep, personal interest in natural science, publishing articles on Hawaiian land shells and evolution. An article he published in *Nature* in 1872 allowed Gulick an introduction to Charles Darwin during a trip to London. "I read your article with the greatest possible interest and admiration," Darwin wrote Gulick.[85]

Gulick's solitary and intellectual nature perhaps influenced his seeming distance from the native populations with whom he worked. Despite writing of Chinese and Japanese friends in his handwritten memoir, he mentions none by name. Instead, Gulick related to people through teaching and writing about biology. Gulick spent much of his adult life attempting to reconcile the evolutionary science he observed in the Hawaiian Islands and the Christian faith he accepted as a child. Gulick believed that the Hawaiian land snails he had studied as a young man demonstrated the principle of evolution by isolation. Although he used the term *species* somewhat loosely, Gulick believed he had categorized over 180 different species of snails, some incapable of interbreeding. Gulick noted that under the same environmental conditions in the Hawaiian Islands, the evolution of snails proved that "there is more happening in evolution than the factors discovered by Darwin can account for."[86] Gulick believed this diversity was "due to release from the standardizing effect of the strenuous competition on continents, and to the increased opportunities to take up new ways of life."[87]

Gulick termed his discoveries *habitudinal* evolution and spent the rest of his life trying to discern the social implications of human isolation and diversity. He also attempted to reconcile his parents' infiltration of Hawaiian culture and his own forceful entry into Japanese and Chinese civilizations. "In biological evolution a new type has influence only as its offspring multiply to the exclusion of other types," Gulick wrote, "but in rational evolution a new character may propagate itself by transforming other types into more or less conformity to its own standards without any infusion of new blood. This is the method of Christ's influence on the world."[88] Choice, even among the lowest snail, suggested that "some future day mankind will execute intelligent plans for influencing its own evolution." Genetics, Gulick wrote in 1907, hid the "secrets of biology."[89]

Gulick spent his last two decades back in the Hawaiian Islands, deconstructing the concept of nationalism using the theory of evolution. For Gulick, who was raised in Hawai'i and lived in Japan, China, and the United States, the question was personal. Gulick believed citizenship was global and international socialism inevitable. Gulick demanded an international response to exploitation, overproduction, waste, and artistic and scientific ignorance. "The socialists are the only political party seeking to attain any of these ends," he wrote. In 1907 Gulick founded the Hawaiian branch of the American Socialist Party.[90]

Gulick's desire to use his Hawaiian and American educations—as well as racial privilege—to influence political, economic, and social conditions throughout the world was no different from the efforts of other missionary children born in the Hawaiian Islands. In Gulick one sees the influence of the islands as an inescapable environmental force propelling him forward and back again.

11. John T. Gulick, 1858. Mission Houses Museum Library.

White missionary children presided over some of the most dramatic environmental changes occurring in the Hawaiian Islands during the nineteenth century. Gone were the *ahupua'a* of traditional Hawaiian society, land grants protecting communal use and water rights from the uplands to the sea. Like the early Hawaiian forests, where ranches and plantations now stood, they had eroded away under decades of legislative and judicial decisions. Industry and international commerce supplanted them.[91] Whereas on square mile of taro could feed over fifteen thousand Hawaiians, one hundred acres of sugar cane required one million gallons a day of irrigated water.[92] As anthropologist Carol MacLennan notes, "Cane sugar production was probably the first true industry of the modern era." Cut cane required immediate milling, and plantations became efficient by bringing field and mill together into one enterprise, which ultimately incorporated transportation, roads, harbors, and shipping for sale overseas.[93]

Yet missionary descendants believed the islands—their topography and geography—had made them who they were. In the absence of a material and social culture, missionary children in the Hawaiian Islands turned to the environment for a sense of identity and fulfillment. "The senses claim Hawaii," explained missionary son Joseph Cooke (1838–79).[94] In nature, John Gulick believed, one obtained "life, pleasure and instruction."[95] Under the stars, another missionary child noted, "he felt himself no longer entirely alone."[96]

As psychologist Alison Gopnik notes, childhood play is both meaningful to children and significant to society: "When we become adults we put all that we've learned and imagined to use."[97] For the white children born to American parents in nineteenth-century Hawai'i, nature became their parent, but they became its master. "Nature is full of antagonistic forces," Andrews argued, "and these are always paired off, and ready to join battle at any provocation."[98] In the end, the missionary children's desire to control the *'āina* (land), which culminated in political revolution, grew out of the children's disproportionate sense of self-reliance, born from a dearth of personal engagements with others, as well as a

**12.** Taro patch, Hawaiian Islands, ca. 1908. By the early nineteenth century, native Hawaiians had learned to cultivate over three hundred varieties of taro on *ahupuaʻa,* the triangle-like wedges that spread from the mountains to the sea. The penalty for wasting water in one's *ahupuaʻa* was death. See Levine, "Lessons from the Taro Patch." Library of Congress, Prints and Photographs Division, LC-USZ62-113415.

sense of rebellion toward the culture and people who, the children believed, had forced their isolation.[99]

Nineteenth-century missionary children in Hawai'i encountered amazing ecological experiences, which few other white children at the time ever would. Yet those missionary children who remained in the Hawaiian Islands—with few exceptions—had little faith in the Hawaiian people or culture.[100] The missionary children had been taught to distrust racial difference and fear acculturation into nonwhite populations. Perhaps the children also desired to prove to themselves that they represented a worthy race. As missionary son William Smith (1848–1929) noted in 1882, missionary parents had made the "sacrifice of family life" and chose the indigenous people instead.[101] This sense of abandonment allowed missionary children to explore places few Americans or Europeans had ever seen. Yet the same independence and insecurities that propelled missionary children toward environmental exploration also inflicted them. Many simply incorporated the tension into the way they understood the world. Their views, as indigenous populations would increasingly discover, coexisted easily with the growing number of nineteenth-century voices who advocated a "white man's burden" of economic exploitation, colonial administration, and suppression of native dissent.

CHAPTER 3

# Schooling Power

*Teaching Anglo–Civic Duty in the Hawaiian Islands, 1841–53*

There's a neat little clock—in the schoolroom it stands, and it points to the time with its two little hands. And may we, like the clock, keep a face clean and bright, with hands ever ready to do what is right.

English nursery rhyme[1]

In the great mansion for men upon earth, we occupy a nursery room, where children may luxuriate and grow into strength.

Missionary son Robert Andrews (Hawaiian Islands, 1865)[2]

Designed to allow American missionary parents in the Hawaiian Islands to avoid sending their children on the six-month voyage around Cape Horn to New England preparatory schools, Punahou School, established outside Honolulu in 1841, accomplished much more than the missionaries could possibly imagine. While Punahou School may have begun as an isolated boarding school for the white children of American Protestant missionaries, Punahou bequeathed a complicated legacy of Anglo-Protestant influence both in the islands and abroad. By combining religious, moral, industrial, and classical training, teachers at Punahou sought to prepare their graduates for leadership positions

within the Hawaiian kingdom. Punahou parents also hoped to transfer the American heritage they had left behind to their children, as
preparation for the children's inevitable journey to the United States
to attend Congregational and Presbyterian colleges and seminaries.

As parents and teachers desired, Punahou was at its heart a religious
institution, yet its initial practice of racial segregation complicated the
white children's practical application of Christianity in the islands and
created tensions between the Anglo-American and indigenous Hawaiian
communities. The closed society within which early Punahou students
learned also created an environment that allowed the children, through
extensive peer networks, to appropriate their schooling for the unique
nineteenth-century historical context in which they lived and against
which they ultimately rebelled. In 1893 Punahou graduates demonstrated the full impact of their missionary education, devising a political
agenda based upon their moral and religious upbringing, a program
that included the revolutionary overthrow of the Hawaiian monarchy.

### Birthing a School

The first American missionaries to arrive in the Hawaiian Islands in 1820
encountered a kingdom very different from the Protestant New England
townships they left behind. Yet the missionaries quickly realized that
long-held Hawaiian customs were not easy to overthrow, and protecting
their children from a "heathen" culture while providing them with an
education became missionary parents' paramount concern. Not only did
parents wish to segregate their children from the Hawaiian language,
which if understood by their children might introduce them to idolatry and promiscuity, but parents also wished their children, especially
their sons, to be prepared to follow in their own footsteps. The ABCFM
expected its missionaries to have college and seminary training, including the ability to translate the Bible from its original Hebrew and Greek
languages, and most ABCFM missionaries held advanced degrees from
New England universities, including Harvard, Yale, and Princeton.[3]

In the mission's first twenty years, these parental considerations,
coupled with the missionaries' unwillingness to be distracted from their
own labors among the Hawaiian people, led to heartbreaking familial

separations. Missionary parents routinely shipped children as young as five years old back to the United States to live among relatives and donors and receive an American education. Many of these children traveled the six-month voyage alone. Some never saw their parents again. With dubious reports of student success reaching them from the United States, missionary parents, by the 1840s, abandoned this practice. In 1841 the parents instead developed a piece of land Oahu governor Boki had gifted them into a boarding school. The school, named Punahou (fresh spring), sat two miles outside the expanding boundaries of Honolulu. Missionary parents convinced new American missionary arrivals Daniel and Emily Dole to serve as principal and teachers to its first class of thirty-four students, including nineteen boarders.[4]

## Punahou-hoe-hoe

From the outset missionary parents demanded Punahou teachers provide their children with superior religious and moral instruction while preparing them to enter elite colleges in the United States. In the early years Punahou teachers attacked these lofty goals through embracing industrial education. In 1844 missionaries William and Mary Rice arrived at the school to help Daniel Dole. As Mary Rice later explained, Punahou was a school that "was intended to be one for manual labor."[5] Over the next ten years, William Rice instructed Punahou boarders in raising *kalo*, sweet potatoes, corn, beans, bananas, and melons. As one missionary parent wrote in 1842, "We trust [our children's] physical, as well as mental powers, may be properly developed."[6]

This educative pedagogy was based upon a simple reality: Punahou needed to control its costs through requiring student boarders to maintain the school. Punahou boarders provided for their own meals by planting, working, and harvesting the school's fields. The results were mixed. "Nothing in their temporal concerns gives me so much uneasiness as the scantiness of their food at Punahou," Abner Wilcox wrote his wife in 1850 about their sons at Punahou. Parents noticed their children had lost weight and often complained of hunger. Yet few parents wanted to jeopardize the school's existence: "Probably you had better say nothing about all this," Wilcox concluded.[7]

For missionary parents, making a New England education affordable in the islands required manual labor and served as an example of agrarian discipline to the indigenous Hawaiian population to whom missionaries hoped to impart agricultural training. For missionary children, the results could be damaging. Student John Gulick, who attended Punahou during the 1840s and 1850s, experienced a physical breakdown due, he later believed, to "the unduly Spartan attitude which his surroundings inculcated." Required to ring the rising bell for fieldwork without an alarm clock, Gulick "went through unnumbered hours of wakefulness for fear that he might accidentally oversleep." In 1846 Gulick withdrew from school due to his poor health, attending only intermittently during the next eight years.[8]

Students called their school "Punahou-hoe-hoe."[9] Rising before daylight, students hoed weeds in the fields until seven in the morning and again for an hour or two after supper until they could see at least two stars. After gathering their own water and changing clothes, students would study until bedtime at nine.[10] Punahou students attempted to adapt to the rationale of their elders and the rigors of their schedule. "If you wish to be happy, keep busy," declared the student-authored *Punahou Gazette* in 1848.[11] "One way to promote happiness is to be industrious," a female student explained in the *Weekly Star*.[12]

What parents and teachers deemed the virtues of an industrious life was evident in Punahou student compositions. The *Punahou Gazette*, running from 1848 to 1852, was a weekly newspaper students published and read publicly every Thursday afternoon. Students also issued the *Critic*, a weekly publication criticizing the *Gazette*. In 1852 the *Weekly Star* replaced both newspapers by combining contributions and criticism in one issue. The preserved newspapers, meticulously copied by hand for consumption among the student body, provide insight into the minds of the young missionary children, as well as the nature of their education. The extent to which missionary habits were transferred to their children, in the midst of an indigenous culture often at odds with these values, demonstrates the success of Punahou as a colonial institution.[13] By keeping busy "the mind is occupied, and we cannot spare time for unpleasant feeling," the *Weekly Star* reporter concluded.[14] Not all observers agreed with such pedagogy. "We are happy all day long," noted an old native woman, "not like white people, happy one moment, gloomy another."[15]

### Dichotomies of Island Learning

In fact moral and religious instruction at Punahou revolved almost exclusively around separating American values from indigenous Hawaiian practice. Time or, more specifically, not wasting one's time, was a constant theme at Punahou during the 1840s and 1850s. While manual labor was necessary for the functioning of the school, parents and teachers stressed to their children that developing industrious minds was the most important responsibility in which missionary children were to engage their time. As one young scholar explained, "'Knowledge is power,'—and the more you have of it, the better."[16]

Yet all around them Punahou children witnessed an indigenous culture tuned to the natural rhythm of the islands and unmoved by the demands of the clock. Punahou teachers attempted to address this dichotomy by contrasting Hawaiian and American cultural practices and erasing any conflict missionary children may have felt about their station in the islands. In reality, Punahou turned out an odd mix of stern instruction in an unorthodox environment.

The school building itself was constructed in island fashion, a one-story, E-shaped adobe structure about two hundred feet in length. Each wing opened into a courtyard surrounded by verandahs. The building was, according to one observer, "purely a native product."[17] The treeless plain between Honolulu and the school allowed an unobstructed view of the ocean. Mountains were the children's backyard. Horseback riding, caving, hiking, and swimming competed for the students' attentions, and weekends were filled with such pursuits. "Children who are kept at continued application to any kind of employment can never enjoy that sprightliness and vigor, which is one of the chief indications of health," a young contributor to the *Gazette* wrote, arguing for more free time. "Their ability to study is diminished." Punahou students learned that securing beloved native pastimes, such as swimming, required utilizing exclusively Anglo-American arguments.[18]

In addition to the distractions of its geographic setting, Punahou's amenities sharply contrasted with parental and teacher messages of cleanliness. Being sent away from the dining room table for one's dirtiness may have seemed unfair to Punahou boarders, since the bathing pond had a foot of mud on its shallow bottom. Students would stir up the water until it was black. "The result of such a state of matters," explained one student, is that "he who bathes [does] not derive very much benefit from it."[19] Student newspapers frequently complained about the bathing pond, a source of stress for some children whose parents had long taught them to despise the levels of cleanliness found in indigenous homes. Punahou living, in reality, had more in common with the "dirty kanaka," in the words of one student, than with the New England standards their parents carried to the islands.[20]

Punahou also decried nineteenth-century American gender roles. Punahou girls and boys spent much more time together in educational pursuits than many midcentury, middle-class youth in the United States.[21] Girls who did not board at Punahou rode their horses to school. Girls served as newspaper editors and contributors and studied Greek. Boys took drawing and music classes. And despite the school's separate aims to prepare boys to "enjoy the privileges of a college and to study any of the learned professions" and to train girls "for the highest usefulness in whatever station Divine Providence may place," Dole supplemented this more meager agenda for females by teaching Punahou girls to "render themselves independent of the assistance of others."[22] In this way Punahou School defied educational gender norms in the United States and contributed to the development of the missionary daughters' pronounced self-assuredness, a confidence seemingly disproportionate to their white minority status within the Hawaiian Kingdom.

Close proximity between genders and extended time away from parental supervision led to peer bonding that often bridged the Puritan gender divide. Punahou girls and boys together visited volcanoes, explored the wilderness, rode horseback around Diamond Head, and visited Waikiki beach. Thirty-four missionary children eventually married each other.[23]

Upon one gender question Punahou boys remained decidedly ortho-dox: women should play no political role in civic life. The Punahou Debating Society attacked the question in the early 1850s, concluding that women were too busy in their domestic sphere to "meddle with politics." Furthermore, the young debaters agreed, the biblical curse precluded a woman from governing a man.[24] Only one male student voted in favor of granting women political rights, and it appears no girls were invited to participate in the debate. In this respect Punahou's gender training mirrored New England values rather than its Hawaiian environment, a strong testament to the influence of missionary teach-ers and parents. The most influential Hawaiian premiers, since the founding of the Hawaiian kingdom, had all been women, and indige-nous women prominently served in the House of Nobles. In 1840, for example, five women sat in the upper chamber. Despite these powerful female examples, the monarch who missionary descendants eventually overthrew was also a woman.[25]

Proximity among Punahou students also stretched across age. Puna-hou's boarding arrangement meant children ranging from ages five to seventeen, and occasionally older, were required to interact as a family, the older students teaching the younger ones and helping them navi-gate critical childhood years away from home. Reality proved crueler. Students repeatedly reminded each other in their newspapers to be kind to younger students. Ignoring the feelings of younger children, according to the *Gazette*, is "frequent here."[26] Daniel Dole once admitted that he "dreaded" a new scholar arriving at Punahou, "knowing the seasoning he was sure to go through despite our utmost vigilance."[27] What parents hoped would be a safe haven for their children in the islands was, according to at least one graduate, a harsher experience than arriving alone in the United States for the first time. Bullying and cruelty at Punahou disrupted parental hopes that peer relationships would adequately supplement the missionary family back home. Instead peer culture at Punahou became an independent force pulling on children in new and, ultimately, political ways.[28]

Perhaps the greatest dichotomy in student learning at Punahou was the persistent loneliness that attacked some students, despite their parents' hopes that keeping their children in the islands would spare them the difficulties of traveling to and studying in the United States. Missionary children in the Hawaiian Islands often suffered extreme emotional distress from prolonged family separations. Henry Lyman, who attended the school from 1846 to 1853, recalled the first time he visited home: "I could only clasp my mother's neck, and weep like an infant in her arms."[29] Orramel Gulick (1830–1923), a contemporary of Lyman, reported home to his mother, "I puke once in a while."[30] Gulick's younger brother Charles died of bulimia in 1854.[31] One female student died of a "lingering illness," perhaps an eating disorder, despite her Punahou teachers' daily commands that she loosen her corset.[32] A female eating disorder would not have been unusual. Missionary Elizabeth Edwards Bishop starved herself to death in 1828, due to an extreme curvature of the spine that made eating painful. Despite the pleas of fellow missionaries, Bishop continued to restrict her diet in an attempt to manage her pain. One lonely student lamented in a school essay, "I once had a happy home."[33]

Loneliness among the scholars also was enhanced by dislike of their teachers. The anticipation of seeing school friends after vacations was, in the words of one student, always "mingled somewhat with the fear of Mr. Dole."[34] Dole, one biographer noted, "made it a point never to spare the rod."[35] Also a firm believer in corporal punishment, teacher Marcia Smith was known for "great physical strength."[36] Ann Eliza Clark remembered, "Her punishments were numerous and frequently applied, and her memory is indelibly stamped on the minds of all those who have enjoyed her instructions." So severe were her memories that Clark, who attended Punahou for only one year, wrote, "I cannot think of her and of those days calmly."[37]

Despite student complaints Punahou School was doing something right, even under Dole, who retired in 1855. Punahou graduates were receiving high honors in U.S. colleges, and even a few American children were moving to Honolulu to attend the school. By 1858 the school had close to eighty pupils. A traveler sighting Honolulu from her ship asked if the city was Punahou.[38] "I feel safe in saying that no school equal, on the whole, to [Punahou] is to be found west of the Alleghenies,"

**13.** Hawaiian children in front of a grass house. Missionary children were not allowed to attend their parents' schools for native Hawaiians. Instead the white children were segregated from the Hawaiian culture and taught to devalue Hawaiian practice. Mission Houses Museum Library.

boasted William Alexander (1833–1913), who left Punahou in 1849 to attend Yale University. Graduating second in his class at Yale, Alexander asserted, "Only in New England would [Punahou] find a few rivals."[39]

More importantly to parents, Punahou students were inheriting the cultural standards of their New England–born elders and preparing themselves for entry into the United States. Few parents in the 1840s and early 1850s saw a future for their children in the Hawaiian Islands and trusted Punahou to make their children's transition into American culture seamless. Taught by their nineteenth-century American primers, Punahou students believed that deportment constituted character. Biting one's nails, swearing, lying, and stealing were bad habits one formed in childhood, just as Sabbath keeping, Bible reading, and prayer were necessary for lifelong success. Gambling, billiards, and theater made the list of "don'ts," as did saying *don't, can't,* and *won't.*[40] As one student attested, "A person's character may often be known by the language he uses."[41]

Most importantly, missionary children learned that filial obedience was necessary for receiving love. "God loves obedient children, but those who are disobedient he does not love," one child summarized. When differences between missionary parents and their indigenous hosts arose, it was clear whose side missionary children were expected to take.[42]

## Raising Race

From their earliest memories missionary children were taught to distrust native Hawaiians. Parents built *kapu* yards within which children played, and from which indigenous people were forbidden. In some missionary homes natives were required to leave the room whenever a child entered. Parents spoke only English to their children. Under no circumstances were missionary children allowed to attend school or fraternize with indigenous children. As a result Punahou School refused to admit indigenous children until 1852, more than a decade after the school's founding.[43] Missionary Dwight Baldwin voiced what nineteenth-century American missionary parents in the Hawaiian Islands all believed: "We must give a knowledge of the world . . . even while we are afraid to have them associate with any of the society around us."[44]

Punahou teachers juxtaposed indigenous Hawaiians to the white Americans whenever refining their lessons of proper industry and use of time. Student papers attest to teacher success. Numerous school compositions contrasted missionary diligence with the dreaded "Kanaka fever." As one student wrote, the illness, also known as "Lazy fever," could only be cured by "Dr. Industry" or "Dr. Birch."[45] Advocating corporal punishment for indigenous practice, Punahou students transferred their own transgressions against Anglo-Protestant norms onto native Hawaiians. In an essay entitled "Evil Tendencies to be Resisted in Procuring an Education at these Islands," another student explained that "the indolent habits of the natives" were caused by a tropical climate and the easy availability of food. Students were to pay special attention to these risks, which could threaten their status in the islands as "respectable" members of society.[46]

Missionary children prized their Punahou education, which set them further apart from the Hawaiian population. As missionary son and

Punahou student Samuel Alexander rhetorically asked, "What is man without a cultivated intellect, but a brute, and what are the majority of men, who live along through life, but a drove of *sensual asses?*"[47] Despite the missionaries' support for numerous indigenous schools, missionary parents could not hide their racism from their own children. Missionaries had designed their native schools to teach the indigenous people a written Hawaiian language and to read a Hawaiian-language Bible. Missionary parents had far loftier goals for their own children, including one day transferring their pastoral and educative responsibilities to their children. As John Gulick noted to his father when Punahou began accepting nonwhite students, "I think perhaps . . . you would find more aversion to such equality than you anticipate, even amongst your good folk."[48]

Punahou students reserved in their minds one exception to their parents' and teachers' views on race. Born into virtual poverty, supported wholly by the goodwill and donations of Americans they had never met, and surrounded by an extravagantly wealthy indigenous elite who had welcomed their births with open arms, missionary children during the early years of Punahou revered the Hawaiian monarchy. Punahou students had a long association with members of the *ali'i* class. In Honolulu several missionary families sent their children to the Hawaiian Chiefs' Children's School (called the Royal School after 1846), prior to their transfer to Punahou. The Royal School, under the administration of missionaries Amos and Juliette Cooke, was designed to teach Hawaiian chiefs and chiefesses the English language, and of the sixteen Hawaiian royal children who boarded at the school, five became Hawaiian monarchs.[49] Students at the Royal School formed significant attachments with missionary children. Elizabeth Judd wrote that the king's sons Lot Kamehameha and Alexander Liholiho "came to our house daily, where we read, sang and played together."[50]

At Punahou students also came into contact with young Hawaiian royalty. Henry Lyman remembered the "cavalcade" of young chiefs who visited the school. "The vivacious young chieftains, resplendent in blue broadcloth and gilt buttons, always made a profound impression on our barefooted squad," he wrote.[51] The two schools would organize wrestling matches and running races in which the missionary children often lost to the six-foot-tall Hawaiians.[52]

Missionary children respected the authority of the Hawaiian monarchy and the grandeur of their Hawaiian schoolmates. Prince Alexander, for instance, had a retinue of twenty-five servants at the Royal School.[53] Punahou students accepted the wealth, privilege, and physical prowess of their future monarchs and admired their skills in memorization, oration, and languages. This respect must have been communicated to the young chiefs, for Lot was shocked when called "nigger" while visiting the United States. "Lot never forgave or forgot it," Elizabeth Judd noted.[54]

Missionary children seemed oblivious to these inconsistent attitudes toward native Hawaiians. From its outset Punahou School employed Hawaiian natives, who lived in separate quarters while maintaining the campus and serving the students. Opuni worked in the Punahou kitchen for ten years. Kahui, the campus carpenter, guided the boys on hiking trips.[55] Yet in four years of weekly Punahou student newspapers, only a handful of contributors refer to non-*ali'i* Hawaiians by name, and only one in a positive manner. "There is now on the Island of Kauai an old woman who was my nurse in younger years," the young author wrote. "I have no doubt but that she would make any sacrifices on my account. That she would risk her life and go through any danger for my sake." Despite this praise, the *Weekly Star* writer apologized: "I do not mean however to say that the Hawaiians are not degraded."[56]

Missionary children's acceptance of Hawaiian elites also extended only so far. While at least six missionary children eventually married native Hawaiians, Punahou student Charles Judd (1835–90) voiced what many of his peers believed: "Do you think I would marry a girl with native blood? . . . [F]ar from it."[57] Judd was discussing the future Queen Emma. Warren Chamberlain neatly summarized where Punahou students obtained such attitudes, noting in 1849—nearly thirty years after missionary arrival to the islands—that missionary parents thought the amalgamation of their white children and native Hawaiians "repugnant."[58]

**14.** Hawaiian man carrying calabashes. Native Hawaiians were instrumental to missionary families. Fetching water, growing food, and washing clothing were just a few of the tasks for which missionaries relied on their indigenous servants. Hawaiian missionaries also used indigenous Hawaiians as wet nurses and nannies for their infants. Mission Houses Museum Library.

## The "Cold Water" Army

Issues of race and class infused the cultural understandings of nineteenth-century missionary youth in the Hawaiian Islands. The children viewed their own whiteness, as well as their parents' close association with the Hawaiian monarchy and *ali'i* class, as distinct identifiers that separated them from the majority native population. Yet missionary children also united around a shared moral code, the prize missionary parents hoped to earn for their children by sending them to Punahou. During Punahou's earliest decades, one Anglo-Protestant value surpassed all: temperance. On every island missionary children joined temperance societies, attended temperance meetings, and debated all facets of the issue. George

Wilcox, who attended Punahou throughout the 1850s, remembered joining a temperance society when he was three years old. Influenced by the American temperance movement, some missionary children also joined the "cold water army" and refused to drink coffee or tea.[59]

So serious were Punahou students regarding the evils of intoxicating drink that in 1846 debaters unanimously voted rum "productive of more evil than war."[60] Missionary children were taught that the "free circulation of spirituous liquors" lessened respect for law, life, and property. Under the influence of the missionaries, thousands of native children also joined temperance societies.[61] At Punahou students learned that alcohol was destroying native lives and culture. "I have not much fear in saying that if it were not for the restraining influence of the present stringent laws with regard to liquor and the good influence of the missionaries," wrote a student in the *Weekly Star*, "that they would soon dwindle away to nothing."[62]

With the missionary children's hatred of liquor came a distrust of foreign visitors. Missionaries had long influenced native rulers to legislate against prostitution and drunkenness—vices encouraged, the missionaries argued, by foreign whalers, merchants, and naval sailors. Missionary son Sereno Bishop noted that almost all foreigners in Honolulu during the first twenty years of the mission were at odds with the missionaries.[63] This ongoing conflict grew stronger when Kauikeaouli (Kamehameha III) issued a law against drunkenness in 1835 and outlawed liquor distillation and importation in 1838. The king also imposed the first Hawaiian duty, a tax on wine imports.[64]

Kamehameha III also sided with the American missionaries on Protestantism, forbidding Roman Catholic missionaries from operating in the islands. As a result of his policies, the nation faced in 1839 the first threat to its independence. Arriving in Honolulu the French frigate *L'Artemise* brought demands from the French government: religious toleration for French Catholic missionaries, as well as limits on Hawaiian duties for French wines and brandies. Kamehameha ultimately acquiesced to French demands, effectively repealing his own liquor laws.[65] To the missionary families, Catholic priests and alcoholic imports represented the worst sort of foreign aggression. As one Punahou student revealed,

"Those who have visited these shores are worse than the Hawaiians themselves."[66]

Of the foreigners increasingly coming to shore, most Punahou students directed their animosity toward the French, whose invasive actions were directly related to the two things their parents most abhorred: liquor and Roman Catholicism. In 1840 Persis and Lucy Thurston's father refused to leave his post and travel with his daughters to college in the United States because "two Catholic priests ha[d] lately established themselves at Kailua." He never saw Lucy again. His daughter contracted a respiratory infection upon arriving in America and died a few weeks later.[67]

Thurston was not the only missionary father concerned with French influence. "Popery and Brandy, as you will see are at the bottom of this whole affair," Ann Eliza Clark's father wrote to the ABCFM board regarding the 1849 incident with France. Punahou students generally agreed with their parents, decrying French influence in the islands. The missionary children never predicted that future Hawaiian monarchs would *willingly* choose to reverse the course their parents had charted for the islands.[68]

## God Save the Queen

By 1865 many missionary descendants were choosing to remain permanently in the islands. Kamehameha III had opened the doors to private land ownership, and the American Civil War had boosted Hawaiian agriculture. Missionary children saw, for the first time, an economic future for themselves in the islands.

Missionary descendants also began to notice the Hawaiian monarchy's progressive repudiation of their parents' missionary efforts. Kalākaua, whose reign began in 1874, distanced his government from the American missionaries and their children by joining the Anglican Church and reinstituting native religious practices. By reviving genealogical *meles* (chants), promoting the hula, and redirecting the Hawaiian Board of Health to license *kāhuna* (native healers), Kalākaua solidified the origins of chiefly power, importance of indigenous ceremonies, and possibilities of priestly medicine. Kalākaua's reign was further marred, in the eyes of the missionary families, by his close association with Walter Murray Gibson, a Mormon.[69]

"Church-going among the Hawaiians is now about as rare as staying away used to be forty years ago," missionary son and Punahou graduate William Castle (1849–1935) lamented in 1881.[70] Castle was right in one respect. The American-founded Congregational church in the islands had lost its hold on the government and the people. By 1896 there were almost as many Catholics as Protestants in the islands, and the number of Protestants included Anglicans. Fully one-sixth of the population adhered to Mormonism.[71] The years of Kalākaua's rule, wrote missionary son and Punahou graduate Joseph Emerson (1843–1930), "mark the lowest stage of corruption reached in church and state in these islands."[72]

Kalākaua's support for removing liquor restrictions, licensing the sale of opium, and chartering a lottery company were untenable political positions to white Punahou graduates, and missionary descendants experienced a major defeat in 1882 when the Hawaiian legislature eliminated prohibition for native Hawaiians. The restriction on giving intoxicating drink to Hawaiian natives had been in place for over three decades and came with steep fines or imprisonment for those who broke the law. In 1886 the Hawaiian legislature further voted to allow the licensing and sale of opium.[73]

William Alexander—who graduated from Punahou School in 1849 and served as the school's president from 1864 to 1871—asserted in his *History of Later Years of the Hawaiian Monarchy and the Revolution of 1893* that opium licensing and its related scandals were directly responsible for the revolution against the Hawaiian monarchy.[74] In 1887 a group calling itself the Hawaiian League demanded through armed force that Kalākaua sign a new constitution that removed his powers to appoint the upper house of the legislature and made his executive cabinet responsible only to the legislature. Of the known organizers of this secret league, all but one had attended Punahou. All were members of American missionary families.[75] "The mad plunge into the abyss was suddenly arrested by the determined efforts of Hawaii's most faithful sons and friends," Joseph Emerson declared. The new legislature immediately revoked the opium licensing law and prohibited the sale of opium in the islands.[76]

Queen Liliʻuokalani took her brother's place after his death in 1891. She reigned for less than two years. An Anglican like her brother, Liliʻuokalani signed new opium licensing legislation and a lottery bill, while presenting to the nation a new constitution, which would restore the monarchical powers lost by her brother and suppress white political power through enlarging the indigenous electorate.[77]

While the influence of white business and agricultural interests would certainly have been checked by the queen's efforts to restore the powers of the monarchy and increase the voting influence of the indigenous population, more worrying to missionary descendants was her rejection of their parents' moral and religious values, passed down in missionary homes, reinforced at Punahou, and commended in New England colleges.[78] Of the twenty-eight men on the Committee of Public Safety that overthrew Liliʻuokalani in 1893, more than one-third were Punahou graduates. Sanford Ballard Dole, the son of Punahou principal Daniel Dole, led the revolution and served as the new Hawaiian Republic's first president.[79]

## Trampling Down the Vineyards

Punahou graduates encouraged each other during the political struggles of the late nineteenth century. Just as their Punahou teachers had done in the classroom, missionary children as adults contrasted their own moral training to the immorality of the indigenous nation. "What now may we naturally expect from the descendants of the American Missionaries?" asked Hiram Bingham Jr. "They have been, are now, and will be trained in the highest schools of the nation."[80] Who better than to lead the nation, Punahou graduate Samuel Damon argued, than the missionary descendants? "In the midst of this new world stands our own group, undoubtedly called to be of influence in the propagation of great and noble ideas," Damon surmised.[81] The growth of the Roman Catholic Church, influence of British Anglicanism and American Mormonism, and resurgence of monarchical support for native religion, liquor, gambling, and opium brought the Punahou graduates to their breaking point.

**15.** Missionary son William Dewitt Alexander (1833–1913) attended Punahou School, graduated from Yale University, and returned to Punahou to serve as a teacher and president. After the revolution, Alexander became minister of public instruction for the Hawaiian Republic and wrote *A Brief History of the Hawaiian People* (1899) for use in the public schools. In the preface Alexander professes to write his history from the perspective of "a patriotic Hawaiian." Alexander married missionary daughter and fellow Punahou student Abigail Baldwin (1833–1913). Mission Houses Museum Library.

**16.** Queen Liliʻuokalani. Mission Houses Museum Library.

The missionary children's outcry against native Hawaiian rule did not occur overnight. Punahou School with its parental directives and secluded environment nurtured a culture that fostered peer networks and utilized peer pressure to reinforce the white minorities' social morals. Vulnerable children, themselves a colonial battleground, lived isolated from the culture of their birthplace and separated from their parents. Formal authoritative structures and informal peer networks instead worked in tension at Punahou to replace traditional familial and community bonds. Through peer culture, students creatively engaged their social world by publicly critiquing each other's work. These "intensive negotiations with and among the students" created what Yitzak Kashti calls a "profound experience of culture."[82] It is not surprising that in such an environment discussions turned political. As one graduate remembered, "What profound discussion we used to have concerning 'the powers that be.'"[83]

White missionary children in the islands coalesced around each other in the decades following their Punahou experiences. Education served as an additional marker to race and religion. Punahou remained a solid indicator of deportment and class, a divider, missionary descendants argued, between those capable of moral and political leadership and the outsiders who were to follow them. That Punahou students would be leaders in the islands the graduates did not question. "Who are better qualified . . . than the children of those who first brought light to the land?" James Alexander (1835–1911) asked.[84] That they would always respect the monarchy was less certain. "We are all as yet good and loyal subjects to his majesty," fifteen-year-old Robert Andrews noted in 1852. When the opportunity came for Punahou graduates to choose sides, they chose revolution.[85]

### Samuel Chapman Armstrong (1839-93)

This revolutionary mindset traveled with the missionary children around the world. Perhaps the best example of Punahou's early and extensive influence is found in the legacy of missionary son Samuel Chapman Armstrong. Armstrong attended the school during its first two decades before traveling to the United States to attend Williams College. When the American Civil War broke out, Armstrong joined the Union Army, earned his U.S. citizenship, and, after the war, founded Hampton Institution to educate former Southern slaves.

In his last report to the Trustees of Hampton Normal and Agricultural Institute, Armstrong estimated that close to 150,000 pupils had been reached by Hampton teacher-graduates during the twenty-five years following the Civil War.[86] More importantly, Armstrong's message of racial uplift through manual labor was adopted by mentee Booker T. Washington at Tuskegee Institute, hundreds of secondary schools in the rural South, and U.S. educators in colonial Hawai'i, Puerto Rico, and the Philippines. Many have argued that Armstrong set in motion a system of training that would dominate U.S. educational models for minority and colonial populations for one hundred years.[87]

Nevertheless, Armstrong's application of manual labor for freed slaves was distinctly rooted in his personal experiences at Punahou and the racialist ideas he and fellow missionary sons and daughters developed as children in the islands. Armstrong explained: "The [N]egro and the Polynesian have many striking similarities. Of both it is true that not mere ignorance, but deficiency of character is the chief difficulty, and that to build up character is the true objective point in education. It is also true that in all men education is conditioned not alone on an enlightened head and a changed heart, but very largely on a routine of industrious habit, which is to character what the foundation is to the pyramid."[88] One can almost hear the earlier battle cry of Armstrong's Punahou instructors in his philosophy of education, as Armstrong urged his charges to appreciate the twin habits of industry and scholarship.

## Teaching Revolution

American missionary parents in the Hawaiian Islands never intended their children to acculturate into indigenous Hawaiian society. Their educative efforts were strictly designed to train their children to assimilate into American society or lead the Hawaiian kingdom in its spiritual and cultural regeneration, a process missionaries designed from the beginning to reflect nineteenth-century, Anglo-Protestant ideals. While parental efforts remained incomplete, and missionary

**17.** Samuel Chapman Armstrong (1839–93). Born in the islands and educated at Punahou School, Armstrong attended Williams College in Massachusetts before joining the U.S. Army and fighting in the American Civil War. After the war Armstrong founded Hampton Institute in Virginia. Image ca. 1860–70, Library of Congress, Prints and Photographs Division, LC-DIG-cwpb-05892.

**18.** Students studying soil formation at Hampton Institute, ca. 1898. At Hampton Institute Samuel Chapman Armstrong combined the manual labor experiences of his childhood at Punahou School with his military training in the U.S. Army during the Civil War. Library of Congress, Johnson (Frances Benjamin) Collection, LC-USZ62-62379.

children maintained a sense of bicultural identity throughout their lives, the segregated nature of their education and their asymmetrical opportunities for advanced education separated them from the larger indigenous society and caused them to form peer attachments almost solely within their racial and religious communities. When these communities appeared threatened by Hawaiian monarchs, the children reacted violently.[89]

Ironically, parallel missionary efforts in Honolulu to separate indigenous children from their Hawaiian caretakers and inculcate them in New England Calvinism and Anglo-American deportment fell far short of missionary goals. After teaching ten years at the Royal School, the Cookes had witnessed few—if any—Christian conversions. Historian

Linda Menton argues that the *aliʻi* children probably did not "internalize the values taught at the school" because they were not isolated from the indigenous Honolulu community.[90] Hawaiian caretakers could always be found on the other side of the wall surrounding the school, often weeping over the separation.[91] White boarders at Punahou had no similar familial outlets for escape. Instead, they turned toward each other and formed their own army of resistance against the indigenous vices that so occupied their parents' attentions.

Punahou School during the 1840s and 1850s provides an example of the highest educational ideals accomplished within a relatively impoverished setting. Missionary parents struggled to pay their children's board, and Punahou children worked in the school's fields to help supply enough food for boarders. That numerous Punahou graduates went on to attend elite U.S. institutions such as Harvard, Mount Holyoke, Williams College, and Yale testifies to the resolve of white parents, teachers, and students in the islands. Nevertheless, Punahou graduates entered Hawaiian civil society with tremendous baggage. Their racialist understanding of morality and culture limited their ability to work with their indigenous Hawaiian neighbors. It is not surprising that white colonial childhood in the islands included such complicated messages. More surprising are the significant efforts missionary children undertook to connect their religious beliefs to political values and, eventually, to revolution—an agenda that went far beyond what their missionary parents had arrived in the islands to accomplish. The 1893 political overthrow of Queen Liliʻuokalani reflects the ability of missionary children in the Hawaiian Islands to appropriate their religious upbringing into a political plan tailored to fit their colonial experience as white, privileged minorities living in a nineteenth-century Christian missionary field.

CHAPTER 4

# Cannibals in America

*U.S. Acculturation and the Construction of National Identity in Nineteenth-Century White Immigrants from the Hawaiian Islands*

Ye parents who have children dear, and ye, too, who have none, if you would keep them safe abroad, pray keep them safe at home.

English nursery rhyme[1]

From birth I was cast upon you; from my mother's womb you have been my God. Do not be far from me, for trouble is near and there is no one to help.

A Psalm of David (22:10–11)[2]

American assimilation has seldom been rapid or absolute, but its complexities have often been ignored. In the nation's earliest period of immigration following the American Revolution, immigrants were usually merchants, tied to bilateral trade agreements and paying for passage aboard trade ships traveling the Atlantic Ocean. Predominantly European, these early "passengers" were usually overlooked and almost never feared once entering the United States. By the mid-nineteenth century, this had changed. American merchants, freed from restrictive mercantile trade practices with Britain, had discovered the Pacific Ocean and shattered the myth of American isolation, as well as the invisibility of immigration. New racial theories based on Darwin's theory of natural selection fell on the heels of U.S. entry into the non-Atlantic world, and just as Americans traveling abroad had little desire to forsake their U.S. citizenship, Americans at home coupled their expanding knowledge of the non-European world with fears that Pacific-based immigrants to the United States would threaten American cultural values at the very time Americans were attempting to transport their cultural institutions abroad.[3]

American missionaries to the Hawaiian Islands were among the earliest waves of Americans living, trading, and proselytizing abroad, and their children were among the earliest foreign exchange students to attend U.S. colleges. The story of ABCFM missionary children entering the United States in some ways supports and in other ways belies studies of nineteenth-century U.S. immigration. As immigrants, missionary children quickly realized American culture was different from their own. The children negotiated this new landscape largely alone, depending upon "chain migration" for emotional and even physical support. And despite their parents' desires to make them Americans, missionary children demonstrated the complex and often ambiguous acculturation process that confirms what historian Paul A. Kramer notes as the limits of U.S. cultural transmission through international college exchange.[4]

Many missionary children utilized their American educations and positions in U.S. society to advocate U.S. policies that benefited their families back home. Many returned to the Hawaiian Islands and participated in political revolution. Yet two events stand out in complicating these immigration stories. The 1809 arrival of the *Triumph* to the United States and the 1861 outbreak of the American Civil War both demonstrate that nineteenth-century immigrants from the Hawaiian Islands also affected the course of U.S. history.

## Dull Strangers

The first children to immigrate to the United States from the Hawaiian Islands were native Hawaiians. Not only did young Henry Obookiah influence American missionary interest in the Hawaiian Islands, but he also set in motion the chain of events that led to the overthrow of the Hawaiian monarchy and the U.S. annexation of the islands. Born around 1792, Obookiah witnessed as a young boy the violent deaths of his parents and infant brother in interisland struggles for *ali'i* dominance. Desiring to leave the islands, Obookiah found refuge with an American ship captain, who transported him to the United States on board the *Triumph*. When he arrived in 1809, Obookiah was around seventeen years old, a child by nineteenth-century legal standards.[5]

Obookiah initially was not well received. Viewed by New Englanders as "unpromising," his countenance "dull and heavy," Obookiah desired to assimilate. It was his ability to learn English that changed the minds of those around him. Eager to learn, Obookiah soon attracted the attention of members of the newly formed ABCFM, who sought Obookiah's company on their 1812 trip around the United States to raise funds for foreign missions. Because he did not yet consider himself a Christian, Obookiah's presence on the trip was meant to solicit sympathy and, of course, donations.[6]

Most significant in Obookiah's recollections of his early experiences in the United States was his desire to become a Christian in the way he had been taught, which meant gaining membership in a New England Congregational church. When he and his Hawaiian shipmate Thomas Hopu prayed together for the first time in their native language rather than in English, Obookiah recorded their surprise in his journal: "We offered up two prayers in our tongue—the first time that we ever prayed in this manner. And the Lord was with us." One week later Obookiah began to plan his return to the Hawaiian Islands to preach "the religion of Jesus Christ" to fellow Hawaiians in their language.[7]

Despite the ABCFM's efforts to educate Obookiah and raise funds to return him to the islands, Obookiah died of typhus fever in 1818. When his memoirs were published the following year, they sold over fifty thousand copies and required twelve editions. Reading his story in 1819, a group of young college graduates decided they needed to complete Obookiah's mission, and the ABCFM's first company of missionaries to the Hawaiian Islands left the United States the same year. While

Obookiah's friend Thomas Hopu was on board the ship transporting the seven white missionary couples, the ABCFM had clearly replaced Obookiah's goal with a new directive: the permanent settlement of American missionaries in the Hawaiian kingdom.[8]

### Superior Adventures

During the 1820s and 1830s missionary parents in the Hawaiian Islands sent almost all missionary children back to the United States by the time they reached age seven. Missionary mother Mercy Whitney explained parental reasoning to her children: to capture "advantages far superior to what you would have had at the Islands."[9] Missionaries recorded many of these parting scenes, including one daughter who screamed from the deck of her ship, "Oh, father, dear father, do take me back!"[10] Missionary parents often made the situation worse by advising their children that they might never see each other again. Indeed, some did not. Whitney, for example, never saw two of her four children again. While nineteenth-century parents in the United States often chose familial separation in order to secure an education or apprenticeship for a child—and had the legal authority to do so—the length of time and the distance missionary parents were willing to put between themselves and their very young children were extreme. That so many missionary parents chose separation from their children demonstrates the power the missionary occupation held over their children's lives.[11]

For the missionary children who traveled to the United States without a parent or guardian, the six-month voyage could be terrifying. Even for American whalers and merchants, traversing the Pacific was a relatively new experience. U.S. trade with China increased after the American Revolution, but Americans had little to offer the Chinese until they discovered that sandalwood from the Hawaiian Islands and seal furs from the Pacific Northwest could help equalize exchange rates. American whalers also began entering the Pacific, as whale oil became a popular lubricant in the growing number of factories and as a better-smelling source of light. The Hawaiian Islands made it possible for Americans to buy sandalwood from the Hawaiian monarchy in order to trade for

**19.** Henry Obookiah. Mission Houses Museum Library.

Chinese goods and resupply whaling and sealing vessels for excursions into the North Pacific.[12]

These Pacific trading ventures brought the first missionaries to the islands in 1820 and took missionary sons Warren and Evarts Chamberlain back around Cape Horn in the 1830s. The boys were ages seven and five. Even at the end of his life, Warren remembered with terror the "monster wave" that filled their cabin one night while they slept.[13] Samuel and Henry Whitney, ages eight and six, remembered being left by their parents under the supervision of an "unkind captain."[14] Henry Obookiah noted the hazing he received from sailors, as well as the general discontent among the crew. Judging from Obookiah's account, as well as lawsuits filed by sailors over inadequate food and water provisions, starvation was a constant concern for sailors on lengthy Pacific voyages. The memoirs of former cabin boys who recounted the physical abuse and neglect they experienced aboard nineteenth-century American merchant and whaling vessels suggest that it would be surprising if missionary children did not experience similar food shortages or mistreatment during their half-year voyages.[15]

Missionary children would have understood the irony of their situation. One of the most vexing attributes of Hawaiian society for missionary parents was its lack of nuclear fidelity. Hawaiian marriage traditionally had been rare outside of the *ali'i* class, and children often changed hands, adopted by grandparents and others.[16] English travel writer Isabella Bird noticed that despite the "capriciousness" of familial ties, Hawaiians were "remarkably affectionate to each other."[17] These relationships, while valued by Hawaiians, were shocking to Americans. Missionary parents who gave up their children, while attempting to teach the Hawaiians to keep their own, demonstrated an amazing ability to compartmentalize their lives.

Missionary parents expected their own children to rejoice in their opportunity to leave the islands to pursue superior advantages in the United States. Advised that the United States was a bastion of religious and educational opportunities, children were admonished by parents to "value your privileges, and to feel grateful for them." Perhaps one day, Samuel and Mercy Whitney wrote their sons, you will be able to "thank your Parents who were willing to part with you."[18]

**20.** Sophia Mosely Bingham (1820–87) was born the same year the first ABCFM missionary company arrived in the Hawtaiian Islands. She was eight years old when she arrived in the United States to live with relatives. Mission Houses Museum Library.

## Trafficking in Children

Missionary children, most of whom were not U.S. citizens due to their birth outside the United States, traveled without currency. Their parents had none. Like the earliest "passengers" across the Atlantic, these children were, in fact, commodities, traded by missionary parents to host families and colleges and expected by parents to be received with reverence and care. Like the textiles, ceramics, and teas making their way from China to Boston and New York, missionary children were a novelty, providing a translation of the Pacific to those whose curiosities had been aroused.[19]

Because missionary parents had eschewed personal property, as well as monetary income, their children entered a nation in which they had no independent legal standing and little ability to earn money. By the 1820s the "assumption of the law had shifted to deny the identity of a child altogether, up to age twenty-one," historian Holly Brewer writes. "The father had to contract on the child's behalf." Employers had little interest in entering into labor or property agreements with missionary children under the age of twenty-one, since such contracts would not be recognized in court, and children would not be held liable for broken agreements.[20]

Consequently, missionary parents placed their children into the hands of the ABCFM board. In 1834 the board began to grant small annual stipends to ABCFM missionary children attending U.S. schools. Until then, missionary children, usually between the ages of six and ten, entered a foreign nation literally destitute and alone. Missionary parents relied on the ABCFM to make sure their children found and maintained proper placement. If no sympathetic supporter could be found, children were, in essence, sold to strangers, the board providing portions of the child's allowance to their guardians as needed.[21] Board secretary Rufus Anderson argued that the system "with few exceptions" worked.[22]

The exceptions, according to Anderson, were "owing to causes which experience will remedy hereafter, or against which no human wisdom can provide in this imperfect world."[23] Such analysis probably was not comforting to the children of whom he spoke and who, like other immigrants to the United States, experienced the first rumblings of American distaste for foreigners. In 1819, the same year the ABCFM sent missionaries to the Hawaiian Islands, Congress placed its first restrictions on Atlantic passenger trade. The Act Respecting Passenger Ships and Vessels (Steerage Act) limited the number of people allowed passage on merchant ships to two persons per five tons. Atlantic seaboard states attempted even more restrictions, causing the Supreme Court to rule that only Congress could regulate foreign commerce. It was a divided court and a controversial decision, as states argued their own resources were being depleted to support newly arriving foreigners. The difference in the case of missionary children from the Hawaiian Islands, is that their parents—U.S. citizens—were among the first to send their poor and uneducated to the United States—the very action Americans feared foreign governments of plotting.[24]

The effect of ABCFM policy toward missionary children was to commodify missionary childhood. The success of the missionary parents' plans for their children depended upon their children being well received by the American public. Two things were required: to project the horrors of childhood in the Hawaiian Islands and to display the successes of their children as they submitted to an American education. This rate of exchange, in turn, provided missionary children with a free education, as well as the necessities of life. For some the exchange rate proved too high. "You probably think I live fancy as I board myself," James Chamberlain wrote to his sister. "Crackers and water is my principal diet."[25] Seven-year old Warren Chamberlain was entrusted to a farmer who required him to rise nearly four hours before dawn, in order to get his chores done before school. "I sleep on straw because . . . there is not a mattress in the house to sleep on," Chamberlain wrote his parents. When a physician advised Chamberlain that the difficult farm work was damaging his health, Chamberlain moved, "as Mr. W. would not keep me without reducing my wages."[26]

Situations such as the Chamberlains were common. Missionary children often were bounced around once inside the United States. Since correspondence between parents and children also took six months, parents sent letters to their child's last known address only to hear six months later that the child had moved families, schools, or even states. Even living with relatives was not always the optimal situation. Maria Whitney, shipped to the United States at age six, was passed from home to home, her relatives deeply disapproving of her parents' decision to send her to them and only agreeing to accept the burden of caring for Maria for short periods of time.[27] Sophia Bingham's guardian believed that the girl's relatives had overindulged the eight-year-old upon her arrival to the United States and spent the next several years attempting "to counteract" the attention Sophia had received.[28]

The psychological costs of such a system were steep. "You will never find persons who will answer the part of parents after you have once left them," Warren Chamberlain wrote his sisters. "Our experience before you convinces us of this."[29] Martha Chamberlain (1833–1913) wrote her mother asking for money so that she and her sister could leave their American home. "Dr. Anderson's family is no home for us," Martha wrote. She was referring to Rufus Anderson, the ABCFM secretary responsible for the placement and care of all ABCFM missionary children entering the United States.[30]

It is not hard to imagine confusion among missionary children over the dictates of a religious faith that required so much sacrifice at such a young age. In turn children were expected to display gratefulness to their parents and American donors for their position. Warren Chamberlain wrote to his sisters regarding relatives with whom he had briefly stayed: "I would not hurt mother's feelings, if it were possible, and I will not say everything that impresses my mind."[31]

Instead missionary children acted out in other ways. Some refused to write to their parents, forcing siblings to communicate basic information on their behalf. Others expressed their dissatisfaction more subtly. When Mercy Whitney eulogized her husband as "*a Father to them all*," she was referring to the indigenous Hawaiians.[32] Henry Whitney responded by naming his firstborn son after his American guardian.[33] Maria Whitney, sent to the United States like her brother, returned to the islands sixteen years later but refused to live with her mother and married without her mother's consent. "She manifests but little affection for, and still less confidence in me," Mercy Whitney complained.

"This seems strange . . . and I cannot account for it, unless I attribute it to her long absence from me."[34]

Others satirized their responsibility to convey the perceived awfulness of life among the native Hawaiians. People came daily to visit Persis and Lucy Thurston's trunk of Hawaiian "curiosities." Persis chose to deal with the scrutiny by dressing in native Hawaiian clothing and parading around the curious visitors.[35] She later did the same for peers at Mt. Holyoke Seminary, conducting a missionary prayer meeting in the Hawaiian language and "in the style of the Islanders, with white long gown, long shawl made of the bark of trees . . . a necklace of human hair taken from the head of captives." Wearing jewelry made of whale and swine teeth, Thurston was, in the words of one observer, "truly comical to see."[36] Missionary daughter Elizabeth Judd dryly recalled her invitation to speak to the hundreds of "eager faces" who had turned out to hear "the woman from the Cannibal Islands."[37]

Missionary children also rebelled against their parents by heading to California. "To our great surprise, we have just heard, that Asa Thurston, son of our honored brother Thurston, is digging gold in California!" one missionary father noted in 1849. "I should hope that none of our children at the Islands will be led in that direction." Thurston was a student in the United States when gold was discovered in California.[38] Missionaries reminded their children about the dangers of pursuing money. "The way of life is filled with temptations," missionary Abner Wilcox told his son Charles, "more I fear in California than elsewhere." Charles Wilcox disagreed and soon moved there.[39]

With California gold rushers spending winters in Honolulu, and Honolulu residents heading to California, the financial world had shrunk overnight. "I will go to California and worship the golden calf for one brief year," a missionary son announced before leaving Punahou School for the United States.[40] His friends followed him. John Gulick convinced his parents to allow him to visit Oregon missionaries, only to immediately head to San Francisco and mine for gold.[41]

California was not the missionary parents' ideal America. Education, not gold mining, Fanny Gulick wrote her son in California, "is the first object."[42] The California gold rush had, however, placed San Francisco at the center of Pacific commerce. By 1850 missionary children and mail from the islands were able to travel to New York through San Francisco, overland to Nicaragua, and up the Atlantic coast, a journey of weeks, not months. Later companies of ABCFM missionary parents benefited from these changes, utilizing California as a mechanism to keep better tabs on their children in the United States.[43]

As a result of increasing U.S. contact with the Hawaiian Islands, missionary children failed in their most significant effort to subvert parental demands: the redefinition of their parents' understanding of a successful education. Despite familial tensions created by distance and time, missionary parents maintained a profound grip on their children's choice of professions. While allowing their children to pursue whatever course of "usefulness" God unveiled to them, missionary parents made clear to their children that becoming a missionary was the highest status one could attain. "Above all," missionary Peter Gulick wrote, "I desire that [my children] become faithful and devoted missionaries."[44] When Lucy Thurston's youngest child returned to the Hawaiian Islands as an ordained minister, years of familial separation melted away in an instant. "A son! Qualified for the gospel ministry," she gushed. "It is enough."[45]

In the face of such expectations, missionary children faced an uphill battle in reclaiming the "useful" life. James Chamberlain wrote to his mother that he wanted to become an artist. Chamberlain's conviction did not last long in the face of parental criticism. He became a minister.[46] Parents squashed several other dreams by correspondence. John Gulick asked permission to become a scientist, and Evarts Chamberlain (1831–82) a sailor: "I was born on an Island. I have sailed thousands of miles on the Ocean, and I have seen some storms that made the ship rock like a cradle," Evarts wrote his parents. Both children were rebuked. Gulick became a missionary. Evarts Chamberlain, after numerous professional failures, settled for journalism.[47] Even forty years later, James Chamberlain reflected, "I ought to have been an artist."[48]

### Warts and Winters

The stakes for missionary parents sending their children to the United States were enormous. Their ability to maintain their chosen missionary

**21.** Jeremiah "Evarts" Chamberlain (1831–82). Named in honor of an early leader of the ABCFM, Chamberlain spent much of his life between locations and occupations. He traveled to the United States unaccompanied by an adult when he was only five years old. Chamberlain wanted to be a sailor, but his mother would not allow it. He served in the U.S. Army on a Mississippi steamboat during the Civil War, wrote a novel that failed to sell, and returned to the Hawaiian Islands only to leave them again. Evarts's siblings noted that he was unsettled and discontent for much of his life. Mission Houses Museum Library.

profession in the Hawaiian Islands rested with the continued goodwill of the Hawaiian people and financial support of the American public. Missionary children became the currency by which Americans understood the value of the missionaries' efforts. Missionary parents viewed their children's failures as their own, and in no greater arena were the successes and failures of their children on display than in New England colleges and seminaries.[49]

Missionary parents expected their college-age children to demonstrate that they were capable of assimilating American standards of success, despite their birth in the Hawaiian Islands. Missionary children were also expected to display a desire to return to the islands to complete their parents' mission to the Hawaiian people. These two goals were often at odds. Americans themselves were entering into a debate about whether those born outside the United States were capable of assimilation. Americans were newly independent and deeply sensitive about their relative position within the "civilized" world, and as Kariann Yokota explains, "American intellectuals linked cultural aspirations to an object already in their possession: whiteness."[50]

Yet there was some confusion among U.S. and British elites about how well whiteness would survive in the more hostile environment of North America. "It was hoped and sometimes legislated, that whiteness was an object that could be possessed but not lost or transferred," Yokota writes. The relative geographical relationship to centers of power "determined how others perceived their level of 'civilization.'" While missionary parents had been born in New England and educated in Boston, Andover, and New York, their children had been born in the Hawaiian Islands. It was unclear to the new purveyors of race what impact this had, although their belief remained strong that over time even "savages" could become refined.[51]

As American intellectuals argued ways to secure their status of whiteness outside the British Empire, Congress succumbed to popularized views of national hierarchy and racial inferiority. Westward expansion became critical to linking U.S. trade in the Pacific to centers of power on the East Coast, but American legislators became increasingly hesitant to allow nonwhite immigrants from China, Japan, and the Hawaiian

Islands the same legal protections that immigrants crossing the Atlantic had enjoyed.[52]

When the United States settled its Oregon boundary with Britain in 1846, hundreds of Hawaiian laborers, formerly employed by the Hudson's Bay Company, sought U.S. naturalization. They were denied by Oregon's territorial governor under legislation limiting citizenship to white males. When Hawaiian Islanders sought Oregon Territory land grants from the U.S. federal government, Oregon's territorial delegate to Congress argued vehemently against including Hawaiians, whom he considered "a race of men as black as your negroes of the South, and a race, too, that we do not desire to settle in Oregon." In 1852 the California senate passed a resolution to restrict the entrance of *kanaka* laborers. In 1866 the Oregon legislature declared it illegal for a person with one-fourth *kanaka* blood to marry a white person.[53]

Missionary children were aware of these debates and desired to prove their membership among civilized races. Punahou students, for example, became upset by news that American visitors reported the students a "more lazy and shiftless set than almost any school in New England."[54] Seventeen-year-old Lucy Thurston, on her way to the United States, worried, "The children of missionaries who have returned from the Sandwich Islands . . . are found fault with for their excessive indolence. . . . All those who return in this vessel will of course be criticized."[55] As missionary children from the Hawaiian Islands began to win top academic awards at schools such as Williams College and Yale University, the *New York Observer* would only call their success "curious."[56]

Missionary children worked hard to dispel such perceptions. In this respect they joined in tandem with their parents' educative goals. Williams College loomed especially large in parental hopes and student aspirations. Nestled deep in the hills of Massachusetts—Samuel Chapman Armstrong called them "nature's warts" compared to the *mauna* (mountains) of the islands—Williams College began educating young men in 1793.[57] Missionary parents were attracted to the college by several important events that had occurred at the institution. In 1810 Williams College and Andover Seminary students led the effort to form the ABCFM, the sending organization for all Congregational missionaries to the Hawaiian kingdom. Over a half-dozen missionary fathers had attended Williams. Most importantly, the college had appointed Mark Hopkins its president in 1836, a position he held for thirty-six years. In 1857 the ABCFM also elected Hopkins as its president, extending to missionary parents the hope their children would be encouraged by the college to follow their parents into missionary service.[58] Williams College was also where board secretary Rufus Anderson sent his own son.[59]

Missionary parents and children generally had chosen wisely in Williams College. President Hopkins became an advocate for the missionary children, reserving special rooms for them and even, as in the case of Armstrong, inviting them to live with his family. "He told me that I should have no college bills whatever to pay, being a descendant of the Hawaiian mission," Armstrong wrote home.[60] The college's moral and religious culture was also generally supportive of parental wishes. "The religious influences here are very good," James Alexander wrote his mother. The college held prayer meetings five days each week and fined students for their absence. Students were required to attend two services each Sunday.[61]

Missionary parents could not control everything, however, and their sons assimilated a different theology than they had received as students. Hopkins was a new breed of theologian and critical of Rufus Anderson's singular focus on teaching indigenous cultures to read the Bible. "We regard destiny as turning upon *character*," Hopkins stated. "All desirable results of political economy and social order, and a high, pure, and permanent civilization, will follow."[62] As historian Paul Harris argues, this focus on character "represented a subtle departure from evangelical rhetoric" that emphasized spiritual conversion and discipline. Hopkins, Harris notes, considered colleges "character-building institutions vital to the creation of an educated elite to guide the process of social change."[63] Hopkins's message was particularly well received by missionary youth whose segregated childhoods had already trained them to expect political and social leadership positions. When founding Hampton Institute, Samuel Chapman Armstrong declared, "Whatever good teaching I may have done has been Mark Hopkins teaching through me."[64]

For missionary daughters, the Mecca of female institutions was Mount Holyoke Female Seminary in South Hadley, Massachusetts. Established in 1837 by Mary Lyon, the college prepared women to be "*educators*," as opposed to "mere teachers," in the words of Lyon.[65] Lyon advocated training young women for usefulness around the world, as well as cultivating the "missionary spirit."[66] She was a personal friend of Rufus Anderson, who sent his daughter to the seminary during the 1840s, and the two cooperated to recruit Americans for missionary work.[67] The ABCFM was, to Lyon, "the glory of our country—the corner stone of all our voluntary benevolent associations."[68] Several missionary mothers in the Hawaiian Islands had attended the seminary, and some of the earliest missionary daughters sent to the United States attended Mount Holyoke. In 1853 five missionary daughters attended the seminary together.[69]

Missionary parents were pleased that Lyon ran a tight ship. Lyon required all students to board at the institution and participate in its domestic upkeep. "All the teachers and pupils, without exception, will constitute one family," she stated. To Lyon the enemies of American civilization were "infidelity and Romanism," and the school required public worship and Bible study, private devotions, prayer meetings, and Sabbath keeping.[70] Mount Holyoke girls also exercised daily. "How I hate winter," Martha Chamberlain complained after a two-mile walk. "Sometimes it seems as though I could not possibly spend another winter in the United States."[71]

Mount Holyoke faculty and students extolled, prayed for, and funded missionaries in the Hawaiian Islands. Teachers solicited missionary donations from all pupils and kept track of individual contributions to both home and foreign missions in a written notebook. In 1853, for example, the school donated over $900 to missions.[72] The pressure to conform must have been great. As one student noted, New England had its Blue Laws, but Mount Holyoke had "*Bluer Laws*."[73]

Lyon treated the missionary daughters from the islands well. The students had their own room and did not have to sleep in public rooms, where many students lived due to overcrowding. At least two missionary daughters were invited to stay and teach at the school after their graduation. But just like missionary sons at Williams, missionary daughters heard new messages at Mount Holyoke. Like other rising female institutions of the mid-nineteenth century, Mount Holyoke was changing the nature of a "woman's profession." As Anne Scott writes, "despite their emphasis upon the importance of woman's sphere, [these colleges] were important agents in that development of a new self-perception and spread of feminist values."[74] Missionary daughters from the Hawaiian Islands became missionaries, teachers, and wives, just as their parents hoped they would, but unlike their mothers, Hawaiian missionary daughters could—and did—return to the islands as single professional women and married their partners for love, not expediency. Like their male counterparts at Williams, Mount Holyoke graduates returned to the Hawaiian Islands ready to take leadership roles within them.[75]

### Marks of Mammon

Despite the support children received from college administrators, missionary children from the Hawaiian Islands did not wish to stay in the United States after graduation. Ann Eliza Clark did not wait for graduation, leaving Mount Holyoke early to return home to the islands. Like many foreign-exchange students, missionary children had every intention of returning home, yet their desire to return to the islands was based upon something more than homesickness, pointing again to the complexities of assimilation.[76]

At Mount Holyoke Mary Lyon feared that the "temptations" to return to the islands to live like aristocracy would cause the young ladies from the Hawaiian Islands to lose their missionary spirit.[77] Part of Lyon's concern may have stemmed from what she saw the girls experience in the United States. Martha Chamberlain, for example, kept a list of those students, "the *aristocracy*," she called them, who invited each other to parties off campus. Martha referred to herself and her sister as the "common people."[78] Similarly, while missionary sons excelled academically at Williams, they also felt they had something to prove. Sanford Dole remarked in 1867 that the Hawaiian delegation at Williams was down to only one "solitary representative from the Islands, to stand up for the reputation of Hawaii during the coming year."[79]

**22.** Maria (1832–1909) and Martha (1833–1913) Chamberlain. The sisters together attended Mount Holyoke Seminary and returned to the Hawaiian Islands in 1853. Mission Houses Museum Library.

Nineteenth-century missionary children from the Hawaiian Islands demonstrated the insecurities and rootlessness noted in other groups of "third-culture" children.[80] They respected the United States as an institution: "The free and just government of the United States is preferable to any other," wrote one student in the *Punahou Gazette*.[81] Missionary children in the islands celebrated George Washington's birthday and the Fourth of July. Yet once arriving in the United States, missionary children found themselves unimpressed by American society, writing home about the intemperance, profanity, novel reading, and Sabbath breaking around them. In 1844 former missionary Gerrit Judd accused his missionary colleagues of trying to "make" their children Americans instead of allowing them to embrace the Hawaiian kingdom as home.[82] In these efforts missionary parents decidedly failed. Their children repetitively complained about cheaters at school, denominationalism in the churches, Democrats who supported slavery, and Unitarians who preached pluralism.[83]

Missionary children detested the number of people living in American cities. In Manhattan, "carts, carriages, horses, men, newsboys, bootblacks, beggars, porters . . . all appeared to see who could make the most noise," William Andrews (1842–1919) described. Andrews called the furrowed brows of New York shipping merchants the "mark of Mammon" and disdained the New Yorkers who traveled to New Jersey every Sunday to frequent liquor stores closed by law across the river. "This leaves us a quiet city on Sundays—something new for New York."[84] In many places, missionary children noted, "religion is almost a dead letter."[85]

Students from the Hawaiian Islands also attacked the American psyche. "It is nothing but hurry, hurry, hurry, hurry, one thing after another all the time. No idle moments here," Martha Chamberlain wrote her mother.[86] "An American tries to be in two places at once," Samuel Armstrong observed.[87] "The imaginary wants of many people in America are quite too numerous," Oliver Emerson remarked.[88] James Chamberlain criticized Americans for "running after each new thing."[89] Immigrants from the Hawaiian Islands conversely sensed a closed-mindedness in Americans. William Alexander disparaged "the shallowness, the slavery to prejudice . . . and narrow views that prevail so much among what are called educated men in this country."[90]

The missionary children's attitudes about the United States often stemmed from their feeling that they were outsiders. By speaking only the Hawaiian language to each other when around Americans who did not understand it, and holding annual conventions across Massachusetts and New York, white immigrants from the Hawaiian Islands demonstrated their frustration with their foreign status. "I feel truly thankful that we have been brought up amidst the good influences of a *heathen* country and not in the U.S.A," James Alexander wrote home in the 1850s.[91] His sister Mary Jane Alexander (1840–1915) concurred, "I am thankful my home is not here, and that I can hope to return to my native land."[92]

Not all were able to return to the Hawaiian kingdom. Passage to the islands could cost as much as $500. James Alexander borrowed money from the ABCFM in order to return home to his parents. The board expected him to pay it back.[93] Evarts Chamberlain borrowed funds at 6 percent interest from a Boston merchant.[94] Henry Lyman left the Hawaiian Islands intending to return as an attorney "to grow rich in the courts of the kingdom." He never did.[95] Missionary sons and daughters who settled in the United States lamented the loss of their native land throughout the remainder of their lives.[96]

## War Comes a Calling

Despite their overwhelming desire to return to the islands, missionary children embraced the Union with the outbreak of the Civil War in 1861. In fact, for missionary children entering the United States during the 1850s and 1860s, the war was the single most important influence in their American acculturation. As staunch opponents of slavery, missionary parents admired the Republican Party and cheered the election of Abraham Lincoln. Missionary sons eagerly joined the Union Army, believing it a way to combine the values they had learned at home with the patriotism around them.

Some missionary sons may have also used the war as a way to demonstrate their independence. Historian Philip Greven argues that many nineteenth-century evangelicals suppressed deep animosity toward parents and authority because they had not been taught how to disagree. "Consequently by becoming soldiers for Christ," Greven proposes, "evangelicals often demonstrated a remarkable capacity for vigorous and sustained aggressiveness." Missionary children living in the United States during the war showed a decided determination to join the Union cause, despite their parents' pleas they remain uninvolved. "We send Nathaniel from us hardly expecting to see his face again," missionary John Emerson worried, "as he goes to our native land at a time when the spirit of war is raging."[97]

At least a dozen missionary sons from the islands enlisted in the Union Army. Brothers William, Theodore, and Joseph Forbes enlisted. "I feel as though I had buried them all in one grave," their mother wrote.[98] William Forbes traveled with General Sherman through Georgia. Theodore Forbes spent six months in a hospital and was permanently disabled. A rebel sharpshooter killed Joseph Forbes.[99]

For his part, Nathaniel Emerson fought at Fredericksburg, Chancellorsville, and Gettysburg before catching fever during the Battles of the Wilderness. Emerson's Punahou friends were impressed, noting to each other that he was "spilling his blood in the glorious cause of universal liberty."[100] Samuel Ruggles, appointed assistant surgeon in the U.S. Army, died in the war. Henry Lyman, also an army surgeon, served casualties after the battle of Shiloh. Titus Coan practiced medicine in the U.S. Navy. Samuel Conde twice escaped being held prisoner by the Confederate Army. James and Evarts Chamberlain served the U.S. Army on Mississippi River steamboats. Siblings Porter and Mary Green and Jennie Armstrong taught freed slaves. Jennie's brother Samuel Armstrong became a brigadier general, his service allowing him to become a naturalized U.S. citizen. Armstrong cited the American Civil War as among the greatest influences upon his life.[101]

Missionary children were caught up in the feeling of being part of something greater than themselves. Mary Jane Alexander described being in New York City after the fall of Sumter: "the scene was grand; the change of men from dollar and cent calculators to enthusiastic patriots was sublime."[102] Samuel Alexander declared, "I am not certain but [war] is my calling."[103] Mary Andrews, lacking a flag, "hung out of a window a red dress, a white one, and a blue one, determined not to be behind in [her] exhibition of patriotism."[104] Supporting the Union was one way missionary children could agree with Yankees and demonstrate they were not like idle Southerners. After all, in his wildly successful *How to Be a Man*, popular nineteenth-century children's author Harvey Newcomb compared children from the tropical climate of the Hawaiian Islands to Southern slaveholders, that "vicious" class of idlers.[105]

## Homefront Battlefields

Like other Western-educated foreigners who returned to their home-lands to appropriate what they had learned, the Hawaiian-born U.S. college students of the 1860s became the middle-aged revolutionaries of the 1890s. But supporting the eventual U.S. absorption of the islands and working toward it initially were considered two different things to missionary descendants returning to the Hawaiian kingdom. Missionary children remained ambivalent about U.S. expansion. English writer Isabella Bird was confused by the "incongruous elements" of Hawaiian culture in which "Republicans by birth and nature" uttered the words "Your Majesty" so easily. Bird noted that although missionary descendants expected U.S. annexation, it was "impious and impolitic to hasten it."[106]

The Union's prosecution of the Civil War gave missionary children from the islands a moral confidence in the United States. Bird, traveling the Hawaiian Islands in 1873, called the small nation thoroughly "Americanized."[107] Missionary children did not agree. Believing themselves Hawaiian, not American, they did not see the cultural and racial superiority by which they lived their Hawaiian lives. Missionary children believed their moral education and appreciation for republican government, which they had received at Punahou and in the United States, elevated their position in the islands. While in the United States, missionary children adopted racial understandings of national behavior. White missionary children distanced themselves from the Hawaiian people and argued for their own ability to rule the island nation based upon race. By lecturing each other not to abuse their superiority, they reaffirmed those beliefs. As missionary son Henry Whitney—who returned to the islands and became editor of the *Pacific Commercial Advertiser*—stated, native Hawaiians were "inferior in every respect to their European and American brethren."[108]

**23.** Louis Dalrymple for *Puck* magazine (January 25, 1899): "School Begins." Cuba, Puerto Rico, Hawai'i, and the Philippines receive the benefits of an American education. The blackboard reads: "England has governed her colonies whether they consented or not. By not waiting for their consent she has greatly advanced the world's civilization. The U.S. must govern its new territories with or without their consent until they can govern themselves." Library of Congress, Prints and Photographs Division, LC-DIG-ppmsca-28668.

"Who are the real people of Hawaii?" Sereno Bishop asked in 1896. "Are they the decadent and dwindling race of aboriginal Hawaiians, who still linger in the land?" Sent to the United States at age twelve, Bishop returned to the islands thirteen years later as an ABCFM missionary. "Or are they not rather the fresh, active, brainy white race?" Bishop used his bully pulpit as editor of the Hawaiian evangelical publication the *Friend* from 1887 to 1902 to argue annexation was necessary for maintaining white political and economic control over the Hawaiian Islands. "Hawaii is to find its unavoidable and certain destiny in the bosom of the American Union," Bishop predicted.[109] By the 1890s Bishop had also convinced Sanford Ballard Dole. Perhaps no Hawaiian-born missionary son better illustrates the complexities of Americanization and what historian Donna Gabaccia calls "immigrant foreign relations" than Dole.[110]

## Sanford Ballard Dole (1844–1926)

Sanford Ballard Dole attended college and law school in the United States with a clear desire to return to the Hawaiian Islands. Despite the U.S. citizenship of his parents and his status as a white native in the islands, Dole never viewed himself as an American, and his life exemplifies a reluctant acceptance of U.S. international power. Born at Punahou School to Emily and Daniel Dole, Sanford Dole's earliest years were marked by tragedy and transiency. Just days after her son's birth, Emily Dole died, and Dole was removed from his father and two-year-old brother George. Shuffled between missionary families, Dole returned to his father and stepmother, Charlotte Knapp Dole, two years later. The one constant in Dole's early life was the presence of a Hawaiian wet nurse. Dole later remarked, "I am of American blood but Hawaiian milk."[111]

As a student at Punahou, Dole imbibed the same messages fellow missionary children did. Principal Daniel Dole's belief that the racial character of the islands was inevitably changing and his desire to teach the missionary children "to become part of a new nation" were not lost on his son Sanford.[112] The younger Dole retained a lifelong respect for the school's mission, later becoming its longest-serving trustee and helping to administer the institution for forty-eight years.[113]

When Sanford Dole arrived at Williams College in 1866, he entered the institution as a senior. Dole was anxious to return home to the Hawaiian Islands, and Williams College president Mark Hopkins encouraged his leanings. "I have decided to study law, with reference to practicing at Honolulu," Dole wrote to his parents in 1866. "I look upon it as a possible stepping stone to influence and power in the Government, where they need good men."[114] The decision deeply disappointed his parents, who wished Dole to return as a pastor to the natives. "It is too late to change my plans," he answered them.[115]

Like Hopkins, Dole was critical of the American missionary experiment in Hawai'i. "I think that the reason that the old missionaries have so little influence . . . is because they thunder at [the people] too much from the pulpit, and shun them too much in the affairs of daily life," Dole wrote his stepmother from the United States in 1868. "A good man could, I think, do more for the nation for morality and justice than preaching to the natives," Dole noted.[116]

Dole was dissatisfied at Williams and in the United States, calling himself a "Hawaiian exile."[117] Yet when he returned to the islands, he often condemned the white residents, who had visibly increased in number during his absence, for what he believed to be their negative influence upon the Hawaiian kingdom of his youth. From his first years back in the islands, Dole was concerned with the issue of Hawaiian labor. In Dole's condemnation of the Masters and Servants Act, Dole compared Chinese contract labor to U.S. slavery. The 1850 act allowed Hawaiian planters to offer foreign labor contracts of up to five years. The contracts were binding even if signed outside the islands.[118] "The words so often heard during the last few years, 'I did not like my Chinaman, so I sold him last week,' or 'I have bought a new cook,' smack too disagreeably of the Southern institution for us to pass lightly by," Dole wrote in 1869.[119] Dole's first issue of the *Punch Bowl*, an anonymous newspaper which ran from July 1869 through October 1870, dealt with the labor question, and his biographer Helen Allen concludes that Dole was "more interested in the workers than the plantation owners."[120]

Dole instead advocated selling individual plots of up to thirty acres of government lands to immigrant settlers and paying for the passages of up to eight hundred families annually. "The children of the immigrants, educated in our schools, would grow up, to all intents and purposes, nationalized Hawaiians," he explained. Dole's view of Hawaiian citizenship was racially expansive but politically restrictive, based upon a degree of commitment and responsibility. In truth it was a blend of his own attachment to the islands as a Hawaiian-born white, but also American influences, including the 1862 Homestead Act.[121]

In 1884 Dole became a member of the Hawaiian legislature and worked to pass the first Hawaiian Homestead Act, designed "to provide many persons of small means who were without permanent homes and are desirous of obtaining homesteads."[122] The Hawaiian government made available for purchase public lands of between two and twenty acres. Individuals, irrespective of race, who paid a $10 filing fee and quarterly interest on the appraised value of the land were freed from paying taxes on the land for five years. Homesteaders could not transfer their land to a third party and were required to pay or mortgage the price of the land at the end of five years. In 1887 King Kalākaua rewarded Dole with an appointment to the Hawaiian Supreme Court, where he served until the 1893 revolution.[123]

Dole held the Hawaiian monarchy in high regard. The fact that the Hawaiian monarchy had willingly created a constitution and legislature limiting its power, and continued to live under it, deeply influenced Dole's thinking. Kamehameha III's 1839 Bill of Rights was "not wrung from an unwilling Sovereign by force of arms, but the free surrender of despotic power by a wise and generous ruler," Dole wrote. The *Māhele*, Dole commended, resulted from "the earnestness and patriotism of the King and chiefs, who cheerfully made great sacrifices of authority."[124] The 1853 Hawaiian constitution forbade slavery, Dole noted, "ten years before this enlightened policy was followed by the United States."[125]

Despite his support for the monarchy, Dole had concerns about its retrenchment. In 1864 King Lot Kamehameha refused to take the oath pledging loyalty to the constitution and unilaterally called a constitutional convention. The changes he ushered through the convention continued to allow the Hawaiian monarch to appoint the house of nobles but reduced the legislature to one chamber, ostensibly to increase the king's influence. All cabinet appointments were made by the king and served at his pleasure. There was no provision for overriding the king's veto. "The constitution was defective," Dole wrote, "in that it lacked restrictions on royal arbitrary power, if the sovereign was bent on attempting to exercise it."[126] Dole's commitment to constitutional law now propelled him in a new direction—toward abolishing the monarchy.

Missionary grandson Lorrin A. Thurston stated that Dole "was the revolution."[127] Yet Dole's leadership in both the 1887 and 1893 revolutions was tentative and ambivalent. Dole advocated a native solution to political unrest, including putting Princess Kaiulani on the Hawaiian throne rather than abolishing the monarchy, but he also continued to support the revolutionaries when they moved against the throne. In a letter to his brother George, Sanford Dole wrote, "Over and over again I pleaded that they consider accepting Kaiulani in a regency. When it proved to be of no avail I felt there was nothing else to do." Dole viewed his own participation in revolution as necessary to safeguarding the Hawaiian kingdom he loved.[128]

In 1887 Dole invited the Hawaiian League to meet at his home to plan revolution. The league illegally forced Kalākaua to sign a new constitution limiting the monarch's power by allowing the election of nobles, separating the legislative houses, and creating a veto override. Dole strongly agreed with these constitutional changes that favored the legislature. When Queen Liliʻuokalani attempted to abrogate this Bayonet Constitution, Dole again assumed leadership in the resistance movement. As he had done before, Dole condemned what he viewed as constitutional proposals that allowed for monarchial abuse of power. Under the queen's proposed constitution, the Hawaiian monarch would be able to remove cabinet officials without legislative approval, ignore a legislative veto override, appoint nobles, and restore a one-house legislature.[129]

Dole's ideas on legislative authority actually ran counter to evolving U.S. constitutional theory. As Fareed Zakaria has pointed out, similar debates were occurring in the United States with the opposite outcome. Post–Civil War presidents flexed their executive muscles by arguing for the unilateral right to remove cabinet members and for an increased use of their veto power. Like the Hawaiian monarchs, U.S. presidents sought greater executive privileges at the expense of legislative power. In the case of the United States, presidents did so in order to move around deeply divided congresses and exert greater national and international influence. Dole did not look to the United States as his guide when attempting to define executive power in the islands, although he utilized the legal training he had received there to assert legislative authority over the monarchy.[130]

As the revolutionaries seized control of government buildings, Dole forced Liliʻuokalani to abrogate the monarchy, and he became the first and only president of the provisional government and Hawaiian republic. In defending the revolutionaries' actions, Dole wrote U.S. minister Albert Willis: "It is difficult for a stranger like yourself . . . to obtain a clear insight into the real state of affairs and to understand the social currents, the race feeling and the customs and traditions which all contribute to the political outlook. We, who have grown up here . . . are conscious of the difficulty of maintaining a stable government here. A community which is made up of five races, of which the larger part but dimly appreciate the significance and value of representative institutions, offers political problems which may well tax the wisdom of the most experienced statesman."[131]

The new constitution of the Hawaiian Republic, which Dole helped draft, maintained property and literacy requirements for the electors of the upper house but also gave the upper house the right to introduce revenue bills. Dole noted that the plan, which reasserted the mostly white, propertied class, would "raise considerable opposition."[132] Liliʻuokalani had endeared herself to her people by promising to disenfranchise white foreigners and reduce the property requirements for the electorate. Dole knew he was diluting the indigenous Hawaiian vote. Although native voters technically maintained their franchise, they were also required to swear allegiance to the new republic, and many refused. Through language requirements for naturalization, the republican government also restricted the franchise of Japanese and Chinese residents who comprised nearly half of the islands' residents.[133]

Dole's biographer called the new constitutional government an "oligarchy."[134] Yet from a comparative perspective, a far different scenario was occurring in the United States as presidents sought to negate ethnic, political, and racial divides by exerting new executive interpretations of formerly legislative prerogatives.[135] Dole chose to divide ethnic political interests by emphasizing legislative power. His ideas were rooted in the political legacy of Kamehameha III, but the new constitution was also a reflection of Dole's confidence in peers living in the islands—white, propertied missionary descendants who shared Dole's love for the land but resistance to indigenous autonomy. Dole called them a new breed of "missionaries."[136]

Dole never escaped from his missionary parents or Punahou education. Dole's respect for Kauikeaouli (Kamehameha III) and the Hawaiian constitution did not override his belief in white superiority and American intellectual and cultural supremacy. Dole had read Columbia University professor John Burgess's *Political Science and Comparative Constitutional*

*Law* (1891) in which Burgess argued that the "Teutonic race" had built the most complex states. In writing to Burgess for advice on the new constitution, Dole complained, "There are many natives and Portuguese who have had the vote hitherto, who are comparatively ignorant of the principles of government and whose vote from its numerical strength as well as from the ignorance referred to will be a menace to good government."[137] Dole's acceptance of American racial ideology, but hesitance toward the expansion of U.S. power in the Pacific, explain why Dole was willing to stare down U.S. authority shortly after the revolution. When President Grover Cleveland ordered U.S. minister to Hawaii Albert Willis to return the throne to Lili'uokalani in 1893, Dole replied to Willis: "We do not recognize the right of the President of the United States to interfere in our domestic affairs. Such right could be conferred upon him by the act of this government, and by that alone, or it could be acquired by conquest. This I understand to be the American doctrine, conspicuously announced from time to time by the authorities of your Government."[138]

While Dole and the Committee of Safety had established the Hawaiian Republic with "the view of eventual annexation to the United States," Dole believed he and fellow missionary descendants were the proper gatekeepers of Hawaiian sovereignty until that time.[139] Like other missionary children, Dole's desire to sway U.S. foreign policy was always on behalf of the islands, yet unlike other nineteenth-century immigrants to the United States, these white missionary children ultimately demonstrated disproportionate influence over their one-time host country. They convinced the U.S. government to annex their nation by congressional joint resolution in 1898.

## Adult Rebellions

It is tempting to view the missionary children's participation in revolution and support for U.S. annexation as the simple product of racial hatred or economic incentive. Queen Lili'uokalani certainly did. It was a "project of many years on the part of the missionary element that their children might some day be rulers of these islands," she argued to the U.S. government after her overthrow.[140] Certainly Sanford Dole was familiar with the interests of sugar planters in the islands, having

**24.** Executive Council of the Republic of Hawai'i. Samuel Mills Damon (*far left*), Sanford Ballard Dole (*middle*), and William Owen Smith (*far right*) were all missionary sons. Mission Houses Museum Library.

served as president of the Planter's Labor and Supply Company in 1885. The group of planters had formed after the United States granted trade reciprocity, in order to cooperate on labor issues and share scientific and technological advancements. The group also had strong ties to the Hawaiian League, which forced the Bayonet Constitution upon Kalākaua in 1887 and was led by Sanford Dole.[141]

Certainly Sereno Bishop's repeated calls for annexation were steeped in the language of white superiority. But when one pictures Bishop as a child watch his mother starve herself to death, rather than return to the United States to seek medical attention, or imagines Bishop arriving in the United States only to realize the "grossness of speech" there was what his parents had shipped him away from the islands to avoid, one begins to understand the complexities of missionary children's attitudes toward the Hawaiian kingdom.[142] For example, missionary son Henry Baldwin (1842–1911), one of the most successful and powerful sugar planters in the Hawaiian Islands, did not want to remove Lili'uokalani from her throne and advocated working within Hawaiian constitutional means to address political conflict. Baldwin's public efforts on her behalf, as well as his peers' response (he was "howled down" at a public meeting), demonstrate that debate over U.S. annexation began in the Hawaiian Islands among the white missionary descendants.[143]

It seems ridiculous that a parent like Peter Gulick could force his children to become missionaries while living six months away by mail or sea. It becomes less amusing when one learns that Gulick's son Charles died of bulimia as a college student in the United States, the illness caused by what biographer Clifford Putney believes was fear of disappointing God and his parents.[144]

While Henry Obookiah may have begun the trajectory toward U.S. annexation in 1812, the American Civil War propelled it forward by giving moral license to a frustration and aggressiveness that many of the missionary children sensed but few could describe. The war allowed them an outlet for supporting a cause independent of their parents—a cause that gave them prestige among their American peers. The frustration missionary children experienced stemmed from their complicated relationships with their parents.

In 1861 President Abraham Lincoln gave young students from the Hawaiian Islands a reason to identify with the American nation. Republican unity against the expansion of slavery and the Northern commitment to fight against secession provided an environment for the acculturation of Hawaiian immigrants, a process affecting not just white children from the islands. Indigenous Hawaiians served in the Union Army, as well. Yet the war affected each group of Hawaiians in dramatically different ways. Among whites from Hawai'i the war fostered loyalty to the United States and a rationale for installing republicanism through violent means. For indigenous Hawaiians the war created a false sense of security, as Queen Lili'uokalani found when she surrendered her island nation to the United States during the 1893 revolution. Hoping for justice, she was met with silence. For nineteenth-century white Americans, ousting a U.S.-educated, white republican government to restore an indigenous monarchy would have been, in fact, truly revolutionary.

CHAPTER 5

# Crossing the *Pali*

*White Missionary Children, Bicultural Identity,*
*and the Racial Divide in Hawai'i, 1820–98*

If all the seas were one sea, what a *great* sea that would be! And if all the trees were one tree, what a *great* tree that would be! . . . And if all the men were one man, what a *great* man he would be!

English nursery rhyme[1]

And today I take up my Hawaiian Bible to read a chapter in preference to the English version. It is beautiful Hawaiian.

Missionary son Sam Wilcox[2]

## Citizenship and Identity

"The children at the Sandwich Islands have nothing to do. Their parents have no employment for them. They grow up in idleness," lectured popular American children's author Harvey Newcomb in 1846. "Idleness also makes these children vicious. Having nothing useful to do, they are always ready for every evil work."[3] It is doubtful Newcomb, whose *How to Be a Man* and *How to Be a Lady* graced the bookshelves of white missionary children in Hawai'i, was referring to the several hundred white missionary children born and raised in the islands during the nineteenth century.[4] Yet Newcomb's statements must have struck the missionary children, for they, too, were Sandwich Islanders. Not only had they been born subjects of the Hawaiian monarch, but through a strange interpretation of U.S. law many were denied American citizenship, despite the fact that their mothers and fathers were U.S. citizens.

In 1790 the U.S. Congress granted natural-born citizenship "to children of Citizens of the United States, that may be born beyond sea, or out of the limits of the United States," as long as their fathers had resided at one time in the United States, and no state had proscribed citizenship. In 1802 Congress amended the law to read, "And the children of persons who now are, or have been citizens of the United States, shall though born out of the limits and jurisdiction of the United States, be considered as citizens of the United States." The effect, although probably not the intent, of the amendment was to deny birthright citizenship to children born overseas to fathers who had been born after the date of the amendment, April 14, 1802.[5] Immigration officials apparently enforced this interpretation, for Horace Binney, a nineteenth-century immigration attorney, published a pamphlet in 1853 arguing for the law's revision. "It does not probably occur to the American families who are visiting Europe in great numbers, and remaining there, frequently, for a year or more, that all their children born in a foreign country, are ALIENS, and when they return home, will return under all the disabilities of aliens," Binney stated. "Yet this is indisputably the case." The Supreme Court upheld Binney's interpretation of the law in *United States v. Wong Kim Ark* (1898), noting that Congress amended the law in 1855 to provide citizenship to children of citizen fathers born overseas.[6]

Missionary fathers in the first two companies of ABCFM missionaries to the Hawaiian Islands were all born before 1802 and so were unaffected by the law, but by the third company's arrival in 1828, the law began to have effect upon the younger missionaries and their children. Compounding the confusion was King Kamehameha III's ambiguous efforts to require foreigners to take an oath of allegiance renouncing their former citizenship before naturalization. Jonathan Osorio writes that the oath was used throughout the 1840s yet was inconsistently worded and applied and, ultimately, was not even binding. By 1850 the Hawaiian legislature reversed course and allowed dual citizenship.[7]

Consequently, Hawaiian-born missionary children were often unclear about their national identities. Elizabeth Judd took the oath of allegiance when her father left the ABCFM mission and entered government service in 1844, even though she was a Hawaiian subject by birth and excluded from American citizenship by his 1803 birth.[8] James Chamberlain wrote of being a "naturalized American" after twenty years living in the United States, even though his father's birth date meant the younger Chamberlain had been a U.S. citizen all his life.[9] Throughout the 1840s missionary parents opposed their children taking the Hawaiian oath of allegiance, not realizing that in some cases it was a moot point.[10] Clearly, missionary parents were just as confused about their children's citizenship status as were the other American expatriates Binney addressed in 1853.

Despite such confusion Binney's interpretation of U.S. citizenship laws seems to have been enforced by the U.S. government, at least by the time of the American Civil War. White missionary children from the Hawaiian Islands, for example, were asked to show their Hawaiian passports when visiting a U.S. armory in 1867.[11] After serving three years in the U.S. Army, Hawaiian-born Samuel Armstrong was proud his military record entitled him to U.S. citizenship, clearly understanding he had not been granted it at birth. Armstrong's father, born in 1805, was residing in the Hawaiian Islands when Armstrong was born.[12]

Just as clearly, an 1850 Hawaiian law mandated that all "native subjects" were required to apply to the Hawaiian minister of foreign relations for passports to leave the kingdom, a law amended two years later to exclude "all members and persons belonging to the Christian missions on the Islands." The Hawaiian government was attempting to stem the number of native Hawaiians leaving the islands, a response to the steep depopulation of natives from foreign diseases. The amendment excluding members of the Hawaiian mission demonstrates that the Hawaiian government considered white missionary children "native subjects."[13]

In fact, when Gerrit Judd took the oath of allegiance in 1844 and became a naturalized subject of the Hawaiian kingdom, he tried to convince other missionaries to follow. "[Your] children are subjects of His Hawaiian Majesty," Judd argued. "The Protection afforded by the United States to its citizens abroad is of little worth." White missionary children born in the Hawaiian Islands had little expectation the United States would come to their rescue. Instead, they grew up looking to parents, peers, and the Hawaiian monarchy for a sense of national security their own parents did not possess.[14]

### Language and Culture

Missionary children not only negotiated between two national identities—the American citizenship their parents assumed they had, and a Hawaiian nationality parents wished their children to avoid—but also contended with bilingual identities. Although missionary parents tried to keep the Hawaiian language from their children in order to shelter them from knowledge of cultural practices that the missionaries deemed heathen and vile, almost all missionary children became fully proficient in the Hawaiian language by their teenage years. Not only had they heard the Hawaiian language spoken by both parents from their mothers' wombs, but some missionary children were surrounded by Hawaiian caretakers who were allowed to speak Hawaiian to the children until the children were old enough to speak, clearly a formative period for language acquisition.[15]

Children called for their *omole* (bottle) and peppered their letters to each other with Hawaiian expressions. Even at Punahou School student compositions contained Hawaiian words, usually crossed out with the corresponding English word written above. Some parents, like Abner and Lucy Wilcox, became less restrictive with each successive child, so that the youngest siblings were the most proficient in the Hawaiian language.[16] Regardless of how it happened, most missionary children understood Hawaiian. As Henry Parker (1834–1927) remembered, the process occurred "unconsciously." Missionary children, "even those under [the] ban, soon acquired a ready use of the language, often to the horror of the parents." Parker recalled one missionary father who began to address fellow parents in the Hawaiian language. Parents became disturbed when hearing laughter from the children present, realizing the missionary children clearly understood what he was saying.[17]

As significant was the importance missionary children gave the Hawaiian language once they arrived in the United States to complete their education. When Sarah Coan (1843–1916) met King Kalākaua on his visit to New York, she called his Hawaiian "indescribably sweet . . . *only a native can say* aloha nui [many greetings]."[18] A group of Hawaiian mission friends, meeting together in Worcester, Massachusetts, in 1864, eschewed the "vulgar English language" and spoke only Hawaiian, using an interpreter to address non-Hawaiian speakers and assert their Hawaiian nationality.[19] Seventeen-year-old Lucy Thurston spoke Hawaiian on her deathbed. "*Auwe, auwe* [oh dear, oh dear]," Thurston repeated after contracting a respiratory infection in the United States.[20] Luther Gulick, sent to the United States at age twelve, returned to the islands twelve years later, still fluent in the Hawaiian language.[21]

Native Hawaiians understood the power of the spoken word. "Saying the word gives power to cause the action," Hawaiian historian Noenoe K. Silva notes. Missionary children, too, understood this power. "In many instances new meanings, or shades of meaning, must be given to natives' words," Hiram Bingham Jr. argued, as he called other missionary children to missionary service throughout Polynesia. Addressing an annual gathering of missionary descendants from across the islands, Bingham advocated in 1873 what his own father had done half a century before. By creating a Hawaiian written language and translating the Bible into Hawaiian, the American missionaries had shifted the Hawaiian language subtly yet unreservedly toward Christianity, forcing native Hawaiians to follow.[22]

When the American missionaries arrived in the islands in 1820, the ancient Hawaiian religious system of *kapu* (taboos), requiring strict segregation of the sexes, extreme deference to the chiefs, and religious sacrifices, had been abolished only the year before. The Protestant missionaries viewed the resultant upheaval in traditional Hawaiian religious practices as fortuitous, substituting Christian "*kapu*," including strict Sabbath keeping and prohibitions against drunkenness, prostitution, and gambling. The missionaries appropriated the term for the domestic sphere as well, calling their segregated yards for missionary children "*kapu* yards," playgrounds forbidden to native Hawaiians.[23]

Bilingual from birth, missionary children understood what their parents did not: language structures shape how different cultures see the world.[24] A native Hawaiian under chiefly rule justified his *ahupua'a* claim by calling himself a *kama'āina* (land child).[25] The word implied that one was native born and had a right to remain on the land. When white missionary children called themselves "loyal sons of the soil,"[26] they were saying the same: they were native-born "land children" who had the right to participate in the future of the nation. At least a few indigenous Hawaiians approved of the missionary children's appropriation of the Hawaiian language as identity. When missionary son William Rice married Mary Waterhouse, the daughter of English missionaries to the islands, the residents of Kauai held a traditional Hawaiian *'aha'aina* (feast) to celebrate. Five hundred native Hawaiians each brought gifts to the couple, "so delighted," in the words of one observer, "that [Rice] had married an island lady who could speak Hawaiian."[27]

Missionary children from Hawai'i seemed to instinctively understand that they were culturally different from their parents and that these differences affected the trajectory of their lives. Language, missionary son John Gulick wrote, "is the chief instrument of thought [and] builds itself out of symbols and metaphors into which higher and lower meanings are read according to the mood of the individual or the age." Missionary children absorbed the Hawaiian language, despite their parents' efforts, and some even preferred it. Missionary children struggled, however, with how to explain these preferences to their parents and, more importantly, how their Christian faith fit within this cultural divide. "Pity that in their boasted enthusiasm for truth the professed champions of ancient faith, often, yes, usually, shut their eyes to everything new that presents itself as truth," Gulick observed.[28] Sam Wilcox was more pragmatic, preferring to read the Hawaiian translation of the Bible over the English version.[29] As twentieth-century psychologists later noted: the acquisition of knowledge contains communal and cultural components. Nineteenth-century missionary children knew what their parents did not: children's understandings of God reflect the cultures in which they are raised.[30]

## Race and Education

Some missionary children took the power of the word further. In a series of articles written for the Washington DC *Evening Star* between 1893 and 1900, missionary son Sereno Bishop argued strenuously for U.S. annexation, trying to convince Americans of their manifest destiny to rule the inferior Hawaiian race. Bishop walked a fine line, not wanting Americans to believe the native Hawaiian people too dark or lowly to become U.S. citizens. He did this by using language as a cultural marker. Requiring all territorial proceedings to be conducted in English "would be an effective obstacle to the election of ignorant natives to the legislature," Bishop argued. "A Hawaiian of their average weakness of intellect is incapable of mastering the use of English." Bishop boasted that English "has wholly supplanted the native tongue, and has become the medium of instruction in all the schools." Controlling who could govern during the interim it took to acculturate native Hawaiian children to the English language would keep U.S. civil society intact.[31]

Bishop signed his articles under the pseudonym "Kamehameha"—the first Hawaiian chief to unite and rule the islands as a kingdom. In doing so Bishop made a profound declaration. He gave himself the authority to speak for the nation as its rightful heir and ruler.

Bishop's appropriation of indigenous Hawaiian language and history for the purpose of advancing notions of white racial superiority was breathtaking in its arrogance. By assuming the name of the Hawaiian kingdom's most beloved ruler for the purpose of negating indigenous Hawaiian autonomy, Bishop demonstrated how absolute some missionary children believed their mandate to speak for the Hawaiian Islands.

Not all missionary children viewed the Hawaiian nation's transition to English-language instruction positively. While Hawaiian chiefs desired their own sons and daughters to learn English as early as the 1840s, and former missionary and Hawaiian minister of education William Armstrong had encouraged the kingdom to adopt English-language instruction for all native children during his tenure in the 1850s, most public schools continued to teach in the native Hawaiian language until 1896, when the newly established Hawaiian Republic mandated

English-only instruction. Nevertheless, for decades prior, parents who could raise private funds for English-language instruction did so, hoping to further their own children's economic opportunities. The result was a two-tiered educational system in which the Hawaiian language became linked to poverty and backwardness, not cultural pride and civic success.[32] Missionary children Orramel Gulick and Ann Eliza Clark Gulick lamented the progressive loss of the native language among young Hawaiians, who increasingly associated the English language with economic advancement. "Of pride or love for his mother tongue he has but little," the couple wrote. "Soon may a small race and its language pass from the earth!"[33]

The ABCFM also considered the growing emphasis on English-language education harmful. In 1863 ABCFM secretary Rufus Anderson required missionary children at Punahou to study the Hawaiian language in order to receive free tuition.[34] Anderson's efforts were designed to maintain the ability of missionary children to carry on their parents' missionary work among non-English speaking natives, as well as to engender a greater willingness among the white children to serve the native population, a willingness Anderson believed lacking after his visit to the islands in 1863. "Do not look down upon them. Do not despise them," Anderson implored the missionary descendants.[35]

Both Anderson and the Gulicks understood that the dominance of the English language reflected the increasing political and economic influence white foreigners and natural-born subjects held in the islands. English-language immersion did more than disadvantage those unable to communicate in it. It damaged Hawaiian cultural identity. By linking English-language instruction to prospects for U.S. annexation, men such as Sereno Bishop also understood the cultural ramifications of doing so. Ultimately those who argued to preserve native Hawaiian identity were fighting a losing battle. Despite his own fluency in the Hawaiian language, missionary son Sanford Dole, as president of the Hawaiian Republic, signed the legislation mandating that all instruction be conducted in the English language in all Hawaiian schools.[36]

White annexationists in the Hawaiian Islands hoped to develop in Hawaiian children a new nationalism, predicating what recent research

**25.** Kealoha, Hawaiian nurse to the Baldwin children, whose parents were missionaries in the Hawaiian Islands. Native Hawaiians often cared for missionary children, and some children developed close attachments to their native caregivers. Mission Houses Museum Library.

has affirmed: a child's sociolinguistic situation is a key marker of his or her national identification. By eradicating the Hawaiian language from the primary mode of public discourse, as well as from public education, the revolutionaries were anticipating a new national identity—an American one. Yet many missionary descendants instinctively realized that changing the language one spoke could never completely erase a person's attachment to early ethnic ties. Neither did speaking English solidify an American identity. In falling on both sides of the English-language debate, missionary children reflected their own life-long struggle for a sense of national and ethnic belonging.

### Cannibals and Cousins

Confusion over personal identity engendered detachment toward the indigenous Hawaiian population and reflected the missionary children's deep-seated questions about their childhoods. Some were more confident than others. Henry Lyman relished striding through the Hawaiian woods dressed in an "unstarched shirt that displayed a wide rolling collar," high boots, a felt hat, and "bright red sash of Chinese silk." When running into a white foreigner, Lyman enjoyed surprising the visitor with his knowledge of Virgil, French, German, and Greek.[37] Others, such as Sanford Dole, wrote private poetry to "The Half-White Girl," perhaps not only a reflection of personal desire, but also of identity.[38] Others retreated into science and nature. "Trees are companions, the mountains are our elder brothers," John Gulick wrote.[39]

Their internal conflict over national belonging is particularly evident in how they referenced themselves and each other.[40] *Exile, stranger, expatriate,* and *Hawaiian* were terms missionary children from the islands used to describe themselves as students in the United States. Yet their most common nomenclature was *cannibal.* Sitting on the floor "a' la Hawaiian," nine "cannibals" met together in 1864 in Worcester, Massachusetts. They were so excited to see each other, speak Hawaiian, and discuss native politics that George Dole (1842–1912) wrote they left each other "feeling that we had enjoyed more happiness than often falls to the lot of man in one evening."[41]

Cannibal "conventions" occurred almost annually and were reported to fellow missionary children back in the islands. Twenty-two cannibals met at Williams College in 1857.[42] William Armstrong's Wall Street office was "a rendezvous for all Cannibals" passing through New York City.[43] "There are strong ties, which ought to bind the 'cannibal islanders' in this country together," James Alexander wrote. At Union Seminary in New York, Alexander roomed with three other Hawaiian mission youth, "a Cannibal throng," he called them.[44]

Indigenous Hawaiians had never been cannibals, and at least one missionary son was quite sensitive about this fact. Dexter Chamberlain (1807–87), whose parents had been part of the first missionary company to the islands, wrote to the *Boston Daily Advertiser* complaining that "Cannibal Islands" was inappropriate nomenclature for the sovereign Hawaiian kingdom. "That they were *Heathen* and pagan no one can doubt, but that they were savages and cannibals I do not believe," Chamberlain, by then in his seventies, stated. "I was a resident of these Islands several years and believe the aborigines of these Islands to have been kind, hospitable . . . and unless driven to the necessity as in the case of Captain Cook, his officers, and crew, would never have harmed any one."[45]

Missionary children did not believe the Hawaiians had been cannibals, but they realized most Americans did. The children's use of the term suggests that they, too, felt judged as uncivilized by their American peers. "I have seen persons who did not know where the Sandwich Islands are . . . I have seen persons who were surprised at my being white," one boy wrote home.[46] "You can imagine then the pleasure I felt when once in a while I would run against a 'Cannibal' and be greeted with *Aloha*," William Andrews explained.[47]

Yet returning to the islands after college, some missionary children struggled to feel at home again. "I know the fault must be mostly in me," wrote Mary Castle (1838–1926). "I long for a resting place, not of body, but of mind and soul, and it seems to me that I shall never reach it," Castle revealed.[48] "I do hope and pray that [Evarts] may become settled and contented," James Chamberlain wrote about his wandering brother. "There is a place for anybody in this big world. May he find it."[49]

*Creole* was the name Robert Andrews believed best described himself—neither Anglo nor Hawaiian.[50] "We, who are such, hold a peculiar position," Joseph Cooke said of the missionary children, "having early recollections of cocoa-nut and kukui groves, and of sea-breezes and balmy trade-winds sweeping through them, of surf-beaten shore ramblings, and canoe voyages with swarthy, half-naked men at the paddles—and yet by some sort of in-bred instinct, taking to all the ways of the Fatherland when we return thither." Speaking of those who had traveled between the Hawaiian Islands and the United States, Cooke revealed, "None of us are earnest but are sad . . . we are divided in our being, either the one or the other part of ourself vainly craving what it has not and cannot have."[51]

The community in which missionary children most often found a sense of belonging was one they created for themselves. Attempting to carve an identity from the larger Hawaiian society, missionary children together formed the Hawaiian Mission Children's Society (HMCS) in 1853. Originally established by Punahou students to raise contributions for Protestant Christian missions, the society quickly became a social network for missionary descendants and, eventually, their allies. Members called each other "cousins," just as their parents had called fellow missionaries "brothers" and "sisters." The "Cousins' Society" became a place through which monthly meetings, regular correspondence, and annual reports could disseminate information about each other, even around the world. The first missionary the Cousins' Society supported was Dr. Luther Halsey Gulick, one of their own. Eventually the group funded Hawaiian schools and paid for the education of native Hawaiian missionary children who remained in the islands while their parents traveled throughout Polynesia. The society also funded several cousins to come back to the islands to teach. By 1883 the society boasted over nine hundred members. What had started as a group of young Punahou students, sewing to raise funds for missionaries, had turned into an influential peer network of adult missionary descendants, families, and friends, together possessing close to $2 million of the estimated $32 million in island property.[52]

The Cousins' Society had a decided influence on its members studying in the United States. "No cousins by lineage, in this country, are more united and interested in each other, than the mission children, the only playmates of each other," wrote James Alexander from Williams College. "I would enjoy infinitely more a sojourn with my Cousins at the Islands than with my best cousins in the States. And I find that I only echo the feelings of my Hawaiian friends there."[53] The constant correspondence, including newsletters, kept interest in the islands alive among the Hawaiian-born college students and encouraged them to return home after graduation.

### Children of Promise

If missionary children struggled with their national identity, they wrestled even more with a constant fear of displeasing their parents. The Hawaiian mission was the ABCFM's most successful missionary enterprise during the nineteenth century. Rufus Anderson declared the islands essentially Christianized by 1863 with "nothing equal to it" in Christian history.[54] Some of the missionary parents were household names in New England. Titus Coan's seven-thousand-member church in Hilo was the largest Protestant church in the world in 1842. When Samuel Armstrong's father died, the news ran in hundreds of U.S. newspapers. Americans avidly read Hiram Bingham's *A Residence of Twenty-One Years in the Sandwich Islands* (1847).[55]

With the pressure children faced from parents to embrace the missionary profession, some missionary children naturally sought to distinguish themselves in the field. Hiram Bingham's own children were profoundly influenced by their father's success. Elizabeth Bingham tried to become a missionary to China by engaging herself to a man commissioned by the ABCFM. When the board refused to sponsor her due to her poor health, her fiancé broke off the engagement. "She will feel it deeply I know, for her heart was set on going as a missionary," a friend wrote.[56] Nearly two decades later, the Cousin's Society invited Elizabeth's sister Lydia to teach at the Kawaiahaʻo Seminary for native Hawaiian girls. A relative guessed she would accept the position: "I know her mind is not

**26.** Natives crossing the *pali*. For missionary children, the *pali* (steep hill or precipice) symbolized the deep cultural divide they balanced as children of American parents and subjects of the Hawaiian kingdom. Mission Houses Museum Library.

at rest on the subject of entering the foreign work *somewhere*."[57] Lydia Bingham arrived in the islands in 1867, after an absence of nearly thirty years. Elizabeth Bingham joined her sister at the seminary in 1869.[58]

Elizabeth and Lydia's brother Hiram Bingham was similarly drawn to the missionary profession. Under relentless pressure from his father, Bingham decided to go someplace no other missionary had gone and translate the Bible into an unwritten language. Initially sent back to the Hawaiian Islands by the ABCFM in 1856, he wrote his sister, "Father's old people are making very strenuous effort to keep me here as their pastor." The Honolulu congregation circulated a petition signed by several hundred people to convince Bingham to stay. Despite calling the Islands his "native soil" and the indigenous people his "countrymen," Bingham was restless. "I have very little inclination to remain," he wrote. Bingham soon moved on to the Gilbert Islands, translating the entire Bible into the Gilbertese language.[59]

Early ABCFM missionaries, such as the elder Binghams, set strenuous and dramatic goals for themselves while living in the islands. Their children witnessed numerous physical and mental breakdowns as a result. Missionary children sometimes referred to themselves as "orphans" and "fatherless," even when both parents were still living. Missionary children were both attracted to and repelled by the missionary mindset, calling it "anxious labor" that "captivated [their parents] as the prospect of gold drew those who were eager for wealth to the mines of California."[60]

Even though missionary children believed that everyone possessed "some great object in life," most believed theirs would "not be in the line of missionary work." One of children's strongest arguments against missionary labor was the "sacrifice of family life so imperatively demanded by such work." Sent to the United States to live among strangers or to boarding school in Honolulu, missionary children as young as five years old spent years apart from their families. Some never saw their parents again. Missionary son William Smith voiced the missionary children's resolve not to enter into a profession by which they themselves had been hurt: "We shrink from repeating our Fathers' experiences, or of placing our children in the same painful conditions."[61]

More significantly, a sizable minority of missionary children rejected their parents' faith altogether. John Gulick described one such missionary son he visited in the United States: "He admitted religious truth but said he did not feel its power and was a stranger to its hopes. . . . Resolved to make the most of life, he passes on to gain the giddy heights of honor and intellectual power."[62] George Wilcox refused to go before his father's congregation to profess a spiritual conversion he did not feel.[63] Missionary children heard their parents complain about the sacrifices they had made on the mission field and instinctively understood that the external pressure they faced to follow in their parents' footsteps was just another way to commend the martyrdom of the missionaries, delineate their successes, and confirm the rightness of their calling.[64]

Missionary parents, as well as their supporters in the United States, believed children served as important markers in nineteenth-century American missionary endeavors. Not only did missionary parents believe success in the islands depended upon their own children continuing the evangelical mission, but missionaries looked to children as the means to shape Hawaiian society into a Christian nation. ABCFM missionaries in the Hawaiian Islands printed their first Hawaiian-language children's book with spelling, reading, songs, and catechism lessons in 1830. Missionaries passed out over 1,100 copies within two months of its first printing.[65] The missionaries also operated schools for native Hawaiian children. Missionary Laura Judd helped organize the first school and wrote, "The children were not yet tamed, and to catch them even was considered an impossibility."[66] The missionaries determined to focus their labor on educating children as the means to influencing the future indigenous leadership of the nation. Over six hundred native children and youth converted to Christianity in 1838 alone.[67] Arrell Morgan Gibson notes that education became British and American missionaries' "most widely accepted offering" throughout the Pacific region.[68]

American missionary societies had an agenda for children in the United States, as well. The American Tract Society's *Tract Primer* asked children, "Do you know that there are some parts of the world where the minds of men are so dark, that they worship the sun, moon, and stars, and call them gods? . . . When you look at the starry heaven, pity the blindness of these people, and give thanks to God that you have been taught the way of life."[69] The Tract Society's *Children's Picture Book* contained pictures of Polynesian islands with captions including "Perhaps missionaries have come to this island. If they have, they will teach the people to love God. . . . Then we shall have nothing to fear."[70] These simple reading books were designed to inculcate a respect for American missionaries and depict a need for foreign missions, both to engender "systematic charity" and to remind children about the realities of sin and demands of piety.[71] When seventeen-year-old missionary daughter Lucy Thurston died in 1841, the American Tract Society published her journal along with its own editorial comments: "Lucy was *an industrious scholar . . .* Lucy was *obedient to her parents . . .* Lucy *reverenced the Sabbath . . .* Lucy *loved the heathen . . .* Lucy died a *happy, peaceful death*."[72]

The American public's long relationship with the Hawaiian Islands began with children. Children read Captain Cook tales, and a stage play about the English captain ran in Boston and starred a Hawaiian youth actor. In 1816 the ABCFM published the *Narrative of Five Youths from the Sandwich Islands* to raise funds to educate young indigenous Hawaiians arriving in the United States aboard New England merchant ships. The ABCFM hoped to return the native students to the Hawaiian Islands as missionaries. The death of one such student, Henry Obookiah, became the springboard for the first American mission to the Hawaiian kingdom.[73]

The ABCFM also encouraged local societies to start juvenile associations. "Who will carry it on when we are dead?" the board argued. "How easy it is to obtain access to a parent, through the medium of a beloved child," one local society argued. New England churches utilized *A Missionary Catechism, for the Use of Children; Containing a Brief View of the Moral Condition of the World, and the Progress of Missionary Efforts among the Heathen*, published by Yale College in 1821. Part of the ABCFM's early fundraising efforts included supplying slates for Hawaiian children. The success of this effort was quickly followed by offering earmarks for children's education. Missionaries in the Hawaiian Islands advocated the "exclusive privilege" of furnishing Hawaiian children with "such books only as were designed to have a salutary tendency, or were, on the whole, favorable to the service of God."[74]

By far the most popular ABCFM fundraising effort was directed at both American and Hawaiian children. In an amazing display of cultural exchange, children bought "stock certificates" in a vessel built to service Protestant missionaries traveling between the Hawaiian and Micronesian Islands. When the *Morning Star* arrived in Honolulu in 1857, native children, who also possessed ownership in the vessel, lined the shore cheering. The Honolulu *Commercial Advertiser* estimated that one hundred thousand children in both the United States and the Islands had contributed to the construction of the $12,000 ship. Successive *Morning Star* ships were built with children's contributions, as earlier vessels were wrecked or wore out. Two thousand Sunday schools worked together to raise funds for the *Morning Star II* in 1866, contributing $24,000 in less than five months. Two thousand Americans came to see the *Morning Star IV*'s Boston launch in 1884. The chairman of the ABCFM wrote the "owners" of the missionary vessel, "I doubt if any ship ever had so many owners, of such age and character. . . . You are all missionaries." So significant was the *Morning Star* to ABCFM efforts in Micronesia that the arrival of the *Morning Star* remains annually celebrated in the Marshall Islands as "Gospel Day."[75]

### Children of the Land

Hawaiian missionary children occupied a strange, in-between place within this cultural exchange. Missionary children, raised in a torrid climate among native "heathens," were suspected by their American peers of tending toward intellectual lethargy and cultural inferiority. By the end of the nineteenth century many native Hawaiians, rallying "Hawai'i for Hawaiians," also viewed the white missionary children with disdain. Queen Lili'uokalani called them the "missionary set," and the term *missionary* became connected to anyone supporting U.S. annexation.[76] Most missionary children were not missionaries, and some questioned annexation, yet their identities remained fused to their American parents, trapped between the United States and Hawaiian kingdom.

Among contemporary Hawaiian historians, missionary descendants have fared no better. Some writers use the term *haole* to describe the white men, including missionary sons, who forced the Bayonet Constitution limiting the monarch's power upon King Kalākaua in 1887 and over-threw Queen Liliʻuokalani in 1893. The Hawaiian word, which initially referred to any foreigner, came to denote exclusively a white person. Jonathan Osorio writes this change occurred after Captain Cook's arrival to the islands in 1778, although the first published Hawaiian-language dictionary, printed by the ABCFM missionaries in 1836, still defined *haole* as "foreigner."[77] Missionary son Samuel Armstrong recorded that *haole* meant "sacred white pig" and had once been a compliment bestowed upon white visitors.[78] Native Hawaiian David Malo, also writing in the nineteenth century, called the *puaa* (pig) the most important animal in the islands, sacrificed at all significant indigenous rituals. Malo noted an "entirely white" *puaa* was called *haole*.[79] "Now, there is nothing sacred about them or their property," Armstrong wrote about white residents and the growing anti-*haole* sentiment around him. Today *haole* is most often used disparagingly, such as to act like a white person, or to be Europeanized or Americanized.[80]

Conflating national identity and race places white missionary children in Hawaiʻi outside the Hawaiian nation, yet a similar problem exists when attempting to limit Hawaiian political legitimacy to indigenous natives. As Lilikalā Kameʻeleihiwa argues, true Hawaiians share a genealogy derived from the land and "distinct from the waves of foreigners that have inundated our islands." Kameʻeleihiwa uses the term *makaʻāinana* (people who attend the land) to refer to the Hawaiian natives who worked the land for their *aliʻi*.[81] Yet as Cari Costanzo Kapur points out, other racial groups, such as the descendants of Japanese laborers brought to the islands during the nineteenth century to work on plantations, believe their generational connection to the land demonstrates cultural and national belonging.[82]

The missionary children's own attitudes toward indigenous Hawaiians does not help their position within the debate over Hawaiian identity. Scholars, such as Osorio and Silva, use the terms *kanaka* (person or Hawaiian) or *kanaka maoli* (real or native Hawaiian) to refer to Hawaiian natives by racial ancestry, and nowhere do missionary children refer to themselves as *kānaka*. In fact, missionary children, as Silva points out, tended to use the term pejoratively.[83] Cooking "a' la *kanaka*" meant burying meat in the ground and sitting on the floor.[84] Living "*kanaka* style" meant sleeping on dirt floors covered with fleas and animals.[85] Missionary children conflated *kanaka* with "heathen," designating the word a behavior associated with race. "How many of them suppose that [Punahou] is for the Kanaka and the Niger?" John Gulick asked his father about fellow missionary families, as Punahou began accepting nonwhites in the 1850s. "I think perhaps . . . you would find more aversion to such equality than you anticipate, even amongst your good folk."[86] In using the word *kanaka* disparagingly, white missionary children placed themselves outside indigenous Hawaiian culture. Silva is blunt: missionary children were "determined to rule over the Kanaka Maoli."[87]

Nevertheless, in 1846 the native Hawaiian government made its intentions clear: "*E manaoia kela haole keia haole hoohiki pela, ua lilo oia ma ke ano pili i na hana a pau, i kanaka maoli o Hawaii nei* [Every foreigner so naturalized, shall be deemed to all intents and purposes, a native of the Hawaiian Islands]." Under the law *haole* could become *kanaka maoli*. A white person could become a "real" Hawaiian. More importantly, Hawaiian law declared "all persons born within the jurisdiction of this kingdom, whether of alien foreigners, of naturalized or of native parents, and all persons born abroad of a parent native of this kingdom . . . shall be amenable to the laws of this kingdom *as native subjects*" (emphasis added).[88] White missionary children living in the nineteenth century believed their "nativeness" assured.

As anthropologists and historians of the Hawaiian people have long noted, "the hallmark of civilization was, and still is, generosity."[89] Nineteenth-century Hawaiian historian John Papa Ii recorded that Kamehameha I traveled with *haole* men and gave them use of Hawaiian lands. "They were like the people who were born in the islands," Ii writes.[90] Also writing in the nineteenth century, Samuel Kamakau noted the dark side of Hawaiian openness: "The strangers call this love ignorance and think it is good for nothing."[91]

Perhaps nineteenth-century missionary children in Hawai'i would best be described as the *hānai* (adopted). Hawaiian generosity included the practice of raising the children of friends and family members. The practice signified the fluidity of familial relationships but also the very real acceptance of other *kānaka* (human beings), including *haole*, as family. Of the *haole* Kamehameha rewarded, Ii writes, "These men were all related to the king in some way."[92] Missionary daughter Elizabeth Judd records that Kinau, the Hawaiian chiefess who served as regent for her brother Kamehameha III, requested to adopt Elizabeth at her birth in 1831. "As I was the first white girl she had ever seen, " Judd explained, "[Kinau] deigned from that time on to show a great interest in me, either visiting me or having me visit her every day." Kamehameha III later approached Judd's father, requesting that Elizabeth and her sister Helen be married to Kinau's sons Lot and Alexander Liholiho. The American missionary's own definitions of openness and family were not so generous. Judd declined. Both young men eventually became Hawaiian kings.[93]

Samuel Armstrong described the deep attachments formed within the *hānai* relationship. "It is their custom to transfer their loyalty to the children of their friends," he wrote. "For these kind Hawaiians, we, their children, feel a deep attachment."[94] When missionary parents began to pass away, and missionary children perceived the Hawaiian monarchy as moving against their influence and position in the islands, they reacted, taking their own steps to separate from the Hawaiian monarchy. The *hānai* became *kamali'i mākua'ole* (orphans).

Missionary children became important tools in the construction of a colonial society in the Hawaiian Islands. Their presence served to bridge the cultural divide. Indigenous Hawaiians welcomed missionary infants into their hearts and homes, even to the point of asking to adopt them. Missionary families used their children to demonstrate proper familial deportment to Hawaiian parents. White missionary children grew up expecting this continued position of privilege, never realizing how subversive it was. As one missionary son described his appointment to the Hawaiian government, "My parents were quite overwhelmed by this unexpected bounty; but to me, in my ignorance of the world, it seemed quite naturally a part of the due order of events."[95]

Hawaiian mission children were white, but they were not foreigners; they were "Hawaiian" by birth but not by race. Missionary children represented a racial minority within the Hawaiian kingdom. In some respects, missionary children who remained in the islands had the freedom to choose on which side of the *pali* (steep hill) they would fall—living as white Hawaiians or as Americanized foreigners. Many wrestled with confusion over their identities for decades. Yet their writings throughout the turbulent decades of the 1870s, 1880s, and 1890s are increasingly filled with disdain for the Hawaiian *ali'i* who rejected missionary influence and sought a greater voice for the indigenous Hawaiian people and greater native control over a legislature dominated by the white, propertied class. Only a few missionary children cautioned humility and restraint. George Dole warned his peers in 1876, "I think it especially true that in the case of the Hawaiians we are too prone to thoughtless and uncharitable condemnation."[96] Dole's brother, Sanford Dole, also questioned the use of force but changed his mind after realizing the revolutionaries would move forward without him. Dole decided to lead the revolution and hoped eventual U.S. annexation would be "an end to our difficulties."[97]

Dole echoed the beliefs of many missionary children. When the United States annexed the Hawaiian Republic during the Spanish-American War and the American flag was raised in front of the Executive Building on August 12, 1898, Orramel and Ann Eliza Clark Gulick gushed, "It was truly an impressive scene. . . . Great hopes were entertained for better things."[98]

Missionary children believed their American Protestant heritage gave them a unique and privileged place in Hawaiian society. The children had grown up under the tutelage of their parents and witnessed their parents' dramatic success in influencing the laws and customs of the Hawaiian monarchy. Never doubting their Hawaiian citizenship, missionary children attached themselves to the land and opportunities around them, cultivating among themselves paternalist feelings toward the indigenous Hawaiian people they, in reality, often

**27.** Annual meeting of the Hawaiian Mission Children's Society ("Cousins Society"), 1918. Mission Houses Museum Library.

disdained. While some held out hope the Hawaiian people would develop into capable republican citizens and successful property owners, others believed the islands would inevitably transfer to whites. When the native population began to exert its own influence upon the Hawaiian monarchy, calling for the revival of ancient Hawaiian religious practices, an end to liquor prohibition, the granting of opium licenses, and the adoption of universal suffrage, missionary children responded with fear and hostility.[99]

Certainly Liliʻuokalani's efforts to expand the electorate promised to dilute the voices of white property owners, including missionary descendants. The economic interests of the descendants—as prosperous landowners, bankers, planters, and entrepreneurs—were closely tied to the United States, which had granted the Hawaiian kingdom trade reciprocity in 1875. U.S. annexation assured the continuation and expansion of Hawaiian commerce. Yet, as John Whitehead has noted, revolutionaries such as Sanford Dole and missionary grandson Lorrin Thurston "were more concerned with the conduct of the monarchy than the financial interests of the sugar planters."[100] Thurston said as much

**28.** Lili'uokalani appeals to the American press in 1897 for aid in restoring her monarchy. Library of Congress, Prints and Photographs Division, LC-USZ62-105893.

in arguing for annexation: "I am firmly convinced that no other way can what is called 'Anglo Saxon,' 'Occidental,' or 'Western' civilization, as distinguished from 'Eastern,' 'Oriental,' or 'Asiatic' civilization, be maintained in this country." Thurston threw down the gauntlet: "Unless it is so to be, we and our descendants cannot live here."[101] Missionary descendants could not sit back and watch the decline of their influence, including their ability to define the religious and cultural values of the Hawaiian monarchy and people.

Ultimately, the missionary children's decision to support revolution was made easier by the close connections they maintained with their "cousins" in the islands. As fellow missionary children, they understood each other, supported each other, and, in the end, jumped off the precipice together. Love for the Hawaiian land, which missionary children had acquired from the native culture around them, did not include respect for the indigenous people on the land, a reflection of the cultural messages the children had received from their American parents, teachers, and peers. Missionary descendants believed the future of the Hawaiian Islands was best held in their hands. The irony is that while missionary children in Hawai'i believed they were identifying with the Hawaiian Islands and acting on their behalf in supporting the 1893 overthrow of the Hawaiian monarchy and 1898 annexation to the United States, the children actually were aligning themselves with white empires around the world in one of the most dramatic periods of colonization in history.

# Conclusion

*White Hawaiians before the World*

The childhood shows the man, as morning shows the day.
John Milton[1]

An exile, wandering o'er the deep, yet often in my dreamful sleep, I am a child once more.
Sanford Ballard Dole[2]

Strangers move about but native sons remain.
Samuel Kamakau[3]

ABCFM missionary parents in the Hawaiian Islands expected their children to use their upbringing and education to benefit the world. Parents exhorted their children to place personal ambition and worldly wealth aside, in order to bring Christian light to dark places and bolster the next generation of Christian missionaries. Missionaries expected their children to lead spiritual, cultural, and institutional transformations wherever they went, as well as to protect the accomplishments of parents back home in the Hawaiian Islands.

Numerous missionary children from Hawai'i achieved professional distinction, and many had a significant impact upon the political and international changes that occurred in the late nineteenth century. As teachers, journalists, ministers, and philanthropists, the missionary children from Hawai'i presaged the next generation of youth who would join the ranks of the Student Volunteer Movement, YMCA, and YWCA—as well as numerous social gospel organizations—to "evangelize the world" in their generation.[4]

Missionary children from the Hawaiian Islands argued they represented evolution at its best. As adults, missionary children chose careers they believed represented "the best vitality." Their choices continued the political and economic divergence between whites and native Hawaiians, as well as the broader patriarchy and paternalism that existed among Euro-American whites toward indigenous peoples at the end of the nineteenth century.[5]

For John Gulick, Samuel Armstrong, and Sanford Dole, a bicultural upbringing was significant to the decisions they made as adults. These men symbolized the importance that masculinity, male leadership, and the education of boys played in nineteenth-century Anglo-American culture. Although missionary daughters sometimes defied their parents and pursued their own careers, missionary sons more decidedly revealed their Anglo-American notions of race and gender in their actions against Lili'uokalani. Despite the Queen's professed Christianity, missionary sons betrayed her with little compunction when given the first opportunity less than two years into her reign. Their experiences as missionary children and education as white elites shaped their belief that they were capable of leading and altering foreign cultures. Although Armstrong stayed in the United States, Dole returned to the Hawaiian Islands, and Gulick traveled the world, each left his mark upon the peoples he encountered.

## Wise Men of Gotham

"As we launch out," Sanford Dole wrote in 1869, "we trust . . . that the story of the three wise men of Gotham, who went to sea in a bowl, may not be unhappily repeated in our experience."[6] Dole had returned to Honolulu to practice law and begin a newspaper, and he reflected hopes for success that were shared by his peers. Because of the widespread influence of missionary sons like Dole, Armstrong, and Gulick, it is tempting to place them, like the mythical men of Gotham, inside a glass bowl and judge them as colonialists of the worst sort. Many have. Samuel Armstrong, notes William H. Watkins, was a "colonizer for the twentieth century."[7] Yet Armstrong also volunteered for a job few wanted—the education of freed slaves in the Reconstruction South. After volunteering to lead a black regiment, Armstrong continued to work after the Civil War to prove that they—and he—were worthy of American citizenship. By establishing Hampton Institute, Armstrong was following his parents' model and demonstrating the "civilizing" effect an American education could have upon nonwhite peoples.

While many have argued that Armstrong's paternal policies toward former Southern slaves kept African American citizens in positions of menial labor, stunted their political voices, and denied their right to choose their own educational goals, this picture is complicated by Armstrong's Hawaiian experiences. The missionary and cultural influences that affected Armstrong during his Hawaiian childhood shaped the directions Armstrong pursued as an adult. "The negro and the Polynesian have many striking similarities," Armstrong explained.[8]

Like other nonwhite races, Armstrong believed African Americans were "two thousand years apart in real civilization" from white Americans.[9] Armstrong's educational philosophy of self-help merged with nineteenth-century Lamarckian ideas of race, which held that moral, behavioral, and cultural traits were hereditary. "Only in generations can [the Negro] develop those guiding instincts and institutions that the Anglo Saxon has reached through ages of hard experience," he argued.[10]

Despite adopting these Anglo-American ideas, Armstrong was critical of the ABCFM project in the Hawaiian Islands. Echoing lessons he had learned at Williams College, Armstrong decried the missionaries who neglected the "practical training of the whole life."[11] Regarding his peers, the sons and daughters of ABCFM missionaries, Armstrong confirmed, "The Puritanical ideas and ways of the missionary fathers have not been generally followed by their children."[12] He summarized, "I would rather *minister* than be a minister."[13]

On the eve of the American Civil War, Armstrong wrote his sister, "Political excitement runs very high here, but I wonder at my own indifference to it. . . . I take less interest in American politics here than I did at the Islands." Armstrong's emotional attachment to the war effort grew after visiting New York City with his sister shortly after the fall of Fort Sumter. Watching the departure of New York's Seventh Regiment from a third-story window, Armstrong recorded it was "perhaps the sublimest spectacle New York ever saw." Caught up in the crowd's excitement, Armstrong declared, "Even we cannibals intend to adopt the red, white and blue ribbon instead of the plain red as our full national costume."[14]

Armstrong decided to join the Union army. With no other business prospects after graduation, Armstrong admitted that he had not "learned to love the negro" but justified his decision to enlist as a "sort of abolition[ism] . . . I go in, then for freeing [the slaves], more on account of their souls than their bodies." Armstrong had been taught abolition as a child in Hawai'i by missionary Jonathan Green, who often preached against U.S. slavery. The first African American minister Armstrong met lived in Honolulu. The Civil War gave Armstrong a reason to ally with the United States.[15]

Two additional events solidified Armstrong's plans to remain in the United States after college. With the ascension of Lot to the Hawaiian throne in 1863, Armstrong believed the islands had inherited a "miserable government." Lot began the monarchy's steady retrenchment away from legislative authority and missionary influence. Armstrong felt so negatively about the turn in Hawaiian politics that he thought "less and less about going back." The same year U.S. president Abraham Lincoln issued the Emancipation Proclamation, elevating war into a cause to which Armstrong could commit. "So long as this war is to sustain the President's proclamation, *I am in for it*," Armstrong wrote.[16]

Armstrong fought at Gettysburg; he earned a promotion to major for his conduct in the battle and requested charge of an African American regiment. He was appointed by President Lincoln as a lieutenant colonel in the Ninth Regiment of U.S. Colored Troops. Armstrong hoped to demonstrate to the nation the bravery of those in his regiment. After two years on the battlefield with his regiment, Armstrong concluded, "The negro rallied grandly to the duty required . . . [and] gave me a basis of hope to begin the work at Hampton."[17]

In 1865, on the day of his third full year of service in the U.S. Army, Samuel Chapman Armstrong became a U.S. citizen. "This is a thought too immense to be grappled at once, but enough to excite the profoundest emotions," Armstrong wrote his sister Carrie. Unconcerned with American politics just four years before, Armstrong now believed "there may be a place for me in the struggle for right and wrong in this country." That place turned out to be Hampton Institute in Virginia, created under the auspices of the American Missionary Association and directed by Armstrong until his death in 1893.[18]

Despite the accolades he received from Americans for his military service, Armstrong's Americanization was never complete. Armstrong detested the profaneness of Union soldiers, the ostentatious displays of money in New York City, and the emasculating schooling of American children, where "shoes and cloth and money are too plenty." He also condemned Northerners for their attitude toward Reconstruction. "It is simply barbaric to whip the South and go home rejoicing to build monuments of victory, leaving one-third of their countrymen in the depths of distress," he complained.[19] Ten years after achieving American citizenship, Armstrong wrote to Punahou students: "A Hawaiian cannot become a thoroughly rooted American. We may be buried in smoke and dust and work for years, but something like the roar of a distant surf is always sounding in our ears."[20]

Just before the stroke that would take his life, Armstrong reflected that he was "most thankful" for his parents, Hawaiian home, war experiences, Williams College, and work at Hampton.[21] While each of these experiences shaped Armstrong in different ways, Armstrong was most decidedly the product of his bicultural upbringing. The question is not whether Armstrong practiced a paternalist educational philosophy. He did. The question is how Armstrong's views compare to those of his white American contemporaries and whether Armstrong's Hawaiian upbringing influenced his educative philosophy.

Armstrong sought to fill his Hampton students "full of the spirit of missionary work."[22] As one alumnus remembered, "General Armstrong always made us feel that Hampton students 'gathered to scatter.'"[23] Sent out to spread a message of Christian character through practical living, Hampton graduates were taking a gospel Armstrong molded according to his experiences in manual labor at Punahou School, as well as his knowledge of American missionary efforts among native Hawaiians. His views of African Americans and Native Americans were intimately linked to what he had been taught about race as a student in the islands and at Williams College. His decisions to fight in the Civil War and found Hampton Institute merged out of an active personality, rejection of the ABCFM experiment in the Hawaiian Islands, and effort to somehow follow in his parents' path.

The practical impact of Armstrong's beliefs has been well documented. While Armstrong would have rejected the suggestion he was establishing a national system of racial subordination, Northern philanthropists, crucial to the support of Hampton, saw in the manual labor model an opportunity for trained, non-unionized, agricultural labor and, thus, a way to maintain a U.S. monopoly on the international cotton trade. "We cannot afford to lose the Negro. We have urgent need of all and of more," stated industrialist Andrew Carnegie.[24] With a declining national will to invest in Southern reconstruction and the rise of Jim Crow in the South, myopic Northern philanthropic investment in rural industrial schools became the primary option for Southern secondary education. By the 1930s industrial training was the "sole source of public secondary education" in nearly a third of all Southern counties.[25]

Manual education became the chosen mechanism for maintaining nonwhite agricultural labor in post-annexation Hawai'i, as well. By 1906 territorial governor George Carter worried that the agricultural wealth of Hawai'i was in jeopardy "as long as the rising generation, in large proportion, is not being bred to cultivation of the soil."[26] After annexation by the United States, Hawaiian planters could no longer import Chinese labor, and the territorial government turned to manual and English education as the means to raising patriotic plantation workers from among the majority nonwhite population, including the islands' Japanese residents, who represented the largest immigrant group in the islands. Hawaii's Department of Public Instruction ensured that all public schools offered manual education and created a Board of Industrial Schools to oversee agricultural training.[27]

U.S. educators also took the Hampton and Tuskegee models overseas to U.S. colonial possessions. Estelle Reel, U.S. superintendent of Indian schools from 1898 to 1910, used Tuskegee as the model for her 1901 *Uniform Course of Study*, standardized curriculum distributed to American Indian schools, as well as colonial schools in Puerto Rico and the Philippines. Yet Armstrong's self-help pedagogy at Hampton also influenced the Indian nationalist movement. By the early twentieth century, Mohandas Gandhi, impressed with Hampton and Tuskegee Institutes as methods of racial uplift, experimented with self-sustaining education, rural training, and manual arts.[28]

"The names of General Armstrong and Booker T. Washington are very great names of service and sacrifice," Gandhi stated in the late 1920s. "I want our educated friends to realize this. I want them also to realize that when they are propagating intellectual culture, they must also inculcate the principle of dignity of labour as is done in those institutions." Gandhi believed that Indian children did not need a liberal arts education. They needed vocational training for their predominantly rural environment. Because the cost of education for a decolonized state was potentially crippling, Gandhi advocated self-supporting education. "[Students] would not only repay the expenses incurred in the schools but would turn that training to use in after life," Gandhi wrote. "No originality is claimed for the method advocated here. Booker T. Washington tried it with considerable success."[29]

Gandhi's educational efforts, which began in South Africa, were intimately linked to his view of nonviolence. "We have to make [Indian children] true representatives of our culture," he said. "We cannot do so otherwise than by giving them a course of self-supporting primary education." Gandhi believed that Armstrong's work at Hampton Institute was "worth studying by all." Hampton and Tuskegee, Gandhi noted, elevated the "dignity of manual labour."[30]

Samuel Armstrong was not the first American to link race, nationhood, and responsible citizenship to agricultural production and land ownership. After all, seventeenth-century New England Puritans and early nineteenth-century Jeffersonian Democrats had argued similarly.[31] Yet Armstrong was the first in the United States to demonstrate the "success" of manual labor education. "We are ahead and alone," he wrote his mother in 1868.[32] The manual education model would continue to influence educational polices into the twentieth century. In the United States and its colonial possessions, Armstrong's advocates infused prejudice into the industrial education system. In South Africa, Gandhi offered hope. Armstrong could not have predicted all the cultural contexts in which a system he advocated would be tried. Yet he would have clearly understood the complicated relationship between nation and race that infused these experiments.

Sanford Dole would have also recognized the complexities of nationalism. Despite the revolutionary political changes instituted by Dole, his public and private life reflected ambivalence toward race, religion, and nationhood. While Dole clearly believed Christianity provided "all civil, commercial and religious prosperity" in the islands, he often seemed dissatisfied with his whiteness. No one "except clergymen, government officials and fools" wore Euro-American attire in the islands, Dole commented. Dole frequently reflected upon the beauty of Hawaiian women as compared to their "stooping and round-shouldered" white counterparts. "Should one of Pele's lava flows wipe out Hilo," Dole remarked of the white merchants who thronged Hilo's harbor, it would be the "retribution of Nature for a community that could only appreciate it for the gold that it lured in its coffers."[33]

Dole also ignored personal attacks directed at him by other whites living in the islands. Without asking his New England wife, Dole adopted Hawaiian native Elizabeth Puiki Napoleon, the daughter of Pamahoʻa Napoleon. The *hānai* (adoption), based upon the Hawaiian custom of allowing a close friend or relative to raise one's child, agitated the white community. Some speculated that Lizzie, the only fair-skinned child of Pamahoʻa's fifteen children, was Dole's own daughter, but Dole ignored the rumors, to the great chagrin of his wife. Dole and Lizzie clearly loved each other. Dole wrote poetry to Lizzie, and Lizzie named her firstborn child, as well as her ninth and last child, after Dole. Dole's political commitment to his birthplace and personal relationship with Lizzie suggests Dole's bicultural identity, unlike Armstrong's, remained firmly rooted in the *'āina* (land) of Hawai'i.[34]

Unlike Armstrong and Dole, John Gulick spent his life wandering, only to return at the end of his life to the Hawaiian Islands. Like Dole, Gulick and his wife adopted three children while in China. All three were Chinese. Despite his professional and personal engagement with the Chinese and Japanese cultures, Gulick preferred to retreat into science and nature. Gulick's adult life reflected the same sense of exploration and adventure that characterized his childhood. Yet Gulick also wrestled with deep emotional conflict in search of his national and spiritual identity. While in college Gulick desperately hoped his father would change his mind and allow him to become a scientist. Gulick wrote to his father:

> We are all fond of the beauties of nature and of the history of past generations and almost everyone from the king to the beggar spends more or less in gratifying this taste; and it was undoubtedly implanted by the Creator. . . . Now all these things are good and not to be frowned upon, if they are kept within proper bounds. . . . Awaken in a young person a disposition to seek the new and wonderful in the hidden mysteries of nature, and he will never be impelled to go to sea or enlist as a soldier . . . for nowhere will he find so broad a tempting a field for adventure, or so many avenues to promotion and honor as in science.[35]

Gulick kept the letter in his desk for three months before mailing it. On the back of the letter Gulick penciled "my philosophy of life and how we may serve the world *even* by starting a Museum" (emphasis added).[36] His father rejected it. Four years later Gulick tried once more to convince his father that scientific study in Europe would be beneficial. His father rebuffed him. "In the first place, I feel persuaded that you can learn all that is requisite to make you a faithful and an efficient *missionary*, as well in the United States as in any part of the Old

World," Peter Gulick wrote. "Then, as life is *short* and souls are *precious,* the next thing is how shall you get well prepared for your work, and *at it?*" Gulick attended seminary instead.[37]

When the Civil War broke out in 1861, Gulick attempted to join the Union Army. His eyesight prevented him. Disappointed and in poor health, Gulick left the seminary hoping to explore New Granada (Colombia) for land shells. Turned away by revolution, Gulick found himself in San Francisco, looking to merge his missionary training with his love for science and exploration. "I love Mystery and Mystery loves me," Gulick wrote. Gulick found partial answers in Japan and China.[38]

It is somewhat difficult to judge the impact of Gulick's decade in China. Looking back in 1907, Gulick credited missionary schools with the "awakening" of China to Western education, democratic government, women's rights, and "Buddhist temples turned to schools and churches." China Inland Mission director Hudson Taylor said that Gulick's early entry into the interior of China enabled him to overcome the objections of the British minister in Beijing and begin work there, as well.[39] Gael Graham has documented the impact of American Protestant mission schools in China, including their influence upon gender and nationalist movements, despite the fact that Chinese modernists eventually diverged from missionary aims, and the Chinese nationalist government ultimately rejected the missionaries.[40]

Gulick was on the forefront of an explosion in U.S. Protestant missionary efforts. Prior to the 1890s there had been fewer than a thousand American missionaries living outside the United States. During the 1890s the number jumped to five thousand, a result of colonization, open-door treaties, and international trade. China quickly became the largest Protestant missionary field.[41]

Gulick was also a leader in an important transcultural exchange that had significant implications for U.S. foreign policy. Missionaries introduced Christianized Asian nationalists to potential U.S. donors. These supporters in the United States advocated for their Asian friends, including for their political support. What followed was a systematic American policy of supporting leaders, such as Sun Yat-sen, Chiang Kaishek, and Ngo Dinh Diem, over their atheist rivals. While Gulick was in

Asia, for example, Sun Yat-sen was a student at missionary schools in the Hawaiian Islands, including Punahou. The future Chinese nationalist leader chose Punahou after embracing Christianity.[42] In 1912 Gulick met Sun Fo, the son of Sun Yat-sen, calling him "the young man whose father has attained such great note."[43]

Gulick was ambivalent about his own role in introducing China and Japan to Western ideals. "I had seen the factories multiply till their smoking chimney clouded the air with ever increasing gloom while thousands of girls were standing and serving through twelve hours of dimmed daylight and other thousands taking their place during the darker hours of night," Gulick wrote. Gulick believed the United States was complicit in these changes. "I see arising vast corporations that become virtual monopolies," Gulick foresaw. "But these corporations bleed the poor and feed the rich."[44]

Gulick predicted that China would one day dominate the world market in manufacturing cheap, surplus products and would turn to socialism to secure the buying power of its own population.[45] He was not alone in his belief. As Sarah R. Mason notes in her study of twentieth-century adult missionary children in China, the missionary children's widespread sympathy toward the People's Republic of China stemmed from their early cultural experiences in China and "identification" with the Chinese people. For many of the missionary children, communist China was "a more moral social system than the United States, both in terms of social equality and ideological commitment."[46]

Gulick's advocacy for Chinese socialism stemmed both from his cultural understanding of China and his early childhood experiences in Hawai'i. His acceptance of Darwinian evolution as a young boy and his own theory of habitudinal evolution allowed Gulick to appreciate the adaptability and unique diversity of human choice in both China and Japan. Gulick's open-mindedness stemmed from his bicultural upbringing. Only his commitment to Christianity complicated Gulick's desire to acculturate globally.

Unlike Gulick, most missionary children from the islands shrank from the missionary profession, realizing the "plain, ugly, unwholesome facts" of that life. Yet more missionary descendants chose the teaching and ministerial professions than all other careers combined, believing these humanitarian occupations the perfect blend of faith and reason.[47] "For intense work as soldier, pioneer, explorer, or missionary, the only rest is in solitude with God," HMCS president and missionary son William Smith remarked in 1882. Missionary descendants largely lived their lives in one place, yet despite distaste for their parents' profession, many felt compelled to demonstrate they had not negated their parents' choices completely.[48]

Samuel Armstrong, Sanford Dole, and John Gulick exemplified the tension of a missionary upbringing. Loyal to their birthplace, they struggled to achieve a level of professional success that would satisfy both their personal longings and parental demands. Armstrong found his "calling" in the United States. Dole secured his missionary parents' legacy in the Hawaiian Islands. Gulick remained restless, stuck between a desire for scientific recognition, which he never truly achieved, and a missionary career he half-heartedly embraced. As a soldier in U.S. Reconstruction, a pioneer in a new Hawaiian republic, and an explorer of East Asian lands, Armstrong, Dole, and Gulick would have been proud to have been ranked alongside their intrepid missionary parents. Their "successes" in unchartered territories, however, left a complicated trail upon which indigenous peoples and historians continue to navigate.

### Family Empires

When taken in isolation, the decisions American missionary parents made in the Hawaiian Islands during the nineteenth century do not seem particularly significant. What parent does not think about his or her children's educational opportunities or worry about the influence peers and culture may have upon sons and daughters? American parents also have had—at least since the nineteenth century—a myriad of professional options for which to train their children. Yet parents—and particularly evangelical parents—have also held an authority over their children that often surpasses other societal influences. Their power is rooted in biblical teachings of honor and obedience and is directly linked to the child's relationship with God. When combined with inflexible cultural norms and an ideology of racial hierarchy, the message of parental obedience can have profound implications for both children and history. Children, in fact, become a field of empire upon which parents plant their dreams and build their futures.[49]

It may seem strange to consider nineteenth-century white children a colonized population, yet taken as a whole, white missionary children in the Hawaiian Islands were utilized by their American parents, as well as ABCFM supporters in the United States, to achieve a fundamental cultural shift in the Hawaiian kingdom. In order to achieve their goals, missionary parents first had to conform their children to their agenda. For Americans living in the Pacific and on the fringe of U.S. power, their children represented perhaps the greatest natural resource to be harnessed and cultivated for the perpetuation of American evangelical authority. Just like California gold and Hawaiian sandalwood, American missionaries in the Pacific held captive their children and, in some cases, exploited them for the sake of an international agenda. In the case of the Hawaiian Islands, missionary parents segregated their children from society and taught them to idealize American institutions and secure the spread of Christian civilization throughout the world.[50]

Nineteenth-century Christians were not unaware of this exploitation. Rufus Anderson, foreign secretary of the ABCFM, was horrified after being told the full extent of missionary efforts in the Hawaiian Islands to control their sons and daughters. "The practice of training the children in utter seclusion from the native society and language, treats them of course as exotics," he chided in 1851. "It sets them up in hot houses." Anderson warned missionary parents that when they finally transplanted their children into the world, the children would not survive intact. "It would be strange if they did. They were not trained for such exposure." Missionary parents remained unconvinced. Their goal was not to acculturate their children to the indigenous Hawaiians but to make Hawaiian culture more like the New England civilization from which the missionaries had come.[51]

Missionary children became important tools in the construction of a colonial society in the Hawaiian Islands. Their presence served to bridge the cultural divide. Indigenous Hawaiians welcomed missionary infants

**29.** Seven Indian children before entering Hampton Institute, ca. 1899 or 1900. Mohandas Gandhi would later advocate similar manual education for South Asians. Library of Congress, Johnson (Frances Benjamin) Collection, LC-USZ62-78702.

into their hearts and homes. Missionary families used their children to demonstrate proper familial deportment to Hawaiian parents. Missionary children in the islands grew up expecting such privilege.

Missionary children remaining in the Hawaiian Islands perpetuated their parents' goals upon entering adulthood. While disavowing their parents' missionary profession, the children nevertheless sought to retain the island image their parents had molded. As one missionary son explained this generational transition, "We lived very much after the manner of missionary itinerants engaged in periodical visitation of their converts; only our discourse with the people was not so much concerning treasure in heaven as of land and worldly property."[52]

The size of American missionary families in the islands and the entrance of white missionary children into adulthood were crucial factors leading to the Hawaiian monarchy's decision to transfer land to the missionaries and employ their children in the islands. Just as other sites of nineteenth-century European and American colonization required the participation of indigenous elites to aid the administration of Western occupation, so, too, did missionary children accept their role as leaders in Hawaiian society and seek to enhance a political system within which they could benefit.

Yet nineteenth-century African American slaves resisted their Southern owners, twentieth-century Native Americans asserted their indigenous rights in U.S. courts, and some native Hawaiians today agitate for sovereign nationhood. As decolonization efforts around the world have demonstrated, European and American colonization was incomplete, and the colonization of white missionary children in the Hawaiian Islands was no different.[53] Missionary children contested their parents' agendas and rejected the sacrifices they had been forced to make in childhood. Many rejected Calvinist orthodoxy, and some rejected Christianity altogether. Almost all rejected the missionary trade.

Nevertheless, what Nancy Rose Hunt has called the "debris" of colonization remained.[54] Confusion over their personal identity, fear of displeasing their parents, and detachment toward the indigenous Hawaiian population reflected the children's deep-seated emotions about their childhoods. Some missionary children entered adulthood insecure, "wanderers," as their parents described them.[55] "My life is fitful, strange, and lacks the essential of permanence," James Chamberlain mused.[56] "I am a pilgrim, still, though in my native land," decided Robert Andrews.[57]

Nineteenth-century missionary children in the Hawaiian Islands seemed to instinctively understand that they were culturally different from their parents and that these differences affected the trajectory of their lives. Missionary children absorbed the Hawaiian language, despite their parents' taboo, and some even preferred it.

The missionary children's cultural education was not the only difference between them and their American parents. The children's formative years were also developmentally dissimilar. Reality, Harvey Newcomb advised nineteenth-century American parents, should be children's chief concern "through the whole of their being."[58] Yet, as scientists now understand, a child's prefrontal cortex, the part of the brain associated with "limiting and focusing experience, action, and thought," is undeveloped during childhood, allowing children to see the world differently from adults and contemplate possibilities that parents have long rejected through planning and inhibition. Childhood play, Alison Gopnik writes, is "the most visible sign of the paradoxically useful uselessness of immaturity."[59] Many missionary children in Hawai'i had great freedom to explore the islands. They relished travel and embraced adventure. Their childhood play allowed them to contemplate change in ways their parents could not.

Ironically native Hawaiian children had the most independence of all—"free and unconstrained," as historian Linda K. Menton describes them.[60] Their boundless childhood perhaps influenced the Hawaiians' easy acceptance of white foreigners. The American missionaries represented new possibilities and a different way to view the world. Unafraid, indigenous Hawaiians made up their own minds about the *haole* missionaries and their children. Tellingly, native Hawaiians also distinguished a substantive difference between the parents and their children. "Your father combined in one person the various vocations which you five brothers have followed, and all of you put together are not equal to the old man," a native Hawaiian told John Emerson's sons.[61]

The Hawaiian Islands, where missionary children spent their earliest and most formative years, possessed them in a way no other geographical space ever did. The path toward U.S. colonialism in the Hawaiian Islands began in white missionary childhood. The American Civil War, by contrast, increased the missionary children's devotion to the United States and gave them a moral license to exploit their insecurity and discontent. For the majority of missionary children, the Christian faith remained their primary source of security—a bridge to their parents, a compass directing them throughout Hawaiian and American cultures. The tenacity with which most missionary children maintained a form of Christianity was witnessed by the populations among whom the children lived as adults. Their religious adherence influenced U.S. foreign policy in China and Japan and, of course, the Hawaiian Islands.

Missionary children represented a white minority within Hawai'i, yet being white in the nineteenth century garnered enormous protection from European and American states. These international powers sent out with their militaries an ideology of racial superiority by which the missionary children benefited. Missionary children utilized their international standing to comb the world. Their attitudes regarding race and religion, as well as their restless action, ultimately shaped nations, overturned governments, and divided cultures. Their strength of will demonstrates the tremendous capacity children have to piece together childhood into meanings that impact history.

# NOTES

INTRODUCTION

1. Hawaiian and English translations found in N. Emerson, *Unwritten Literature of Hawaii*, 80–81.

2. On the early history of the ABCFM in the Hawaiian Islands, see R. Anderson, *Sandwich Islands Mission*.

3. Dwight Baldwin, correspondence, October 15, 1847, Hawaiian Islands Mission, 1824–1909 (ABC 19.1), American Board of Commissioners for Foreign Missions Archives, Houghton Library, Harvard University (hereafter cited as ABCFMA). Regarding the use of nineteenth-century American missionary and missionary children's manuscripts, I have corrected minor spelling and punctuation discrepancies to conform to modern usage and to make the children and their parents' writings more accessible to a contemporary audience. I have also included biographical dates after the names of all missionary children to differentiate them from other persons mentioned in the text.

4. On missionary family demographics in the Hawaiian Islands, see *Missionary Album*.

5. Whitney, *Hawaiian Guide Book*, 14.

6. Conroy-Krutz, *Christian Imperialism*, 8.

7. Domestic missionary practice in Hawai'i is depicted by Grimshaw, *Paths of Duty*. Kashay introduces the Hawaiian mission children in "Problems in Paradise," 81–94.

8. Igler, *Great Ocean*, 27–29.

9. Daws, *Shoal of Time*, 65–66.

10. Hiram Bingham quoted in Andrew, *Rebuilding the Christian Commonwealth*, 154.

11. *Translation of the Constitution*, 10.

12. Walters, *American Reformers*, 33–35. By 1850 the ABCFM was ordaining 40 percent of all U.S. missionaries, yet its membership had declined from 20 percent of the U.S. public in 1776 to just 4 percent. See Kling, "New Divinity."

13. Andrew, *Rebuilding the Christian Commonwealth*, 119.

14. Rufus Anderson, correspondence, October 24, 1849, Foreign Letters (ABC 2.1.1), ABCFMA.

15. Andrew, *Rebuilding the Christian Commonwealth*, 145–46.
16. Andrew, *Rebuilding the Christian Commonwealth*, 130.
17. Whitehead, "Noncontiguous Wests," 320.
18. Bingham, *Residence of Twenty-One Years*, 355–56.
19. Repousis, "'Devil's Apostle,'" 812.
20. Pratt, *Story of Mid-Pacific Institute*, 28.
21. Whitehead, "Hawaii," 160.
22. Whitehead, "Hawaii," 164.
23. Whitehead, "Hawaii," 164.
24. Sereno Bishop coined the phrase "crossroads of the Pacific." See Bishop, *Reminiscences of Old Hawaii*, 9.
25. Sanford Dole, born and raised in the Hawaiian Islands, should not be confused with his cousin James Dole, founder of Dole Pineapple. James Dole arrived in Honolulu in 1899 at the age of twenty-four. See Cumings, *Dominion from Sea to Sea*, 182–83. Gary Okihiro discusses the influence of Samuel Armstrong in *Island World*, 129–30.
26. Missionary children left a prolific written record, much of which can be accessed in the Children of the Mission Collection, 1830–1900, Hawaiian Mission Children's Society Library, Honolulu, Hawai'i (hereafter cited as HMCS), and *Punahou Gazette* and *Critic*, September 7, 1848–August 13, 1851 (Box 1–5) and *Weekly Star*, February 25, 1852–February 16, 1853 (Box 1–3), Cooke Library Archives, Punahou School, Honolulu, Hawai'i (hereafter cited as CL). The *Annual Report of the Hawaiian Mission Children's Society* contains annual addresses by missionary descendants to their peers, as well as printed correspondence among the missionary children.
27. I would like to thank Gary Okihiro for his insights on the Hawaiian League.
28. Key texts include Osorio, *Dismembering Lāhui*; Silva, *Aloha Betrayed*; Kame'eleihiwa, *Native Land*; Trask, *From a Native Daughter*.
29. Trask, *From a Native Daughter*, vi.
30. Unless otherwise noted I have used Mary Kawena Pukui and Samuel H. Elbert's Hawaiian dictionary for my translations. See Pukui and Elbert, *New Pocket Hawaiian Dictionary*. Missionary translation projects are complicated by the indigenous appropriation of missionary discourses for their own cultural usage, missionary mistranslation of indigenous concepts into Western-oriented ideals, and emergence of new or hybrid meanings created out of a transcultural "middle ground." See Bhabha, "Signs Taken for Wonders," 163–84. Richard White explores the "middle ground" of Jesuit missionaries, French traders, and Native Americans in *Middle Ground*. The problem of hybridity or colonial "debris" is outlined by Nancy Rose Hunt in her study of British missionaries in

the Congo in *Colonial Lexicon*. On cultural (mis)readings of missionary Bible translations, see Peterson, "Rhetoric of the Word," and Peterson, "Translating the Word."

31. John Papa Ii lived through tremendous cultural and political changes affecting his Hawaiian people. Throughout his writings John Papa Ii laments the loss of Hawaiian history through chanting. See Ii, *Fragments of Hawaiian History*.

32. Kameʻeleihiwa, *Native Land*, 315.

33. The Hollywood movie *The Descendants* (2011), directed by Alexander Payne and starring George Clooney, was based on the bestselling novel by Kaui Hart Hemmings. The Obama administration pursued executive action to recognize Native Hawaiians as a tribe. See Akina, "The Racial Spoils System," A13.

34. More recently, Nancy Shoemaker counted as many as twelve differing forms of colonialism within the United States and Pacific. See Shoemaker, "Typology of Colonialism," 29–30. Paul Kramer argues that the "imperial is a necessary tool for understanding the United States' global history, with both prospects and limits." See Kramer, "Power and Connection," 1349.

35. Jennifer Fish Kashay shows that American missionaries and merchants in the Hawaiian Islands shared many concerns by the mid-nineteenth century in "Agents of Imperialism." Ian Tyrell demonstrates that post-1898 American missionary efforts in the Philippines were influential in forming "webs of communication" between international Protestant reformers and U.S. diplomats in *Reforming the World*. Similarly, Emily Rosenberg has explored the influence of American nongovernmental forces in spreading Protestant "liberal-developmentalism" in East Asia at the turn of the twentieth century in *Spreading the American Dream*. Michael Hunt argues that Protestant "moralism" shaped all American encounters with foreign populations throughout the nineteenth century in *Ideology and U.S. Foreign Policy*.

36. Conroy-Krutz, *Christian Imperialism*, 10.

37. Children as fields of colonization or agents of imperialism have remained relatively unexplored outside basic colonial and parental concerns related to the preservation of white society. See, for example, M. Jacobs, *White Mother*, and Stoler, *Carnal Knowledge*. Sara Fieldston notes the role American sponsorship of Vietnamese children played in Cold War propagandizing in "Little Cold Warriors," 240–50. Paula Fass explores the development of the U.S. educational system as a mechanism for the Americanization of nineteenth-century immigrant families in *Children of a New World*.

38. Missionary Hiram Bingham quoted in Andrew, *Rebuilding the Christian Commonwealth*, 152–54. On the ABCFM practice of putting cultural artifacts sent by missionaries on display in Boston, see Andrew, *Rebuilding the Christian*

*Commonwealth*, 126. Sally Engle Merry discusses missionary perceptions of the Hawaiian body in *Colonizing Hawai'i*, 236–37. For a domestic theory of mission among missionary wives in Hawai'i, see Robert, "Evangelist or Homemaker?," 127–30. Early nineteenth-century British evangelical missionaries in Tahiti inspected native homes to make sure they were "plastered in and out, have doors and windows, bedrooms with doors and shutters, and a garden encircling the house." See Stanley, *Bible and the Flag*, 158. On the politics of missionary exhibitions, see Lawson, "Collecting Cultures."

39. Timothy Dwight quoted in Drinnon, *Facing West*, 66.
40. Southern slave owner quoted in Bailey and Kennedy, *American Spirit*, 359.
41. Ephraim Clark, correspondence, June 18, 1857, Hawaiian Islands Mission (ABC 19.1), ABCFMA.
42. Silva, *Aloha Betrayed*, 70.
43. Luther Gulick quoted in Putney, *Missionaries in Hawai'i*, 190n21. Missionaries considered native children intellectually bright but morally damaged. See Merry, *Colonizing Hawai'i*, 237.

1. BIRTHING EMPIRE

1. Wright, *Real Mother Goose*, 106.
2. Amos Cooke quoted in B. Smith, *Yankees in Paradise*, 292.
3. Andrew, *Rebuilding the Christian Commonwealth*, 108, 131–32.
4. Rufus Anderson, correspondence, April 10, 1846, Foreign Letters (ABC 2.1.1), ABCFMA.
5. Missionary Hiram Bingham quoted in Zwiep, *Pilgrim Path*, 137–38.
6. Lydia Bingham Coan, in *Annual Report* (1887), 23–33.
7. American Board, "Report of the American Board," 234.
8. American Board, "Report of the American Board," 234.
9. M. Alexander and Dodge, *Punahou*, 6–7.
10. Lucy G. Thurston, *Life and Times*, 101–2.
11. Frear, *Lowell and Abigail*, 210–13.
12. Correspondence, June 5, 1841, Hawaiian Islands Mission (ABC 19.1), ABCFMA.
13. Bingham, *Residence of Twenty-One Years*, 331.
14. Not all Christian denominations required such high educational standards for their missionaries. See Robert, *American Women in Mission*, 131.
15. M. Alexander and Dodge, *Punahou*, 21.
16. Ephraim Clark, correspondence, June 28, 1853, Hawaiian Islands Mission (ABC 19.1), ABCFMA.
17. Dwight Baldwin, correspondence, June 22, 1848, Hawaiian Islands Mission (ABC 19.1), ABCFMA.

18. Jeremiah Evarts, correspondence, October 27, 1827, Preliminary series (ABC 2.01), ABCFMA.

19. Evarts, October 27, 1827 (ABC 2.01), ABCFMA.

20. Evarts, October 27, 1827 (ABC 2.01), ABCFMA.

21. American Board, "Report of the American Board," 334–36; Rufus Anderson, correspondence, September 5, 1834, Preliminary series (ABC 2.01), ABCFMA; M. Alexander and Dodge, *Punahou*, 6; Zwiep, *Pilgrim Path*, 247.

22. On the concept of disinterested benevolence, see Brekus, "Children of Wrath," 315; Walters, *American Reformers*, 27–28.

23. Peter Gulick, correspondence, August 30, 1842, Hawaiian Islands Mission (ABC 19.1), ABCFMA. Jennifer Fish Kashay notes the role of the 1830s financial panic on contributions to the ABCFM in "Agents of Imperialism."

24. *General Meeting Minutes*, 1832, Hawaiian Islands Mission (ABC 19.1), ABCFMA.

25. B. Smith, *Yankees in Paradise*, 217.

26. Dwight Baldwin, correspondence, October 15, 1847 (ABC 19.1), ABCFMA.

27. Levi Chamberlain, correspondence, December 21, 1847, Hawaiian Islands Mission (ABC 19.1), ABCFMA.

28. Zwiep, *Pilgrim Path*, 247.

29. Damon, *Letters from the Life*, 289.

30. On nineteenth-century gender spheres, see Cott, *Bonds of Womanhood*; or Welter, "Cult of True Womanhood."

31. Horace Bushnell quoted in Bendroth, "Horace Bushnell's *Christian Nurture*," 356.

32. Grimshaw, *Paths of Duty*, 129–30.

33. Correspondence, July 20, 1840, Hawaiian Islands Mission (ABC 19.1), ABCFMA. Missionary Peter Gulick, for instance, called the United States the "land of temptations, and seducers," August 30, 1842 (ABC 19.1), ABCFMA.

34. Correspondence, July 20, 1840, Hawaiian Islands Mission (ABC 19.1), ABCFMA.

35. John S. Emerson, correspondence, July 27, 1840, Hawaiian Islands Mission (ABC 19.1), ABCFMA.

36. *Translation of the Constitution*, 10.

37. Quoted in Hobbs, *Hawaii*, 28–29.

38. Whitehead, "Noncontiguous Wests," 321.

39. Resolutions adopted at meeting of Sandwich Islands Mission, June 1838, Hawaiian Islands Mission (ABC 19.1), ABCFMA.

40. Correspondence, June 1, 1840, Hawaiian Islands Mission (ABC 19.1), ABCFMA.

41. J. Emerson, July 27, 1840 (ABC 19.1), ABCFMA.

42. Correspondence, June 5, 1841, Hawaiian Islands Mission (ABC 19.1), ABCFMA.

43. Hobbs, *Hawaii*, 34; Bradley, *American Frontier in Hawaii*, 341–60.

44. Emily Dole quoted in M. Alexander and Dodge, *Punahou*, 61.

45. Dotts and Sikkema, *Challenging the Status Quo*, 20.

46. Grimshaw, *Paths of Duty*, 103–4.

47. P. Gulick, August 30, 1842 (ABC 19.1), ABCFMA.

48. Richard Armstrong, correspondence, March 21, 1841, Hawaiian Islands Mission (ABC 19.1), ABCFMA.

49. Sarah Andrews quoted in B. Smith, *Yankees in Paradise*, 25.

50. Lorrin Andrews quoted in M. Alexander and Dodge, *Punahou*, 12–13.

51. Wight, *Memoirs of Elizabeth Kinau Wilder*, 55.

52. Bishop, *Reminiscences of Old Hawaii*, 44. The economies of herding are discussed in B. Smith, *Yankees in Paradise*, 25, 291–92.

53. R. Anderson, April 10, 1846 (ABC 2.1.1), ABCFMA.

54. Levi Chamberlain, correspondence, December 16, 1847, Hawaiian Islands Mission (ABC 19.1), ABCFMA.

55. Newspaper clipping, January 1, 1859, Hawaiian Islands Mission (ABC 19.1), ABCFMA.

56. Correspondence, June 1, 1840, Hawaiian Islands Mission (ABC 19.1), ABCFMA.

57. Levi Chamberlain, correspondence, August 22, 1848, Hawaiian Islands Mission (ABC 19.1), ABCFMA.

58. L. Chamberlain, August 22, 1848 (ABC 19.1), ABCFMA.

59. Rufus Anderson, correspondence, October 22 and 24, 1849, Foreign Letters (ABC 2.1.1), ABCFMA.

60. Rufus Anderson, correspondence, July 19, 1848, Foreign Letters (ABC 2.1.1), ABCFMA.

61. R. Anderson, July 19, 1848 (ABC 2.1.1), ABCFMA.

62. On the *Māhale*, see Kenui, "Concerning Foreigners," 119; Hobbs, *Hawaii*, 39–41; Kameʻeleihiwa, *Native Land*, 12.

63. Ii, *Fragments of Hawaiian History*, 50.

64. Kameʻeleihiwa, *Native Land*, 15.

65. Kameʻeleihiwa, *Native Land*, 304.

66. Kamakau, *Ruling Chiefs of Hawaii*, 335.

67. Ministry of Interior quoted in Hobbs, *Hawaii*, 100.

68. Ephraim Clark, correspondence, May 10, 1849, Hawaiian Islands Mission (ABC 19.1), ABCFMA.

69. Rufus Anderson, correspondence, December 3, 1851, Foreign Letters (ABC 2.1.1), ABCFMA.

70. Richard Armstrong to Samuel Chapman Armstrong, correspondence, January 15, 1850, quoted in Kuykendall, *Hawaiian Kingdom*, 1:326n. See also Samuel Castle, correspondence, February 27, 1852, Hawaiian Islands Mission (ABC

19.1), ABCFMA; Peter Gulick, correspondence, April 29, 1852, Hawaiian Islands Mission (ABC 19.1), ABCFMA.

71. Rufus Anderson, correspondence, December 3, 1851, Foreign Letters (ABC 2.1.1), ABCFMA.

72. Kameʻeleihiwa, *Native Land*, 305.

73. Abigail Smith quoted in Frear, *Lowell and Abigail*, 210–13.

74. William P. Alexander, correspondence, August 15, 1859, Hawaiian Islands Mission (ABC 19.1), ABCFMA.

75. On U.S. slavery and American Protestant denominations, see Conkin, *Uneasy Center*; R. Anderson, *Sandwich Islands Mission*, 289. The ABCFM reduced missionary Abner Wilcox's salary during the Civil War, believing his seven sons could support him. See Damon, *Letters from the Life*, 381–82.

76. Levi T. Chamberlain, correspondence and papers, n.d., Children of the Mission Collection, HMCS.

77. Editorial, *Punahou Gazette* and *Critic*, September 7, 1848–March 30, 1849 (Box 1), CL.

78. James Chamberlain, correspondence, late 1850, February 21, 1851, and April 20, 1852, HMCS.

79. Lyman, *Hawaiian Yesterdays*, 219–21. Under 1851 legislation the government appointed land agents for each island. Agents had the responsibility to survey and sell government lands. They received a commission on each sale. See MacLennan, *Sovereign Sugar*, 254.

80. J. Chamberlain, late 1850 and February 21, 1851, HMCS.

81. Warren Chamberlain, correspondence, October 17, 1849, HMCS. Just a few of the missionary sons who sought to benefit from their parents' relationship to the monarchy were Henry Lyman, Henry Whitney, William Armstrong, and Sanford Dole.

82. On missionary sons engaged in sugar planting, see Daws, *Shoal of Time*, 174–75; B. Smith, *Yankees in Paradise*, 327; Piercy, *Hawaii's Missionary Saga*, 179; Grimshaw, *Paths of Duty*, 190; O. Emerson, *Pioneer Days in Hawaii*, 205.

83. Lucy and Edward Wilcox quoted in Damon, *Letters from the Life*, 375–80.

84. Krauss and Alexander, *Grove Farm Plantation*, 94.

85. Rufus Anderson, correspondence, October 22, 1849, Foreign Letters (ABC 2.1.1), ABCFMA.

86. Maria Whitney, correspondence, 1878, HMCS.

87. R. Anderson, *Sandwich Islands Mission*, 330.

88. Hobbs, *Hawaii*, 101; Osorio, *Dismembering Lāhui*, 96–98; B. Smith, *Yankees in Paradise*, 323.

89. J. Chamberlain, late 1850, HMCS.

90. Sanford Dole, in *Annual Report* (1888), 35.
91. On missionary sons appointed to government positions, see O. Emerson, *Pioneer Days*, 229–30; W. Alexander, *Brief History of the Hawaiian People*, 340–45; B. Smith, *Yankees in Paradise*, 342–25; Osorio, *Dismembering Lāhui*, 247.
92. David Igler discusses the catastrophic demographic changes in the Hawaiian Islands in "Diseased Goods," 693–719. Between 1840 and 1860, the native Hawaiian population fell from one hundred thousand to seventy thousand. The number would continue to decline throughout the nineteenth century. See Daws, *Shoal of Time*, 167–68; Amos Cooke quoted in B. Smith, *Yankees in Paradise*, 292.
93. Bird, *Six Months*, 192.
94. Sanford Dole, in *Annual Report* (1888), 36.
95. Anderson Forbes, in *Annual Report* (1863), 25.
96. Asa Thurston, in *Annual Report* (1853), 18.
97. Pratt, *Story of Mid-Pacific Institute*, 2.
98. W. Alexander, *History of Later Years*, 8.
99. Lili'uokalani developed a close relationship with German medium Fraulein Wolf. See Daws, *Shoal of Time*, 264–69.
100. W. Alexander, *History of Later Years*, 12.
101. Bishop, *Reminiscences of Old Hawaii*, 22.
102. Missionary son W. D. Alexander discusses white attitudes toward the last two Hawaiian monarchs in *Brief History of the Hawaiian People*, 308–9, 314–15.
103. O. Emerson, *Pioneer Days in Hawaii*, 242.
104. Sereno Bishop, scrapbook, April 29, 1897, HMCS.
105. Samuel Damon, in *Annual Report* (1882), 32, and *Annual Report* (1886), 32.
106. O. Emerson, *Pioneer Days in Hawaii*, 256.
107. R. Anderson, *Sandwich Islands Mission*, 339–40; Bishop, "Are Missionaries' Sons Tending?," 2–3.
108. Albert Lyons, in *Annual Report* (1883), 33, and *Annual Report* (1890), 35.
109. On births and deaths in missionary families in the Hawaiian Islands, see *Annual Report* (1853), 7–9; Grimshaw, *Paths of Duty*, 89; R. Anderson, *Sandwich Islands Mission*, 240–42.
110. Kennedy, *Magic Mountains*, 130.
111. Cultural anthropologist Robert A. LeVine argues parents across cultures pursue parental goals in a three-part hierarchy: physical survival and health are paramount, followed by economic independence and, lastly, the transmission of cultural values, including religious piety and intellectual achievement. See Rogoff, *Cultural Nature*, 109–16.

112. R. Anderson quoted in Harris, *Nothing but Christ*, 34.

2. PLAYING WITH FIRE

1. Wright, *Real Mother Goose*, 7.
2. Twain, *Roughing It*, 211.
3. Twain, *Roughing It*, 211.
4. Howard Chudacoff argues that nature and family remained the most important influences upon childhood play in the early nineteenth century. Peer culture among the American middle class would begin to supplant such forces by the end of the century. See Chudacoff, *Children at Play*, 50–51.
5. Lyman, *Hawaiian Yesterdays*, 17.
6. Kameʻeleihiwa, *Native Land*, 23–24.
7. Kamakau, *Ruling Chiefs of Hawaii*, 230–31.
8. Missionary Lucy Thurston quoted in Menton, "'Everything That Is Lovely,'" 212.
9. MacLennan, *Sovereign Sugar*, 18–22.
10. On restrictions related to contact with native Hawaiians, see Lucy G. Thurston, *Life and Times*, 128–29. George Wilcox quoted in Damon, *Letters from the Life*, 261.
11. Bishop, *Reminiscences of Old Hawaii*, 14; Malo, *Hawaiian Antiquities*, 75, 109.
12. Linnekin, *Sacred Queens*, 15, 21, 70; MacLennan, *Sovereign Sugar*, 28.
13. On imperial senses, see Rotter, "Empires of the Senses," 3–19.
14. O. Gulick and A. Gulick, *Pilgrims of Hawaii*, 52.
15. Wight, *Memoirs of Elizabeth Kinau Wilder*, 68.
16. Lydia Bingham Coan discusses her parents' early years in Hawaiʻi in *Annual Report* (1887), 23–33.
17. Malo, *Hawaiian Antiquities*, 94.
18. William Smith, in *Annual Report* (1883), 43.
19. Lucy G. Thurston, *Life and Times*, 101–2, 126–27. On the missionaries' use of native domestic servants in the Hawaiian Islands, see Grimshaw, *Paths of Duty*, 138. On domestic service in other colonial contexts, see, for example, Locher-Scholten, "So Close," 131–53; M. Jacobs, "Working on the Domestic Frontier," 165–99. See also Kennedy, *Islands of White*, 153–54.
20. Bingham, *Residence of Twenty-One Years*, 333.
21. Lyman, *Hawaiian Yesterdays*, 13.
22. West, *Growing Up*, 45.
23. Lyman, *Hawaiian Yesterdays*, 49.
24. Bishop, *Reminiscences of Old Hawaii*, 18.
25. Student editorials and essays at Punahou are filled with descriptions of their outdoor adventures. See Editorial, *Punahou Gazette* and *Critic*, September 7,

1848–March 30, 1849 (Box 1), CL. See also Helen W. Ludlow, ed., "Personal Memories and Letters of General S. C. Armstrong," 5 vols. (typescript), Archives and Special Collections, Williams College, Williamstown MA, 42.

26. Damon, *Letters from the Life*, 261.

27. Lucy G. Thurston, *Life and Times*, 123–24.

28. Wight, *Memoirs of Elizabeth Kinau Wilder*, 74–75.

29. British missionary William Ellis quoted in MacLennan, *Sovereign Sugar*, 26–27.

30. Whitney, *Hawaiian Guide Book*, 27.

31. Bishop, *Reminiscences of Old Hawaii*, 49.

32. Wight, *Memoirs of Elizabeth Kinau Wilder*, 72, 101–2. Missionary daughters are described in Frear, *Lowell and Abigail*, 228, 246.

33. Ludlow, "Personal Memories and Letters," 37.

34. Chudacoff, *Children at Play*, 59.

35. Chudacoff, *Children at Play*, 49, 61.

36. John Thomas Gulick, correspondence, April 4 and June 5, 1854, Children of the Mission Collection, HMCS.

37. Wight, *Memoirs of Elizabeth Kinau Wilder*, 11.

38. John Gulick's scientific discoveries and letters to Darwin are recorded in J. Gulick and A. Gulick, *Evolutionist and Missionary*, 477.

39. Damon, *Letters from the Life*, 259, 263; Editorial, *Punahou Gazette* and *Critic*, August 13, 1851–January 27, 1852 (Box 5), CL.

40. O. Emerson, *Pioneer Days in Hawaii*, 157.

41. Chudacoff, *Children at Play*, 64–65.

42. Wight, *Memoirs of Elizabeth Kinau Wilder*, 18–19.

43. Thigpen, *Island Queens*, 91.

44. Twain, *Roughing It*, 274–75, 264.

45. Lyman, *Hawaiian Yesterdays*, 91; Damon, *Letters from the Life*, 261.

46. Cummings, *Missionary's Daughter*, 113. LaRue W. Piercy describes Thurston's trip to the volcano in *Hawaii's Missionary Saga*, 49.

47. Samuel Chapman Armstrong, "Editorial Correspondence," 1880, Samuel Chapman Armstrong Collection, Archives and Special Collections, Williams College, Williamstown MA.

48. Wight, *Memoirs of Elizabeth Kinau Wilder*, 101–3.

49. Weaver, "Memories," 106.

50. For an early and detailed analysis of Hawaiian land divisions, see Hobbs, *Hawaii*. For a discussion on land ownership and foreign influence, see Osorio, *Dismembering Lāhui*.

51. "King's Speeches at the Opening of the Hawaiian Legislature," May 28, 1847, Hawaiian Materials, Rare Manuscript Division, Library of Congress.

52. The Hawaiian Legislature published its rationale in Kenui et al., "Concerning Foreigners," 119.

53. The 1848 whooping cough and measles epidemics hit native populations particularly hard. Missionary children would have seen this in their parents' church congregations. Missionary Lowell Smith reported his congregation fell from 1,500 to 100. See B. Smith, *Yankees in Paradise*, 287–88. Jocelyn Linnekin writes that missionaries reported an infant mortality rate as high as 50 percent and a birthrate of one for every eleven women in the 1850s in *Sacred Queens*, 210. Disease affected the Hawaiian landscape as well. In 1865 the Hawaiian government began quarantining all leprosy patients on the island of Molokai. See Inglis, *Maʻi Lepera*.

54. Igler, "Diseased Goods," 704. Native historian Samuel Kamakau noted the influence of disease on pregnancy and infant mortality in *Ruling Chiefs of Hawaii*, 237.

55. Editorial, *Punahou Gazette* and *Critic*, July 6, 1849–September 27, 1849 (Box 2), CL.

56. Igler, "Diseased Goods," 717–18.

57. "Anglo-Hawaiian" is found throughout the missionary children's writings. See, for example, Whitney, *Hawaiian Guide Book*, 14.

58. Samuel Alexander, in *Annual Report* (1864), 19.

59. Hiram Bingham Jr., in *Annual Report* (1857), 19.

60. Chudacoff, *Children at Play*, 11.

61. Samuel Alexander, in *Annual Report* (1864), 17.

62. Elliott West notes that frontier characteristics, such as a drive to accomplish and control, were common traits among white children born in the American West. West, *Growing Up*, 252.

63. MacLennan, *Sovereign Sugar*, 31–32.

64. On Castle & Cooke's relationship with missionary sons and the missionary sons' later investments, see J. Smith, *Big Five*, viii–xii.

65. In 1876 the Hawaiian legislature allowed for eminent domain over water and land for agricultural purposes. See MacLennan, *Sovereign Sugar*, 149.

66. On contemporary landholdings, see Siler, "Hawaiian History, Housed in a Ranch," M3. Carol MacLennan investigates the webs of missionary-descendant holding companies and trusts in *Sovereign Sugar*, 100–101.

67. Cushman, *Guano and the Opening*, 82–83. Samuel Chapman Armstrong discusses the nitrate trade in Ludlow, "Personal Memories and Letters," 46. Missionary children reported on peers working on the guano islands in *Annual Report* (1859), 9. The account of George Wilcox's experience as an overseer is found in Krauss and Alexander, *Grove Farm Plantation*, 80–83. By 1870 the United

States claimed sovereignty over seventy such guano islands. These uninhabited atolls contained enough "nitrate-rich" guano to appear as several feet of snow. Americans hired Hawaiian labor to collect and load shipments. The relationship between contract labor and the Pacific guano trade is discussed in Melillo, "First Green Revolution," 1028–60.

68. On Anglo-Saxon manhood in the 1890s, see Hoganson, *Fighting for American Manhood*, 34–35, 212n14; Bederman, *Manliness & Civilization*, 11–15, 118–20.

69. Sereno Bishop, in *Annual Report* (1872), 18.

70. For a missionary son's account of the Hawaiian Revolution, see W. Alexander, *Brief History of the Hawaiian People*. Missionary son Sereno Bishop gave strenuous arguments in favor of U.S. annexation that were published in American newspapers. See Sereno Bishop, scrapbook, April 29, 1897, HMCS. U.S. ambassador to the United Kingdom John Hay notoriously referred to the Spanish-American War as a "splendid little war" in a private communication to Theodore Roosevelt. See Millis, *Martial Spirit*, 340.

71. John Gulick, memoir manuscript, HMCS.

72. J. Gulick, memoir manuscript, HMCS.

73. Fanny Gulick quoted in J. Gulick and A. Gulick, *Evolutionist and Missionary*, 11.

74. J. Gulick and A. Gulick, *Evolutionist and Missionary*, 55.

75. John Gulick, correspondence, June 30, 1848, HMCS; J. Gulick, journal, January 18, 1849, HMCS; J. Gulick, memoir manuscript, HMCS; J. Gulick and A. Gulick, *Evolutionist and Missionary*, 320–21.

76. J. Gulick and A. Gulick, *Evolutionist and Missionary*, 121.

77. J. Gulick, memoir manuscript, HMCS.

78. John Gulick, June 5, 1854, HMCS.

79. J. Gulick, memoir manuscript, HMCS; Finn, "Guests of the Nation," 35.

80. J. Gulick and A. Gulick, *Evolutionist and Missionary*, 177.

81. John Gulick, 1880 notes, HMCS.

82. J. Gulick, 1880 notes; J. Gulick, memoir manuscript, HMCS; J. Gulick and A. Gulick, *Evolutionist and Missionary*, 185–92. For a discussion on the relationship between the language of photography and imperialism, see Wexler, *Tender Violence*.

83. J. Gulick and A. Gulick, *Evolutionist and Missionary*, 231–32.

84. J. Gulick and A. Gulick, *Evolutionist and Missionary*, 231–32; J. Gulick, memoir manuscript, HMCS.

85. J. Gulick and A. Gulick, *Evolutionist and Missionary*, 234.

86. J. Gulick and A. Gulick, *Evolutionist and Missionary*, 484.

87. J. Gulick and A. Gulick, *Evolutionist and Missionary*, 462.

88. J. Gulick and A. Gulick, *Evolutionist and Missionary*, 293.

89. J. Gulick and A. Gulick, *Evolutionist and Missionary*, 351, 493.

90. J. Gulick, memoir manuscript, HMCS.

91. On traditional land use, see Fisher, "Hawaiian Culture," 7–27. On the transformation to plantation agriculture, see Jones and Osgood, *From King Cane*.

92. Jones and Osgood, *From King Cane*, 9, 75.

93. MacLennan, *Sovereign Sugar*, 9.

94. Joseph Cooke, in *Annual Report* (1868), 17.

95. John Gulick, *Punahou Gazette* and *Critic*, August 13, 1851–January 27, 1852 (Box 5), CL.

96. Editorial, *Punahou Gazette* and *Critic*, July 6, 1849–September 27, 1849 (Box 2), CL.

97. Gopnik, *Philosophical Baby*, 11.

98. Robert Andrews, correspondence, October 31, 1862, HMCS.

99. Gopnik, *Philosophical Baby*, 163.

100. For opposing revolution against the monarchy, missionary son Henry Baldwin was shouted down by his peers at a mass meeting during the constitutional crisis of 1893. So ubiquitous was the white sentiment for revolution and U.S. annexation that native Hawaiians derogatorily called anyone in favor of annexation a "missionary." See Daws, *Shoal of Time*, 273–74, 292.

101. William Smith, in *Annual Report* (1882), 41.


3. SCHOOLING POWER

1. Wright, *Real Mother Goose*, 2.

2. Robert Andrews, correspondence, February 12, 1865, HMCS.

3. On American missionaries and higher education, see Robert, *American Women in Mission*, 131.

4. Mary Charlotte Alexander, a missionary descendant and Punahou graduate, and Charlotte Peabody Dodge, a Punahou alumna and teacher, extensively catalogued Punahou School history for the school's one hundredth anniversary. Their work is a thoroughly researched yet uncritical look at the school. See M. Alexander and Dodge, *Punahou*, 4–5, 94.

5. Mary Rice, in *Annual Report* (1887), 187.

6. Peter Gulick to Board, correspondence, August 30, 1842, Hawaiian Islands Mission (ABC 19.1), ABCFMA.

7. Damon, *Letters from the Life*, 292.

8. J. Gulick and A. Gulick, *Evolutionist and Missionary*, 22.

9. M. Alexander and Dodge, *Punahou*, 84.

10. Lyman, *Hawaiian Yesterdays*, 130.

11. Editorial, *Punahou Gazette* and *Critic*, September 7, 1848–March 30, 1849 (Box 1), CL.

12. Editorial, *Weekly Star*, February 25, 1852–April 14, 1852 (Box 1), CL.

13. The *Punahou Gazette* and *Critic* were separate student newspapers but are currently archived together. See *Punahou Gazette* and *Critic*, 1848–1852 (Boxes 1–5) and *Weekly Star*, 1852–1853 (Boxes 1–3), CL.

14. Editorial, *Weekly Star*, February 25–April 14, 1852 (Box 1), CL.

15. Bird, *Six Months*, 134.

16. Editorial, *Weekly Star*, February 25–April 14, 1852 (Box 1), CL.

17. M. Alexander and Dodge, *Punahou*, 66.

18. Editorial, *Punahou Gazette* and *Critic*, September 7, 1848–March 30, 1849 (Box 1), CL.

19. Editorial, *Weekly Star*, September 1, 1852–December 22, 1852 (Box 2), CL.

20. *Kanaka* is the Hawaiian word for "person" or "Hawaiian." Missionary children used the word disparagingly. Wight, *Memoirs of Elizabeth Kinau Wilder*, 15.

21. Before the Civil War only a few women went to boarding academies or colleges, and the curriculum was always different from that in male institutions. Only a few coeducational opportunities existed, and in those schools women were usually placed on a separate track. See Cremin, *American Education*, 397.

22. Daniel Dole quoted in M. Alexander and Dodge, *Punahou*, 68–69.

23. Grimshaw, *Paths of Duty*, 190.

24. Editorial, *Weekly Star*, February 16, 1853–April 20, 1853 (Box 3), CL.

25. George Wilcox voted in favor of granting political rights to women. He further defied American gender norms by never marrying. Wilcox become one of the most successful planters in the islands. See M. Alexander and Dodge, *Punahou*, 226. On Hawaiian women serving in government, see Silva, *Aloha Betrayed*, 43–44.

26. Editorial, *Punahou Gazette* and *Critic*, September 7, 1848–March 30, 1849 (Box 1), CL.

27. D. Dole quoted in M. Alexander and Dodge, *Punahou*, 153.

28. D. Dole quoted in M. Alexander and Dodge, *Punahou*, 206.

29. Lyman, *Hawaiian Yesterdays*, 143.

30. Orramel Gulick, correspondence, January 9, 1844, HMCS.

31. Charles Gulick, correspondence, February 16, 1844, HMCS. Clifford Putney argues that bulimia, caused by fear of disappointing God and his parents, led to Charles Gulick's lengthy illness and death. Charles was a student at Punahou from 1842 to 1853 and died in the United States attending college. See Putney, *Missionaries in Hawai'i*.

32. M. Alexander and Dodge, *Punahou*, 77.

33. *Weekly Star*, February 25–April 14, 1852 (Box 1), CL.

34. Editorial, *Punahou Gazette* and *Critic*, July 6, 1849–September 27, 1849 (Box 2), CL.

35. Damon, *Sanford Ballard Dole*, 17.

36. M. Alexander and Dodge, *Punahou*, 78.

37. Ann Eliza Clark, correspondence, n.d., HMCS.

38. Editorial, *Punahou Gazette* and *Critic*, July 6, 1849–September 27, 1849 (Box 2), CL.

39. William Alexander quoted in M. Alexander and Dodge, *Punahou*, 201.

40. Punahou student newspapers are replete with American standards of deportment. See, for example, Editorial, *Punahou Gazette* and *Critic*, July 6, 1849–September 27, 1849 (Box 2), CL. The popular *Girl's Own Book* taught children to "have a scrupulous regard to neatness of person. Broken strings and tangled hair are signs that children are not very industrious in any of their habits." See Child, *Girl's Own Book*, 286.

41. Editorial, *Punahou Gazette* and *Critic*, July 6, 1849–September 27, 1849 (Box 2), CL.

42. Editorial, *Punahou Gazette* and *Critic*, July 6, 1849–September 27, 1849, CL. McGuffey Readers, for example, admonished children: "Do always as your parents bid you. Obey them with a ready mind and a pleasant face." McGuffey, *Eclectic Third Reader*, 66.

43. Emma and Angelina Metcalf were the first students of Hawaiian ancestry to attend Punahou, entering the school in 1852. See Foster, *Punahou*, 34.

44. Dwight Baldwin, correspondence, 1835, HMCS.

45. *Punahou Gazette* and *Critic*, September 7, 1848–March 30, 1849 (Box 1), CL.

46. Editorial, *Punahou Gazette* and *Critic*, August 13, 1851–January 27, 1852 (Box 5), CL. Haunani-Kay Trask writes that missionary histories of Hawaii were often "the West's view of itself through the degradation of my [Hawaiian] past." See Trask, *From a Native Daughter*, 117.

47. Samuel Alexander quoted in M. Alexander and Dodge, *Punahou*, 211.

48. John Gulick quoted in Putney, *Missionaries in Hawai'i*, 121.

49. On the Royal School, see Menton, "'Everything That Is Lovely'"; Menton, "Christian and 'Civilized' Education," 213–42.

50. Wight, *Memoirs of Elizabeth Kinau Wilder*, 72–79.

51. Lyman, *Hawaiian Yesterdays*, 139.

52. M. Alexander and Dodge, *Punahou*, 157–58, 191–98. The discrepancy in sizes could be pronounced. Missionary son Warren Chamberlain called himself a "great fat fellow" at 120 pounds. See Warren Chamberlain, correspondence, January 24, 1845, HMCS.

53. B. Smith, *Yankees in Paradise*, 225–26.

54. Wight, *Memoirs of Elizabeth Kinau Wilder*, 95.

55. M. Alexander and Dodge, *Punahou*, 77–78, 131.

56. Editorial, *Weekly Star*, February 16, 1853–April 20, 1853 (Box 3), CL.

57. B. Smith, *Yankees in Paradise*, 316.

58. Warren Chamberlain, correspondence, October 17, 1849, HMCS.

59. On the temperance movement in the Hawaiian Islands, see James Chamberlain, correspondence, March 7, 1845, HMCS; Levi T. Chamberlain, correspondence, March 12, 1845, HMCS. See also Damon, *Letters from the Life*, 260; Cummings, *Missionary's Daughter*, 51.

60. Editorial, *Punahou Gazette and Critic*, July 6, 1849–September 27, 1849 (Box 2), CL. Students were well aware of the indigenous population decline occurring around them, ruminating frequently about the reasons for it.

61. Menton, "'Everything That Is Lovely,'" 164.

62. Editorial, *Weekly Star*, February 25–April 14, 1852 (Box 1), CL.

63. Bishop, *Reminiscences of Old Hawaii*, 50.

64. Kuykendall, *Hawaiian Kingdom*, 1:162–63.

65. Kuykendall, *Hawaiian Kingdom*, 1:165–66.

66. Editorial, *Weekly Star*, February 16, 1853–April 20, 1853 (Box 3), CL.

67. Cummings, *Missionary's Daughter*, 134.

68. Ephraim Clark, correspondence, August 28, 1849, Hawaiian Islands Mission (ABC 19.1), ABCFMA. On Punahou students and France, see Editorial, *Punahou Gazette and Critic*, August 13, 1851–January 27, 1852 (Box 5), CL; Levi Chamberlain, papers, n.d., HMCS.

69. On Kalākaua's reign, see Osorio, *Dismembering Lāhui*, 184, 199, 225, 284ff, 287fn.

70. William Castle, in *Annual Report* (1881), 26.

71. Latourette, *Great Century*, 254.

72. Joseph Emerson, in *Annual Report* (1898), 51.

73. *Penal Code of the Hawaiian Islands*; Kuykendall, *Hawaiian Kingdom*, 3:257, 302.

74. W. Alexander, *History of Later Years*, 11.

75. Lorrin Thurston, Sanford Dole, Sereno Bishop, Nathaniel Emerson, W. E. Rowell, and William Castle formed the Hawaiian League, which eventually had over four hundred Honolulu members. The group organized a mass public meeting of Honolulu residents that passed resolutions demanding the king sign a new constitution under threat of force. See MacLennan, *Sovereign Sugar*, 235; Osorio, *Dismembering Lāhui*, 235–38. For a partial list of attendees—including former Punahou teachers and students—at the June 30, 1887, mass meeting, see Hewett, *A Sketch of Recent Events*. See also *Oahu College Directory*.

76. Joseph Emerson, in *Annual Report* (1898), 51.
77. Kuykendall, *Hawaiian Kingdom*, 3:581; W. Alexander, *History of Later Years*, 28.
78. Whitehead, "Noncontiguous Wests," 326.
79. Menton, "'Everything That Is Lovely,'" 232–33.
80. Hiram Bingham Jr, in *Annual Report* (1857), 20.
81. Samuel Damon, in *Annual Report* (1886), 29.
82. Kashti, *Boarding Schools*, 79.
83. William D. Alexander, correspondence, January 6, 1851, HMCS.
84. James Alexander, correspondence, October 12, 1859, HMCS.
85. Robert Andrews, correspondence, April 6, 1852, HMCS.
86. Armstrong made this analysis shortly before his death in May 1893 in Ludlow, "Personal Memories and Letters," 1396–97.
87. Arguments regarding the colonial aspects of Armstrong's educational ideology include J. Anderson, "Northern Foundations," 307; Okihiro, *Island World*, 129–30; Watkins, *White Architects*, 60.
88. Armstrong, *Lessons from the Hawaiian Islands*, 213.
89. Menton, "'Everything That Is Lovely,'" 229–33.
90. Menton, "Christian And 'Civilized' Education," 239–40.
91. On Hawaiian caretakers, see B. Smith, *Yankees in Paradise*, 225–27.

## 4. CANNIBALS IN AMERICA

1. Wright, *Real Mother Goose*, 3.
2. *Holy Bible, New International Version*.
3. For an excellent discussion on early U.S. immigration, see Gabaccia, *Foreign Relations*.
4. Kramer, "Is the World Our Campus?," 782.
5. See Dwight, *Memoirs of Henry Obookiah*. An excellent analysis on the impact of Henry Obookiah can be found in Okihiro, *Island World*. On the legal status of children in nineteenth-century America, see Brewer, *By Birth or Consent*.
6. Dwight, *Memoirs of Henry Obookiah*, 18–19.
7. Dwight, *Memoirs of Henry Obookiah*, 60.
8. Andrew, *Rebuilding the Christian Commonwealth*, 98–102.
9. Mercy Whitney, letters to children, August 18, 1834, and October 18, 1841, HMCS.
10. Missionary daughter quoted in Grimshaw, *Paths of Duty*, 133–34.
11. M. Alexander and Dodge, *Punahou*, 15–16; Zwiep, *Pilgrim Path*, 247. Brewer discusses nineteenth-century apprenticeships in *By Birth or Consent*, 277–78.
12. Creighton, *Rites and Passages*, 23; Yokota, *Unbecoming British*, 149–50; Zwiep, *Pilgrim Path*, 247.

13. Warren Chamberlain, personal papers, circa 1909–1910, HMCS.
14. M. Alexander and Dodge, *Punahou*, 14.
15. Dwight, *Memoirs of Henry Obookiah*, 14–16; Vickers, *Young Men*, 191, 238–39.
16. Linnekin, *Children of the Land*, 61–64; Menton, "'Everything That Is Lovely,'" 190–91; M. Alexander and Dodge, *Punahou*, 13.
17. Bird, *Six Months*, 191–92.
18. Mercy Whitney, letters to children, August 18, 1834, and October 18, 1841, HMCS.
19. Through a strange amendment added to U.S. naturalization law in 1802, children born overseas to fathers who had been born after the date of the amendment, April 14, 1802, were excluded from birthright citizenship. The law was amended in 1855 to correct what was perceived as the unintended consequences of the amendment and to allow citizenship to children born overseas to citizen fathers. See McFarland, "Derivative Citizenship," 467–510; Binney, *Alienigenae of the United States*, 5.
20. Brewer, *By Birth or Consent*, 266.
21. American Board, "Report of the American Board," 334–36.
22. Rufus Anderson, September 5, 1834, Preliminary series (ABC 2.01), ABCFMA.
23. R. Anderson, September 5, 1834 (ABC 2.01), ABCFMA.
24. Gabaccia, *Foreign Relations*, 57–65.
25. James Chamberlain, correspondence, March 27, 1856, HMCS.
26. Warren Chamberlain, correspondence, January 19, 1846, and July 17, 1848, HMCS.
27. Grimshaw, *Paths of Duty*, 134.
28. Sophia Bingham, correspondence, May 31, 1831, HMCS.
29. Warren Chamberlain, correspondence, March 5, 1846, HMCS.
30. Martha Chamberlain, correspondence, November 30, 1850, HMCS.
31. Warren Chamberlain, correspondence, July 17, 1848, HMCS.
32. Mercy Whitney, letters to children, February 23, 1846, HMCS.
33. Mercy Whitney, correspondence, August 14, 1847, HMCS.
34. Cochran Forbes, correspondence, March 9, 1849, HMCS.
35. Lucy Thurston quoted in Cummings, *Missionary's Daughter*, 181.
36. Jerusha Babcock, March 14, 1844, Alumnae Biographical Files, Archives and Special Collections, Mount Holyoke College, South Hadley MA (hereafter cited as MHC).
37. Wight, *Memoirs of Elizabeth Kinau*, 170.
38. Ephraim Clark, May 10, 1849, Hawaiian Islands Mission (ABC 19.1), ABCFMA.
39. Abner Wilcox quoted in Damon, *Letters from the Life*, 355–56.
40. Samuel Alexander quoted in M. Alexander and Dodge, *Punahou*, 211.

41. John Gulick, memoir manuscript, circa 1912, HMCS.

42. Fanny Gulick quoted in J. Gulick and A. Gulick, *Evolutionist and Missionary*, 37.

43. Whitehead, "Noncontiguous Wests," 325.

44. Peter Gulick quoted in O. Gulick and A. Gulick, *Pilgrims of Hawaii*, 193–94.

45. Lucy G. Thurston, *Life and Times*, 180.

46. James Chamberlain, correspondence, February 15, 1856, HMCS.

47. Evarts Chamberlain, correspondence, April 1845, HMCS; John Gulick, correspondence, April 4, 1854, HMCS.

48. James Chamberlain, correspondence, January 1, 1898, HMCS.

49. The importance missionaries placed on obtaining a college education can be seen in their chartering of Punahou School as a college in 1853. Even after this noteworthy goal, many missionary parents preferred a U.S. college education. In 1878, for example, ninety-seven mission descendants were studying in the islands, and eighty-seven were in the United States. See *Annual Report* (1879), 6.

50. Yokota, *Unbecoming British*, 219.

51. Yokota, *Unbecoming British*, 224, 238.

52. Gabaccia, *Foreign Relations*, 138.

53. On U.S. legal restrictions toward native Hawaiians, see Barman, "Whatever Happened to the Kanakas," 12–20; Koppel, *Kanaka*, 62.

54. Editorial, *Punahou Gazette* and *Critic*, October 25, 1849–May 3, 1850 (Box 3), CL.

55. Lucy Thurston quoted in Cummings, *Missionary's Daughter*, 169–70, 199.

56. *New York Observer* quoted in M. Alexander and Dodge, *Punahou*, 171.

57. Ludlow, "Personal Memories and Letters," 114.

58. On Mark Hopkins and Williams College, see Marsden, *Evangelical Mind*, 15; Hopkins, *Discourse Delivered at Williamstown*, 5; Durfee, *History of Williams College*, 244.

59. James Alexander, correspondence, September 30, 1854, HMCS.

60. Ludlow, "Personal Memories and Letters," 126.

61. James Alexander, correspondence, February 11, 1855, HMCS.

62. Mark Hopkins quoted in Harris, *Nothing but Christ*, 156.

63. Harris, *Nothing but Christ*, 156.

64. Ludlow, "Personal Memories and Letters," 96.

65. Mary Lyon Collection, Mary Lyon, Circular 7, 1837, MHC.

66. Mary Lyon, Circular 1, June 15, 1845, MHC.

67. Harris, *Nothing but Christ*, 33.

68. Lyon, *Missionary Offering*, 14–16.

69. *Annual Report* (1853), 8–9.

70. Lyon, Circular 7, 1837, MHC.

71. Martha Chamberlain, correspondence, December 18, 1850, and February 20, 1851, HMCS.

72. Records of Contributions Supporting Missionary Work, circa 1841–1902, Missionaries Collection, MHC.

73. Jerusha Babcock letter, March 14, 1844, Alumnae Biographical Files, circa 1831–present, MHC.

74. Scott, "Ever-Widening Circle," 153.

75. Many marriages of early ABCFM missionaries started as a means to achieving missionary status because the ABCFM initially required its missionaries to be married. See Grimshaw, *Paths of Duty*, 6–7.

76. Ann Eliza Clark, "Around Cape Horn in 1850," October 1929, Alumnae Biographical Files, MHC.

77. Lyon, *Missionary Offering*, 248–49.

78. Martha Chamberlain, correspondence, December 23, 1851, HMCS.

79. Sanford Dole, correspondence, July 1867, HMCS.

80. In the 1950s sociologists John and Ruth Hill Useem developed the concept of "third culture" in order to describe children born into a culture different from their parents' place of origin. Because those children often displayed an understanding of global events but also a tendency to suffer insecurity and dissatisfaction, the Useems explained this displacement as an "interstitial" culture, a "culture between cultures." See Pollock and Van Reken, *Third Culture Kids*, 20–21.

81. Editorial, *Punahou Gazette* and *Critic*, October 25, 1849–May 3, 1850 (Box 3), CL.

82. Gerrit Judd, correspondence, September 5, 1844, Hawaiian Islands Mission (ABC 19.1), ABCFMA.

83. For missionary children's discontent, see, for example, James Chamberlain, correspondence, September 6, 1861, HMCS.

84. William Andrews, correspondence, June 15, 1861, October 22, 1865, and May 30, 1866, HMCS.

85. Evarts Chamberlain, correspondence, January 12, 1849, HMCS.

86. Martha Chamberlain, correspondence, December 18, 1850, HMCS.

87. Armstrong writing in 1881 in Ludlow, "Personal Memories and Letters," 865.

88. O. Emerson, *Pioneer Days in Hawaii*, 91–92.

89. James Chamberlain, correspondence, July 1875, HMCS.

90. William Dewitt Alexander, correspondence, circa 1856 and 1857, HMCS.

91. James Alexander, correspondence, October 12, 1859, HMCS.

92. Mary Jane Alexander, correspondence, October 8, 186-, HMCS.

93. James Alexander, correspondence, October 31, 1860, HMCS.

94. Evarts Chamberlain, correspondence, October 13, HMCS.

95. Lyman, *Hawaiian Yesterdays*, 242.

96. James Alexander called those white islanders still in the United States "few." He also said they looked "worn and wrinkled." Alexander contrasted their "decay" to the "growth" those able to return to the Hawaiian Islands would experience once there. See Alexander, correspondence, October 12, 1859, HMCS. For correspondence from adult missionary children in the United States to peers in the Hawaiian Islands, see *Annual Report* (1875), 10, and *Annual Report* (1885), 16.

97. Greven, *Protestant Temperament*, 110, 117.

98. Rebecca Forbes, in *Annual Report* (1862), 11.

99. The *Annual Report* published detailed updates on missionary children serving in the Civil War. See, for example, the "Report of the Corresponding Secretary" in the *Annual Report* (1862, 1863, 1864, and 1865).

100. George Dole, correspondence, October 7, 1864, HMCS.

101. Armstrong cited his parents, the Hawaiian Islands, and the U.S. Civil War as the three greatest influences upon his life. See Ludlow, "Personal Memories and Letters," 1407.

102. Mary Jane Alexander, correspondence, October 8, 186-, HMCS.

103. Samuel Alexander, in *Annual Report* (1861), 11.

104. See Mary Andrews, correspondence, *Annual Report* (1864), 10.

105. Newcomb, *How to Be a Man*, 117–18.

106. Examples of Western-educated nationalists include Sun Yat-sen, Kwame Nkrumah, Sayyid Qutb, and Isoroku Yamamoto. The limits of American acculturation are discussed in Kramer, "Is the World Our Campus?" Gabaccia explores the influence Sun Yat-sen—who received his education in the Hawaiian Islands—had upon China in *Foreign Relations*. See also Bird, *Six Months*, 121, 172.

107. Bird, *Six Months*, 166.

108. Henry Whitney, March 5, 1857, quoted in Silva, *Aloha Betrayed*, 80.

109. Sereno Bishop, scrapbook, November 24, 1896, and January 21, 1898, HMCS.

110. Gabaccia describes "immigrant foreign relations" as those ways in which immigrants influence foreign policy. See Gabaccia, *Foreign Relations*, 1.

111. Sanford Ballard Dole quoted in Allen, *Sanford Ballard Dole*, 19–20.

112. Daniel Dole, correspondence, July 1844, Hawaiian Islands Mission (ABC 19.1), ABCFMA.

113. *Oahu College Directory.*

114. S. Dole quoted in Allen, *Sanford Ballard Dole*, 40.

115. S. Dole quoted in Damon, *Sanford Ballard Dole*, 2.

116. S. Dole quoted in Allen, *Sanford Ballard Dole*, 40, 55.

117. Sanford Dole, correspondence, November 29, 1867, HMCS.

118. *Penal Code of the Hawaiian Islands.*

119. *Punch Bowl*, July 1869, HMCS.

120. Allen, *Sanford Ballard Dole*, 137.

121. S. Dole, "Systems of Immigration and Settlement."

122. W. Alexander, *Brief History of Land Titles.*

123. W. Alexander, *Brief History of the Hawaiian People*, 347.

124. S. Dole, "Evolution of Hawaiian Land Tenures," 12, 18.

125. S. Dole, "Hawaii before the World," 169–70.

126. Dole, *Memoirs of the Hawaiian Revolution*, 45.

127. Lorrin A. Thurston, introduction to Dole, *Memoirs of the Hawaiian Revolution*, ix–x.

128. S. Dole quoted in Allen, *Sanford Ballard Dole*, 245.

129. On the Bayonet Constitution, see Dole, *Memoirs of the Hawaiian Revolution*, 72–73; W. Alexander, *History of Later Years*, 47, 57–58; Osorio, *Dismembering Lāhui*, 241.

130. Zakaria, *From Wealth to Power*, 106–27.

131. S. Dole, *Memoirs of the Hawaiian Revolution*, 122–23.

132. Sanford B. Dole to John William Burgess, March 31, 1894, John William Burgess Papers, [ca. 1873]–1930, Rare Book and Manuscript Library, Butler Library, Columbia University, New York.

133. On Dole's participation in drafting the new republican constitution, see S. Dole to Burgess, March 26, 1894, Burgess Papers, Columbia University; Castle, "Advice for Hawaii," 28–29; S. Dole, *Memoirs of the Hawaiian Revolution*, 164–68; Allen, *Sanford Ballard Dole*, 211. See also Stratton, *Education for Empire*, 87, 94–95.

134. Allen, *Sanford Ballard Dole*, 223.

135. Zakaria, *From Wealth to Power*, 106–27.

136. *Punch Bowl*, March 1870, HMCS.

137. S. Dole to Burgess, March 31, 1894, Burgess Papers, Columbia University.

138. S. Dole, *Memoirs of the Hawaiian Revolution*, 113.

139. S. Dole, *Memoirs of the Hawaiian Revolution*, 76–77.

140. Queen Liliʻuokalani quoted in Silva, *Aloha Betrayed*, 170.

141. Jones and Osgood, *From King Cane*, 39. See also MacLennan, *Sovereign Sugar*, 45, 235.

142. Eating caused Bishop extreme pain. Some believe she may have had a severe spine curvature. See Zweip, *Pilgrim Path*, 238; Bishop, *Reminiscences of Old Hawaii.*

143. Daws, *Shoal of Time*, 273–74.

144. Putney, *Missionaries in Hawai'i*, 110.

### 5. CROSSING THE *PALI*

1. Wright, *Real Mother Goose*, 43.

2. Sam Wilcox quoted in Damon, *Letters from the Life*, 276.

3. Newcomb, *How to Be a Man*, 116–17. Punahou teacher Marcia Smith gave Newcomb's popular *How to Be a Man* to graduating students, advising, "It will greatly increase your ability to do good and give you power over other minds."

4. See M. Alexander and Dodge, *Punahou*, 165.

5. For citation, probable intent and impact of the law, and the U.S. Supreme Court's 1898 interpretation, see McFarland, "Derivative Citizenship," 467–510.

6. Binney, *Alienigenae of the United States*, 5.

7. Osorio, *Dismembering Lāhui*, 57–63.

8. Wight, *Memoirs of Elizabeth Kinau Wilder*, 55.

9. James Chamberlain, correspondence, November 25, 1875, HMCS.

10. Missionary son Warren Chamberlain discussed the views of most missionary parents regarding the Hawaiian oath of allegiance in Warren Chamberlain, correspondence, October 17, 1849, HMCS.

11. Sanford Dole, correspondence, November 29, 1862, HMCS.

12. Ludlow, "Personal Memories and Letters," 480–81.

13. *Statute Laws*, 76, 125–26; Forbes et al., *Act to Prohibit Hawaiians*.

14. "Early Missionaries," 350.

15. The number of missionary children who spoke Hawaiian despite their parents' wishes is noted in O. Gulick and A. Gulick, *Pilgrims of Hawaii*, 52. Recent studies suggest newborns cry in the language their mothers speak and prefer the language and voices they have heard in the weeks before birth. See Kaplan, "Babies Are Found to Cry in Their Mother's Tongue," 16. Infants can also differentiate between languages by five months old. See Feldman, *Development across the Life Span*, 143.

16. Damon, *Letters from the Life*, 102, 261.

17. Henry Parker, "Old Mission School Home," 294–95.

18. Sarah Coan, in *Annual Report* (1875), 10.

19. George Dole, correspondence, October 7, 1864, HMCS.

20. Cummings, *Missionary's Daughter*, 189. Jennifer Kashay first brought Lucy Thurston's short life to my attention in Kashay, "Problems in Paradise," 81–94.

21. J. Gulick and A. Gulick, *Evolutionist and Missionary*, 54.

22. Hiram Bingham Jr., in *Annual Report* (1873), 23.

23. M. Alexander and Dodge, *Punahou*, 16.

24. The relationship between language and cognitive thinking is discussed in Boroditsky, "Lost in Translation."

25. Linnekin, *Children of the Land*, xiii.

26. O. Emerson, *Pioneer Days in Hawaii*, 246.

27. Bird, *Six Months*, 190–91.

28. J. Gulick and A. Gulick, *Evolutionist and Missionary*, 142, 298.

29. Sam Wilcox quoted in Damon, *Letters from the Life*, 276.

30. Contemporary missionary methodology utilizes Lev Vygotsky, a Russian psychologist who studied the relationship between community, culture, and education. See Shaw, "Beyond Contextualization."

31. Sereno Bishop, scrapbook, May 4, 189, and August 1900, HMCS.

32. Dotts and Sikkema, *Challenging the Status Quo*, 20–23.

33. O. Gulick and A. Gulick, *Pilgrims of Hawaii*, 323–24.

34. M. Alexander and Dodge, *Punahou*, 276.

35. Rufus Anderson, in *Annual Report* (1863), 40.

36. Act 51, Section 30, *Laws of the Republic of Hawaii*, 189.

37. Lyman, *Hawaiian Yesterdays*, 232.

38. Allen, *Sanford Ballard Dole*, 277.

39. J. Gulick and A. Gulick, *Evolutionist and Missionary*, 151.

40. On national identity and childhood, see Barrett, "Children's Understanding," 279. Developmental researchers have noted that "children can show preference behavior for some national groups long before they develop any knowledge of these groups." See Coco, Inguglia, and Pace, "Children's Understanding of Ethnic Belonging," 244.

41. George Dole, correspondence, October 7, 1864, HMCS.

42. *Annual Report* (1857), 9.

43. William Andrews, correspondence, May 30, 1866, HMCS.

44. James Alexander, correspondence, October 31, 1860, and October 12, 1859, HMCS.

45. Dexter Chamberlain, correspondence and papers, circa 1880–1881, HMCS.

46. D. Dole, *Monitor*.

47. William Andrews, correspondence, October 22, 1865, HMCS.

48. Mary Castle quoted in Grimshaw, *Paths of Duty*, 189–90.

49. James Chamberlain, correspondence, August 3, 1863, and November 28, 1859, HMCS.

50. Robert Andrews, correspondence, September 30, 1852, HMCS.

51. Joseph Cooke, in *Annual Report* (1868), 17.

52. For histories of the Hawaiian Mission Children's Society, see *Annual Report* (1853, 1880, 1882, 1883).

53. James Alexander, correspondence, March 17, 1858, and October 12, 1859, HMCS.

54. Rufus Anderson, in *Annual Report* (1882), 40.

55. Gibson, *Yankees in Paradise*, 274–75; Ludlow, "Personal Memories and Letters," 120.

56. Martha Chamberlain, correspondence, December 23, 1851, HMCS.

57. Clara Bingham quoted in Pratt, *Story of Mid-Pacific Institute*, 6.

58. Pratt, *Story of Mid-Pacific Institute*, 13–15.

59. Hiram Bingham, correspondence, May 19, 1857, HMCS.

60. One of the most telling arguments against missionary service is found in president William Smith's address to fellow Hawaiian Mission Children's Society members in 1882. His remarks are reprinted in the *Annual Report* (1882), 35–44.

61. William Smith, in *Annual Report* (1882), 35–44.

62. John Gulick describes meeting his friend Nevins Armstrong at Andover in 1854 in J. Gulick and A. Gulick, *Evolutionist and Missionary*, 141–42.

63. Krauss and Alexander, *Grove Farm Plantation*, 100.

64. According to the 1853 HMCS report, "twenty-two of eighty-six mission children over the age of twelve did not profess the Christian faith." See *Annual Report* (1853), 9. In 1846 the ABCFM assumed that twelve of twenty-eight older mission children in the United States had no profession of the Christian faith. See American Board, "Report of the American Board."

65. Bingham, *Residence of Twenty-One Years*, 369.

66. Judd, *Honolulu*, 105.

67. Bradley, *American Frontier in Hawaii*, 346–47; R. Anderson, *Sandwich Islands Mission*, 168.

68. Gibson, *Yankees in Paradise*, 295.

69. American Tract Society's *Tract Primer* inscribed to Richard Baxter Armstrong, correspondence and papers, 1849, HMCS.

70. *Children's Picture Book*, Children of the Mission Collection, n.d., HMCS.

71. Andrew, *Rebuilding the Christian Commonwealth*, 121.

72. Cummings, *Missionary's Daughter*, 193–209.

73. Andrew, *Rebuilding the Christian Commonwealth*, 98–102.

74. ABCFM mission societies and missionary Hiram Bingham are quoted in Andrew, *Rebuilding the Christian Commonwealth*, 144–45, 162.

75. Bingham, *Story of the Morning Stars*, 23–24, 75–76, 95–97; American Board of Commissioners for Foreign Missions, *The Morning Star at Honolulu*; Schwartz, "Resounding the Gospel."

76. Lili'uokalani quoted in Kame'eleihiwa, *Native Land*, 315.

77. Noenoe K. Silva writes that the *haole* were motivated by a belief in their own superiority and created an oligarchy of "haole planters and businessmen." See Silva, *Aloha Betrayed*, 125–26. In reference to missionary son and 1887 Hawaiian League member William Castle, who claimed his status as a Hawaiian, Osorio writes, "For haole to claim that they were also Hawaiian was another very significant appropriation of what had once been an exclusively Native possession." See Osorio, *Dismembering Lāhui*, 237, 290. Andrews, *Vocabulary of Words*.

78. Armstrong, "Editorial Correspondence," 17.

79. Malo, *Hawaiian Antiquities*, 61.

80. Armstrong, "Editorial Correspondence," 17.

81. Kameʻeleihiwa, *Native Land*, 2–3.

82. Kapur, "Gender and Memory," 168–90.

83. My definitions here are taken from Mary Kawena Pukui and Samuel H. Elbert. *Kānaka* is the plural of *kanaka*. See Pukui and Elbert, *New Pocket Hawaiian Dictionary*. Silva discusses the missionary children's racist discourse in *Aloha Betrayed*, 90.

84. Editorial, *Weekly Star*, February 1852–April 1852 (Box 1), CL.

85. Wight, *Memoirs of Elizabeth Kinau Wilder*, 15.

86. John Gulick quoted in Putney, *Missionaries in Hawaiʻi*, 121.

87. Silva, *Aloha Betrayed*, 126–27.

88. *Statute Laws*, 76, 79.

89. Kameʻeleihiwa, *Native Land*, 11.

90. Ii, *Fragments of Hawaiian History*, 105.

91. Samuel Kamakau quoted in Kameʻeleihiwa, *Native Land*, 318.

92. Ii, *Fragments of Hawaiian History*, 105.

93. Wight, *Memoirs of Elizabeth Kinau Wilder*, 7–8, 72.

94. Ludlow, "Personal Memories and Letters," 44.

95. Henry Lyman on being appointed a government surveyor in Lyman, *Hawaiian Yesterdays*, 219.

96. George Dole, in *Annual Report* (1876), 31.

97. S. Dole, *Memoirs of the Hawaiian Revolution*, 76–77.

98. O. Gulick and A. Gulick, *Pilgrims of Hawaii*, 309–11.

99. The most profound debates over the future of the Hawaiian people occur in the missionary children's writings at Punahou during the 1840s and 1850s. See the *Punahou Gazette* and *Critic*, September 7, 1848–August 13, 1851 (Box 1–5), and *Weekly Star*, February 25, 1852–February 16, 1853 (Box 1–3), CL. Missionary son William Dewitt Alexander chronicles the road to revolution from a missionary-descendant perspective in Alexander, *Brief History of the Hawaiian People* and Alexander, *History of Later Years*. Noenoe K. Silva provides valuable

insight into the native revival of traditional cultural and political practices in *Aloha Betrayed.*

100. Whitehead, "Noncontiguous Wests," 326.
101. Thurston, *Hand-book on the Annexation.*

CONCLUSION

1. Milton, *Paradise Regain'd, Book 4,* 220–21.
2. *Punch Bowl,* December 1869, Children of the Mission Collection, HMCS.
3. Kamakau, *Ruling Chiefs of Hawaii,* 377.
4. The Student Volunteer Movement for Foreign Missions (SVM) was formed in 1886 to recruit college students for Protestant missionary work. By the First World War the SVM had sent over 5,800 American missionaries around the world. The organization's agenda was to see "the evangelization of the world in this generation." See *Student Volunteer Movement.*
5. Sereno Bishop, in *Annual Report* (1872), 19. For a discussion on manliness and civilization in late nineteenth-century American culture, see Bederman, *Manliness & Civilization.*
6. Sanford Dole quoted in Allen, *Sanford Ballard Dole,* 68.
7. Watkins, *White Architects,* 60. More recent discussions of Armstrong as southern colonizer include Fear-Segal, *White Man's Club.*
8. Armstrong, *Lessons from the Hawaiian Islands,* 213.
9. Armstrong, *Lessons from the Hawaiian Islands,* 219.
10. Ludlow, "Personal Memories and Letters," 916–17.
11. Armstrong, *Lessons from the Hawaiian Islands.*
12. Armstrong, "Editorial Correspondence," 17.
13. Ludlow, "Personal Memories and Letters," 488.
14. Ludlow, "Personal Memories and Letters," 125, 141–42.
15. Ludlow, "Personal Memories and Letters," 28, 228, 283.
16. Ludlow, "Personal Memories and Letters," 193, 294.
17. Ludlow, "Personal Memories and Letters," 351–52, 499.
18. Ludlow, "Personal Memories and Letters," 480–81.
19. Ludlow, "Personal Memories and Letters," 753.
20. Samuel Armstrong quoted in M. Alexander and Dodge, *Punahou,* 314–15.
21. Ludlow, "Personal Memories and Letters," 1407.
22. Beyer, "Connection of Samuel Chapman Armstrong," 43.
23. Engs, *Educating the Disfranchised,* 135.
24. In his last report to Hampton Trustees, Armstrong wrote, "No one who has taught them doubts the capacity of the Negroes for higher education. . . . There was and is no need of the higher education here when every northern

college is, open to the capable earnest colored student." See Ludlow, "Personal Memories and Letters," 1398. Andrew Carnegie quoted in J. Anderson, "Northern Foundations," 293.

25. J. Anderson, "Northern Foundations," 307.
26. George Carter quoted in Stratton, *Education for Empire*, 106.
27. Stratton, *Education for Empire*, 96–97, 105–7.
28. Okihiro, *Island World*, 129; Nelson, "Tradition of Non-Violence," 121–36.
29. Mohandas Gandhi quoted in Gandhi, *Collected Works*, vol. 39 (June 4, 1927–September 1, 1927), 333, and vol. 46 (May 12, 1929–August 31, 1929), 257–58.
30. Mohandas Gandhi quoted in Gandhi, *Collected Works*, vol. 72 (July 6, 1937–February 20, 1938), 361–62, and vol. 61 (April 27, 1933–October 7, 1933), 287–88.
31. For Puritan New Englanders' views of land use, see, for example, Drinnon, *Facing West*. For a discussion on early Jeffersonian Democrats, see Hietala, *Manifest Design*.
32. Ludlow, "Personal Memories and Letters," 628–29.
33. Sanford Ballard Dole quoted in Allen, *Sanford Ballard Dole*, 66, 73, 276. Allen, too, notes Dole's ambivalence toward cultural difference.
34. Allen, *Sanford Ballard Dole*, 158–67, 215, 279–90.
35. J. Gulick and A. Gulick, *Evolutionist and Missionary*, 151.
36. John Gulick, correspondence, April 4 and June 5, 1854, HMCS.
37. J. Gulick and A. Gulick, *Evolutionist and Missionary*, 152.
38. J. Gulick and A. Gulick, *Evolutionist and Missionary*, 161.
39. John Gulick, 1880 notes, HMCS.
40. Graham, *Gender, Culture, and Christianity*.
41. Porterfield, *Mary Lyon*, 21.
42. Sun Yat-sen married Song Qingling, and Chiang Kai-shek married her younger sister, Song Meiling. The Song family was a prominent Chinese Christian family who were educated in the United States and closely associated with the American missionary community in China. See Bergère, *Sun Yat-Sen*, 25, 250–51. See also Spence, *Search for Modern China*, 385–86. On the volatile U.S. relationship with Chiang Kai-shek, see Westad, *Decisive Encounters*. For the complicated U.S. relationship with Ngo Dinh Diem, see S. Jacobs, *America's Miracle Man*.
43. J. Gulick and A. Gulick, *Evolutionist and Missionary*, 365–66.
44. John Gulick, memoir manuscript, circa 1912, HMCS.
45. J. Gulick and A. Gulick, *Evolutionist and Missionary*, 358.
46. Mason, "Missionary Conscience," 10, 393.

47. The Hawaiian Mission Children's Society printed its occupational findings in *Annual Report* (1879), 6.

48. William Smith, in *Annual Report* (1882), 43.

49. On the psychological impact of Protestant parenting, see Greven, *Protestant Temperament.*

50. The London Missionary Society efforts in Tahiti were derailed, in part, due to the British missionaries' inability to control their own children. The missionaries gave up their post after numerous problems, including their inability to segregate and educate their children. See Latourette, *Great Century*; Gunson, *Messengers of Grace.*

51. Rufus Anderson, correspondence, July 14, 1851, Foreign Letters (ABC 2.1.1), ABCFMA.

52. Lyman, *Hawaiian Yesterdays*, 205.

53. For an excellent introduction to decolonization theory, see Le Sueur, *Decolonization Reader.*

54. Hunt describes the Congolese birthing practice of throwing hot water onto mothers who have just delivered babies, a conflation of Western medical practice and Christian missionary cleanliness in the absence of Western medicines. See N. Hunt, *Colonial Lexicon.*

55. Mercy Whitney, correspondence, April 18, 1850, HMCS.

56. James Chamberlain, correspondence, August 3, 1863, HMCS.

57. Robert Andrews, correspondence, December 24, 1878, HMCS.

58. Newcomb, *How to Be a Lady*, 10–11.

59. Gopnik, *Philosophical Baby*, 12–14.

60. Menton, "'Everything That Is Lovely,'" 201–2.

61. O. Emerson, *Pioneer Days in Hawaii*, 169.

# BIBLIOGRAPHY

ARCHIVAL SOURCES

Butler Library, Rare Book and Manuscript Library, Columbia University, New York
    John William Burgess Papers, [ca. 1873]–1930
Cooke Library, Punahou School, Honolulu
    *Punahou Gazette* and *Critic* and *Weekly Star*, 1848–53
Hawaiian Mission Children's Society Library, Honolulu
    Children of the Mission Collection, 1830–1900
Hawaiian Mission Houses Museum Library, Honolulu
Houghton Library, Harvard University, Cambridge MA
    American Board of Commissioners for Foreign Missions Archives
        Foreign Letters, Transcript series, 1836–1875 (ABC 2.1.1)
        Hawaiian Islands Mission, 1824–1909 (ABC 19.1)
        Preliminary series, 1827–1836 (ABC 2.01)
Huntington Library, Rare Books Collection, San Marino CA
Library of Congress, Rare Manuscript Division, Washington DC
    Hawaiian Materials
Mount Holyoke College, Archives and Special Collections, South Hadley MA
    Alumnae Biographical Files
    Mary Lyon Collection
    Missionaries Collection
Williams College, Archives and Special Collections, Williamstown MA
    Samuel Chapman Armstrong Collection, 1826–1947

PUBLISHED SOURCES

Akina, Keliʻi. "The Racial Spoils System Invents a Tribe for Native Hawaiians." *Wall Street Journal*, December 19–20, 2015.
Alexander, Mary Charlotte, and Charlotte Peabody Dodge. *Punahou, 1841–1941.* Berkeley: University of California Press, 1941.
Alexander, W. D. *A Brief History of Land Titles in the Hawaiian Kingdom*, 1891. Available at www.hawaiiankingdom.org/land-system.shtml.
———. *A Brief History of the Hawaiian People.* New York: American Book, 1899.

————. *History of Later Years of the Hawaiian Monarchy and the Revolution of 1893.* Honolulu: Hawaiian Gazette, 1896.

Allen, Helena G. *Sanford Ballard Dole: Hawaii's Only President, 1844–1926.* Glendale CA: A. H. Clark, 1988.

American Board of Commissioners for Foreign Missions. *The Morning Star at Honolulu, Sandwich Islands.* Boston, 1857.

————. "Report of the American Board of Commissioners for Foreign Missions." Boston: The Board, 1846.

Anderson, James D. "Northern Foundations and the Shaping of Southern Black Rural Education, 1902–1935." In *The Social History of American Education,* edited by B. Edward McClellan and William J. Reese, 287–312. Urbana: University of Illinois Press, 1988.

Anderson, Rufus. *History of the Sandwich Islands Mission.* Boston: Congregational Publishing Society, 1870.

Andrew, John A., III. *Rebuilding the Christian Commonwealth: New England Congregationalists and Foreign Missions, 1800–1830.* Lexington: University Press of Kentucky, 1976.

Andrews, Lorrin. *Vocabulary of Words in the Hawaiian Language.* Lahainaluna HI: Press of the High School, 1836.

*Annual Report of the Hawaiian Mission Children's Society.* Honolulu: Government Press, 1853–1937.

Armstrong, Samuel Chapman. *Lessons from the Hawaiian Islands.* Hampton VA, 1884.

Bailey, Thomas A., and David M. Kennedy. *The American Spirit.* 9th ed. Vol. 1. Boston: Houghton Mifflin, 1998.

Barman, Jean. "Whatever Happened to the Kanakas." *Beaver* 77, no. 6 (December 1997/January 1998): 12–20.

Barrett, Martyn. "Children's Understanding of, and Feelings about, Countries and National Groups." In Barrett and Buchanan-Barrow, *Children's Understanding of Society,* 251–86.

Barrett, Martyn, and Eithne Buchanan-Barrow, eds. *Children's Understanding of Society.* Hove, UK: Psychology Press, 2005.

Bederman, Gail. *Manliness & Civilization: A Cultural History of Gender and Race in the United States, 1880–1917.* Chicago: University of Chicago Press, 1995.

Bendroth, Margaret. "Horace Bushnell's *Christian Nurture.*" In *The Child in Christian Thought,* edited by Marcia J. Bunge, 350–64. Grand Rapids MI: William B. Eerdmans, 2001.

Bergère, Marie-Claire. *Sun Yat-Sen.* Translated by Janet Lloyd. Stanford CA: Stanford University Press, 1998.

Beyer, Carl Kalani. "The Connection of Samuel Chapman Armstrong as Both Borrower and Architect of Education in Hawai'i." *History of Education Quarterly* 47, no. 1 (2007): 23–48.

Bhabha, Homi K. "Signs Taken for Wonders: Questions of Ambivalence and Authority under a Tree outside Delhi, May 1817." In *"Race," Writing and Difference*, edited by Henry Louis Gates Jr., 163–84. Chicago: University of Chicago Press, 1985.

Bhana, Surendra. "The Tolstoy Farm: Gandhi's Experiment in 'Co-Operative Commonwealth.'" *South African Historical Journal* 7, no. 1 (1975): 88–100.

Bingham, Hiram. *A Residence of Twenty-One Years in the Sandwich Islands, or the Civil, Religious, and Political History of Those Islands: Comprising a Particular View of the Missionary Operations Connected with the Introduction and Progress of Christianity and Civilization among the Hawaiian People.* 2nd ed. New York: Sherman Converse, 1848.

Bingham, Hiram, Jr. *Story of the Morning Stars, the Children's Missionary Vessels, with Sequels.* Boston: American Board, 1897.

Binney, Horace. *Alienigenae of the United States under the Present Naturalization Laws.* Philadelphia: C. Sherman, 1853.

Bird, Isabella. *Six Months in the Sandwich Islands.* Honolulu: University of Hawai'i Press, 1964.

Bishop, Sereno Edwards. "Are Missionaries' Sons Tending to America a Stolen Kingdom?" *Friend* (Honolulu) 52, no. 1 (1894): 2–3.

———. *Reminiscences of Old Hawaii with a Brief Biography by Lorrin A. Thurston.* Honolulu: Hawaiian Gazette, 1916.

Boroditsky, Lera. "Lost in Translation: New Cognitive Research Suggests That Language Profoundly Influences the Way People See the World; A Different Sense of Blame in Japanese and Spanish." *Wall Street Journal*, July 24–25, 2010.

Bradley, Harold Whitman. *The American Frontier in Hawaii: The Pioneers, 1789–1843.* Stanford: Stanford University Press, 1942.

Brekus, Catherine A. "Children of Wrath, Children of Grace: Jonathan Edwards and the Puritan Culture of Child Rearing." In *The Child in Christian Thought*, edited by Marcia J. Bunge, 300–328. Grand Rapids MI: William B. Eerdmans, 2001.

Brewer, Holly. *By Birth or Consent: Children, Law, and the Anglo-American Revolution in Authority.* Chapel Hill: University of North Carolina Press, 2005.

Burgess, John W. *Political Science and Comparative Constitutional Law: Sovereignty and Liberty.* Vol. 1. Boston: Ginn, 1891.

Castle, Alfred L. "Advice for Hawaii: The Dole-Burgess Letters." *Hawaiian Journal of History* 15 (1981): 24–30.

Child, Lydia Maria Francis. *The Girl's Own Book.* Boston: Carter and Hendee, 1832. Reprint, New York: Clark, Austin, 1883.

Chirico, Jennifer, and Gregory S. Farley, eds. *Thinking Like an Island: Navigating a Sustainable Future in Hawai'i.* Honolulu: University of Hawai'i Press, 2015.

Chudacoff, Howard P. *Children at Play: An American History.* New York: New York University Press, 2007.

Coco, Alida Lo, Cristiano Inguglia, and Ugo Pace. "Children's Understanding of Ethnic Belonging and the Development of Ethnic Attitudes." In Barrett and Buchanan-Barrow, *Children's Understanding of Society,* 223–50.

Conkin, Paul K. *The Uneasy Center: Reformed Christianity in Antebellum America.* Chapel Hill: University of North Carolina Press, 1995.

Conroy-Krutz, Emily. *Christian Imperialism: Converting the World in the Early American Republic.* Ithaca: Cornell University Press, 2015.

Cott, Nancy F. *The Bonds of Womanhood: "Woman's Sphere" in New England, 1780–1835.* New Haven: Yale University Press, 1977.

Creighton, Margaret S. *Rites and Passages: The Experience of American Whaling, 1830–1870.* Cambridge: Cambridge University Press: 1995.

Cremin, Lawrence. *American Education: The National Experience, 1783–1876.* New York: Harper & Row, 1980.

Cumings, Bruce. *Dominion from Sea to Sea: Pacific Ascendancy and American Power.* New Haven: Yale University Press, 2009.

Cummings, A. P. *The Missionary's Daughter: A Memoir of Lucy Goodal Thurston of the Sandwich Islands.* New York: American Tract Society, 1842.

Cushman, Gregory T. *Guano and the Opening of the Pacific World: A Global Ecological History.* New York: Cambridge University Press, 2013.

Damon, Ethel M., ed. *Letters from the Life of Abner and Lucy Wilcox, 1836–1869.* Honolulu: Honolulu Star-Bulletin, 1950.

——. *Sanford Ballard Dole and His Hawaii: With an Analysis of Justice Dole's Legal Opinions by Samuel B. Kemp.* Palo Alto CA: Pacific Books, 1957.

Daws, Gavan. *Shoal of Time: A History of the Hawaiian Islands.* New York: Macmillan, 1968.

Dole, Daniel, ed. *The Monitor: A Monthly Journal, Devoted to Parents and Children* 1, no. 4. Honolulu, Oahu, Sandwich Islands, 1845.

Dole, Sanford B. "Hawaii before the World." *Friend,* June 1920.

——. "Systems of Immigration and Settlement." *Pacific Commercial Advertiser,* November 16, 1872.

Dole, Sanford Ballard. "Evolution of Hawaiian Land Tenures Read before the Hawaiian Historical Society, December 5, 1892." In *Papers of the Hawaiian Historical Society.* Milford NY: Kraus Reprint, 1978.

——. *Memoirs of the Hawaiian Revolution.* Honolulu: Advertiser, 1936.

Dotts, Cecil K., and Mildred Sikkema. *Challenging the Status Quo: Public Education in Hawaii 1840–1980*. Honolulu: Hawaii Education Association, 1994.

Drinnon, Richard. *Facing West: The Metaphysics of Indian-Hating and Empire-Building*. Minneapolis: University of Minnesota Press, 1980.

*D's Spelling Book: Calculated to Render Reading Completely Easy to Little Children; To Impress upon Their Minds the Importance of Religion, and the Advantages of Good Manners*. Hartford: Increase Cooke, 1802.

Durfee, Calvin. *A History of Williams College*. Boston: A. Williams, 1860.

Dwight, Edwin Welles. *Memoirs of Henry Obookiah: A Native of Owhyhee, and a Member of the Foreign Mission School; Who Died at Cornwall, Conn. Feb. 17, 1818 Aged 26 Years*. Philadelphia: American Sunday School Union, 1830.

"Early Missionaries Who Became Hawaiian Citizens." *Friend* 104, no. 7 (July 1934): 350.

Emerson, Nathaniel Bright. *Unwritten Literature of Hawaii: The Sacred Songs of the Hula*. Edited by Smithsonian Institution Bureau of American Ethnology. *Bulletin*, vol. 38. Washington DC: Government Printing Office, 1909.

Emerson, Oliver Pomeroy. *Pioneer Days in Hawaii*. Garden City NY: Doubleday, Doran, 1928.

Engs, Robert Francis. *Educating the Disfranchised and Disinherited: Samuel Chapman Armstrong and Hampton Institute, 1839–1893*. Knoxville: University of Tennessee Press, 1999.

Fass, Paula S. *Children of a New World: Society, Culture, and Globalization*. New York: New York University Press, 2007.

Fear-Segal, Jaqueline. *White Man's Club*. Lincoln: University of Nebraska Press, 2007.

Feldman, Robert S. *Development across the Life Span*. 3rd ed. Upper Saddle River NJ: Pearson Prentice Hall, 2005.

Fieldston, Sara. "Little Cold Warriors: Child Sponsorship and International Affairs." *Diplomatic History* 38, no. 2 (April 2014): 240–50.

Finn, Dallas. "Guests of the Nation: The Japanese Delegation to the Buchanan White House." *White House History* 12 (2003): 14–38.

Fisher, Scott. "Hawaiian Culture and Its Foundation in Sustainability." In Chirico and Farley, *Thinking Like an Island*, 7–27.

Forbes, David W., Kamehameha, King of the Hawaiian Islands, Zamorano Club, and Roxburghe Club of San Francisco. *An Act to Prohibit Hawaiians from Emigrating to California "Where They May Die in Misery," 1850*. San Francisco: Paul Markham Kahn, 1986.

Foster, Nelson. *Punahou: The History and Promise of a School in the Islands*. Honolulu: Punahou School, 1991.

Frear, Mary Dillingham. *Lowell and Abigail: A Realistic Idyll.* New Haven CT: Privately printed, 1934.

Gabaccia, Donna R. *Foreign Relations: American Immigration in Global Perspective.* Princeton: Princeton University Press, 2012.

Gandhi, Mahatma. *Collected Works of Mahatma Gandhi Online.* New Delhi: Publications Division, Ministry of Information and Broadcasting, Govt. of India, 1990.

Gibson, Arrell Morgan. *Yankees in Paradise: The Pacific Basin Frontier.* Completed with the assistance of John S. Whitehead. Histories of the American Frontier series. Albuquerque: University of New Mexico Press, 1993.

Gopnik, Alison. *The Philosophical Baby: What Children's Minds Tell Us about Truth, Love, and the Meaning of Life.* New York: Farrar, Straus and Giroux, 2009.

Graham, Gael. *Gender, Culture, and Christianity: American Protestant Mission Schools in China, 1880–1930.* New York: Peter Lang, 1995.

Greven, Philip J. *The Protestant Temperament: Patterns of Child-Rearing, Religious Experience, and the Self in Early America.* New York: Alfred A. Knopf, 1977.

Grimshaw, Patricia. *Paths of Duty: American Missionary Wives in Nineteenth-Century Hawaii.* Honolulu: University of Hawai'i Press, 1989.

Gulick, John Thomas, and Addison Gulick. *Evolutionist and Missionary, John Thomas Gulick: Portrayed through Documents and Discussions.* Chicago: University of Chicago Press, 1932.

Gulick, Orramel Hinckley, and Ann Eliza Clark Gulick. *The Pilgrims of Hawaii; Their Own Story of Their Pilgrimage from New England and Life Work in the Sandwich Islands, Now Known as Hawaii; with Explanatory and Illustrative Material Compiled and Verified from Original Sources.* New York: Fleming H. Revell, 1918.

Gunson, Neil. *Messengers of Grace: Evangelical Missionaries in the South Seas, 1797–1860.* Melbourne: Oxford University Press, 1978.

Harris, Paul William. *Nothing but Christ: Rufus Anderson and the Ideology of Protestant Foreign Missions.* Oxford: Oxford University Press, 1999.

Hemmings, Kaui Hart. *The Descendants.* New York: Random House, 2007.

Hewett, A. M. *A Sketch of Recent Events: Being a Short Account of the Events Which Culminated on June 30, 1887, Together with a Full Report of the Great Reform Meeting, and the Two Constitutions in Parallel Columns.* Honolulu: Hawaiian Gazette Print, 1887.

Hietala, Thomas R. *Manifest Design: American Exceptionalism & Empire.* Rev. ed. Ithaca: Cornell University Press, 2003.

Hobbs, Jean. *Hawaii: A Pageant of the Soil.* Stanford: Stanford University Press, 1935.

Hoganson, Kristin L. *Fighting for American Manhood: How Gender Politics Provoked the Spanish-American and Philippine-American Wars.* New Haven: Yale University Press, 1998.

*The Holy Bible, New International Version.* Colorado Springs: International Bible Society, 1973.

Hopkins, Mark. *A Discourse Delivered at Williamstown June 29, 1886 on the Fiftieth Anniversary of His Election as President of Williams College.* New York: Charles Scribner's Sons, 1886.

Hunt, Michael H. *Ideology and U.S. Foreign Policy.* New Haven: Yale University Press, 1987.

Hunt, Nancy Rose. *A Colonial Lexicon of Birth Ritual, Medicalization, and Mobility in the Congo.* Durham NC: Duke University Press, 1999.

Igler, David. "Diseased Goods: Global Exchanges in the Eastern Pacific Basin, 1770–1850." *American Historical Review* 109, no. 3 (June 2004): 693–719.

———. *The Great Ocean: Pacific Worlds from Captain Cook to the Gold Rush.* Oxford: Oxford University Press, 2013.

Ii, John Papa. *Fragments of Hawaiian History as Recorded by John Papa Ii.* Translated by Mary Kawena Pukui. Edited by Dorothy B. Barrère. Honolulu: Bishop Museum Press, 1959.

Inglis, Kerri A. *Maʻi Lepera: Disease and Displacement in Nineteenth-Century Hawaiʻi.* Honolulu: University of Hawaiʻi Press, 2013.

Jacobs, Margaret D. *White Mother to a Dark Race: Settler Colonialism, Maternalism, and the Removal of Indigenous Children in the American West and Australia, 1880–1940.* Lincoln: University of Nebraska Press, 2009.

———. "Working on the Domestic Frontier: American Indian Domestic Servants in White Women's Households in the San Francisco Bay Area, 1920–1940." *Frontiers: A Journal of Women Studies* 27, no. 1–2 (2007): 165–99.

Jacobs, Seth. *America's Miracle Man in Vietnam: Ngo Dinh Diem, Religion, Race, and U.S. Intervention in Southeast Asia.* Durham NC: Duke University Press, 2004.

Jones, C. Allan, and Robert V. Osgood. *From King Cane to the Last Sugar Mill: Agriculture Technology and the Making of Hawaiʻi's Premier Crop.* Honolulu: University of Hawaiʻi Press, 2015.

Judd, Laura Fish. *Honolulu: Sketches of Life in the Hawaiian Islands from 1828 to 1861.* Chicago: Lakeside Press, 1966.

Kamakau, Samuel Manaiakalani. *Ruling Chiefs of Hawaii.* Rev. ed. Honolulu: Kamehameha Schools Press, 1992.

Kameʻeleihiwa, Lilikalā. *Native Land and Foreign Desires: Pehea Lā E Pono Ai? How Shall We Live in Harmony?* Honolulu: Bishop Museum Press, 1992.

Kaplan, Karen. "Babies Are Found to Cry in Their Mother's Tongue." *Los Angeles Times,* November 7, 2009.

Kapur, Cari Costanzo. "Gender and Memory in the Pacific: Contemporary Hawaiian Nationalism and the Memorialization of Plantation Workers at the Japanese Cultural Center of Hawai'i." *Amerasia Journal* 35, no. 2 (2009): 168–90.

Kashay, Jennifer Fish. "Agents of Imperialism: Missionaries and Merchants in Early Nineteenth-Century Hawaii." *New England Quarterly* 80, no. 2 (2007): 280–98.

———. "Problems in Paradise: The Peril of Missionary Parenting in Early Nineteenth-Century Hawaii." *Journal of Presbyterian History* 77, no. 2 (Summer 1999): 81–94.

Kashti, Yitzhak. *Boarding Schools at the Crossroads of Change: The Influence of Residential Education Institutions on National and Societal Development.* New York: Haworth Press, 1998.

Kennedy, Dane. *Islands of White: Settler Society and Culture in Kenya and Southern Rhodesia, 1890–1939.* Durham NC: Duke University Press, 1987.

———. *The Magic Mountains: Hill Stations and the British Raj.* Berkeley: University of California Press, 1996.

Kenui, Tiona, Nawaakoa, et al. "Concerning Foreigners Taking the Oath of Allegiance." *Friend*, August 1845: 118–19.

Kipling, Rudyard. "The White Man's Burden." *McClure's Magazine* 12, no. 4 (February 1899): 290–91.

Kling, David W. "The New Divinity and the Origins of the American Board of Commissioners for Foreign Missions." In *North American Foreign Missions, 1810–1914: Theology, Theory and Policy,* edited by Wilbert R. Shenk, 11–38. Grand Rapids MI: William B. Eerdmans, 2004.

Koppel, Tom. *Kanaka: The Untold Story of Hawaiian Pioneers in British Columbia and the Pacific Northwest.* Vancouver: Whitecap Books, 1995.

Kramer, Paul A. "Is the World Our Campus? International Students and U.S. Global Power in the Long Twentieth Century." *Diplomatic History* 33, no. 5 (2009): 775–806.

———. "Power and Connection: Imperial Histories of the United States in the World." *American Historical Review* 116, no. 5 (December 2011): 1348–91.

Krauss, Bob, and William P. Alexander. *Grove Farm Plantation: The Biography of a Hawaiian Sugar Plantation.* Palo Alto CA: Pacific Books, 1965.

Kuykendall, Ralph S. *The Hawaiian Kingdom.* Vol. 1, *1778–1854, Foundation and Transformation.* Honolulu: University of Hawai'i Press, 1938. Reprint, 1968.

———. *The Hawaiian Kingdom.* Vol. 2, *1854–1874, Twenty Critical Years.* Honolulu: University of Hawai'i Press, 1966.

———. *The Hawaiian Kingdom.* Vol. 3, *1874–1893, The Kalakaua Dynasty.* Honolulu: University of Hawai'i Press, 1967.

Latourette, Kenneth Scott. *The Great Century in the Americas, Austral-Asia, and Africa, A.D. 1800–A.D. 1914.* Vol. 5, *A History of the Expansion of Christianity.* New York: Harper & Brothers, 1943.

*Laws of the Republic of Hawaii Passed by the Legislature at Its Session, 1896.* Honolulu: Hawaiian Gazette, 1896.

Lawson, Barbara. "Collecting Cultures: Canadian Missionaries, Pacific Islanders, and Museums." In *Western Women and Imperialism: Complicity and Resistance,* edited by Nupur Chaudhuri and Margaret Strobel. Bloomington: Indiana University Press, 1992.

Le Sueur, James D., ed. *The Decolonization Reader.* New York: Routledge, 2003.

Levine, Penny. "Lessons from the Taro Patch." In Chirico and Farley, *Thinking Like an Island,* 79–124.

Linnekin, Jocelyn. *Children of the Land: Exchange and Status in a Hawaiian Community.* New Brunswick NJ: Rutgers University Press, 1985.

———. *Sacred Queens and Women of Consequence: Rank, Gender, and Colonialism in the Hawaiian Islands.* Ann Arbor: University of Michigan Press, 1990.

Locher-Scholten, Elsbeth. "So Close and Yet So Far: The Ambivalence of Dutch Colonial Rhetoric on Javanese Servants in Indonesia, 1900–1942." In *Domesticating the Empire: Race, Gender, and Family Life in French and Dutch Colonialism,* edited by Julia Clancy-Smith and Frances Gouda, 131–53. Charlottesville: University Press of Virginia, 1998.

Lyman, Henry M. *Hawaiian Yesterdays: Chapters from a Boy's Life in the Islands in the Early Days.* Chicago: A. C. McClurg, 1906.

Lyon, Mary. *Missionary Offering, or Christian Sympathy, Personal Responsibility, and the Present Crisis in Foreign Missions.* Boston: Crocker and Brewster, 1843.

MacLennan, Carol A. *Sovereign Sugar: Industry and Environment in Hawai'i.* Honolulu: University of Hawai'i Press, 2014.

Malo, David. *Hawaiian Antiquities (Moolelo Hawaii).* Translated from the Hawaiian by Dr. N. B. Emerson, 1898. Honolulu: Hawaiian Gazette, 1903.

Marsden, George M. *The Evangelical Mind and the New School Presbyterian Experience: A Case Study of Thought and Theology in Nineteenth-Century America.* New Haven: Yale University Press, 1970.

Mason, Sarah R. "Missionary Conscience and the Comprehension of Imperialism a Study of the Children of American Missionaries to China, 1900–1949." PhD diss., Northern Illinois University, 1978.

McFarland, Michael G. "Derivative Citizenship: Its History, Constitutional Foundation, and Constitutional Limitations." *New York University Annual Survey of American Law* 63, no. 3 (2008): 467–510.

McGuffey, William H. *The Eclectic Third Reader: Containing Selections of Prose and Poetry, from the Best American and English Writers.* Cincinnati: Truman and Smith, 1837.

Melillo, Edward D. "The First Green Revolution: Debt Peonage and the Making of the Nitrogen Fertilizer Trade, 1840–1930." *American Historical Review* 117, no. 4 (October 2012): 1028–60.

Menton, Linda K. "A Christian and 'Civilized' Education: The Hawaiian Chief's Children's School, 1839–50." *History of Education Quarterly* 32, no. 2 (1992): 213–42.

Menton, Linda Kristeen. "'Everything That Is Lovely and of Good Report': The Hawaiian Chiefs' Children's School, 1839–1850." PhD diss., University of Hawaii, 1982.

Merry, Sally Engle. *Colonizing Hawai'i: The Cultural Power of the Law.* Princeton: Princeton University Press, 2000.

Millis, Walter. *The Martial Spirit: A Study of Our War with Spain.* Boston: Houghton Mifflin, 1931.

Milton, John. *Paradise Regain'd, Book 4.* 1671.

*Missionary Album: Portraits and Biographical Sketches of the American Protestant Missionaries to the Hawaiian Islands.* Honolulu: Hawaiian Mission Children's Society, 1969.

Nelson, William Stuart. "The Tradition of Non-Violence and Its Underlying Forces." *Journal of Religious Thought* (Summer–Autumn 1959): 121–36.

Newcomb, Harvey. *How to Be a Lady: A Book for Girls, Containing Useful Hints on the Formation of Character.* 5th ed. Boston: Gould, Kendall and Lincoln, 1848.

———. *How to Be a Man: A Book for Boys, Containing Useful Hints on the Formation of Character.* 11th ed. Boston: Gould, Kendall and Lincoln, 1853.

*Oahu College Directory, Seventy-Fifth Anniversary, 1841–1916.* Honolulu HI, 1916.

Okihiro, Gary Y. *American History Unbound: Asians and Pacific Islanders.* Oakland: University of California Press, 2015.

———. *Island World: A History of Hawai'i and the United States.* Berkeley: University of California Press, 2008.

———. "Toward a Pacific Civilization." *Japanese Journal of American Studies,* no. 18 (2007): 73–85.

Osorio, Jonathan Kay Kamakawiwo'ole. *Dismembering Lāhui: A History of the Hawaiian Nation to 1887.* Honolulu: University of Hawai'i Press, 2002.

Parker, Henry. "Old Mission School Home of Free Kindergarten and Children's Aid." *Friend* 93 (December 1924): 294–95.

*Penal Code of the Hawaiian Islands, Passed by the House of Nobles and Representatives on the 21st of June, A.D. 1850.* Honolulu: Government Press, 1850.

Peterson, Derek. "The Rhetoric of the Word: Bible Translation and Mau Mau in Colonial Central Kenya." In *Missions, Nationalism, and the End of Empire*, edited by Brian Stanley, 165–79. Grand Rapids MI: William B. Eerdmans, 2003.

———. "Translating the Word: Dialogism and Debate in Two Gikuyu Dictionaries." *Journal of Religious History* 23, no. 21 (1999): 31–50.

Piercy, LaRue W. *Hawaii's Missionary Saga: Sacrifice and Godliness in Paradise*. Honolulu: Mutual, 1992.

Pollock, David C., and Ruth E. Van Reken. *The Third Culture Kids: The Experience of Growing Up among Worlds*. Yarmouth ME: Intercultural Press, 2001.

Porterfield, Amanda. *Mary Lyon and the Mount Holyoke Missionaries*. Oxford: Oxford University Press, 1997.

Pratt, Helen Gay. *The Story of Mid-Pacific Institute*. Honolulu: Tongg, 1957.

Pukui, Mary Kawena, and Samuel H. Elbert. *Hawaiian Dictionary*. Honolulu: University of Hawai'i Press, 1971.

———. *New Pocket Hawaiian Dictionary with a Concise Grammar and Given Names in Hawaiian*. With Esther T. Mookini and Yu Mapuana Nishizawa. Honolulu: University of Hawai'i Press, 1975, 1992.

Putney, Clifford. *Missionaries in Hawai'i: The Lives of Peter and Fanny Gulick, 1797–1883*. Amherst: University of Massachusetts Press, 2010.

Repousis, Angelo. "'The Devil's Apostle': Jonas King's Trial against the Greek Hierarchy in 1852 and the Pressure to Extend U.S. Protection for American Missionaries Overseas." *Diplomatic History* 33, no. 5 (2009): 807–37.

Robert, Dana L. *American Women in Mission: A Social History of Their Thought and Practice*. Macon GA: Mercer University Press, 1996.

———. "Evangelist or Homemaker? Mission Strategies of Early Nineteenth-Century Missionary Wives in Burma and Hawaii." In *North American Foreign Missions, 1810–1914: Theology, Theory and Policy*, edited by Wilbert R. Shenk, 116–32. Grand Rapids MI: William B. Eerdmans, 2004.

Rogoff, Barbara. *The Cultural Nature of Human Development*. Oxford: Oxford University Press, 2003.

Rosenberg, Emily S. *Spreading the American Dream: American Economic and Cultural Expansion, 1890–1945*. New York: Hill and Wang, 1982.

Rotter, Andrew J. "Empires of the Senses: How Seeing, Hearing, Smelling, Tasting, and Touching Shaped Imperial Encounters." *Diplomatic History* 35, no. 1 (2011): 3–19.

Schwartz, Jessica. "Resounding the Gospel: Examining the Influence of the Missionary Encounter in the Marshall Islands." Paper presented at the Annual Meeting of the American Historical Association, Chicago, January 6, 2012.

Scott, Anne Firor. "The Ever-Widening Circle: The Diffusion of Feminist Values from the Troy Female Seminary, 1822–1872." In *The Social History of American Education*, edited by B. Edward McClellan and William J. Reese, 137–59. Urbana: University of Illinois Press, 1988.

Shaw, R. Daniel. "Beyond Contextualization: Toward a Twenty-First-Century Model for Enabling Mission." *International Bulletin of Missionary Research* 34, no. 4 (2010): 208–15.

Shoemaker, Nancy. "A Typology of Colonialism." *Perspectives on History* 53, no. 6 (October 2015): 29–30.

Siler, Julia Flynn. "Hawaiian History, Housed in a Ranch: Fourth-, Fifth-, and Sixth-Generation Descendants of Powerful Patriarch H. P. Baldwin Live in a Compound on One of the State's Largest Working Cattle Ranches; Family Reunions under the Camphor Tree." *Wall Street Journal*, April 25, 2014.

Silva, Noenoe K. *Aloha Betrayed: Native Hawaiian Resistance to American Colonialism.* Durham NC: Duke University Press, 2004.

Smith, Bradford. *Yankees in Paradise: The New England Impact on Hawaii.* Philadelphia: J. B. Lippincott, 1956.

Smith, Jared G. *The Big Five: A Brief History of Hawaii's Largest Firms.* Honolulu: Advertiser, 1942.

Spence, Jonathan D. *The Search for Modern China.* New York: W. W. Norton, 1990.

Stanley, Brian. *The Bible and the Flag: Protestant Missions and British Imperialism in the Nineteenth and Twentieth Centuries.* Leicester, UK: Apollos, 1990.

*Statute Laws of His Majesty Kamehameha III, King of the Hawaiian Islands, Passed by the House of Nobles and Representatives, during the Twenty-First Year of His Reign, and the Third and Fourth Years of His Public Recognition, A.D. 1845 and 1846.* Vol. 1. Honolulu: Government Press, 1846.

Stoler, Ann Laura. *Carnal Knowledge and Imperial Power: Race and the Intimate in Colonial Rule.* Berkeley: University of California Press, 2002.

Stratton, Clif. *Education for Empire: American Schools, Race, and the Paths of Good Citizenship.* Oakland: University of California Press, 2016.

*The Student Volunteer Movement for Foreign Missions.* New York: Association Press, 1946.

Thigpen, Jennifer. *Island Queens and Mission Wives: How Gender and Empire Remade Hawai'i's Pacific World.* Chapel Hill: University of North Carolina Press, 2014.

Thurston, Lorrin A. *A Hand-book on the Annexation of Hawaii.* St. Joseph MI: A. B. Morse, 1897.

Thurston, Lucy G. *Life and Times of Mrs. Lucy G. Thurston, Wife of Rev. Asa Thurston, Pioneer Missionary to the Sandwich Islands, Gathered from Letters and Journals Extending over a Period of More Than Fifty Years.* Ann Arbor MI: S.C. Andrews, 1882.

*Translation of the Constitution and Laws of the Hawaiian Islands, Established in the Reign of Kamehameha III.* Translated by William L. Richards. Lahainaluna HI: Press of the High School, 1842.

Trask, Haunani-Kay. *From a Native Daughter: Colonialism and Sovereignty in Hawai'i.* Rev. ed. Honolulu: University of Hawai'i Press, 1999.

Twain, Mark. *Roughing It.* Vol. 1. New York: Harper & Row, 1913.

Tyrrell, Ian. *Reforming the World: The Creation of America's Moral Empire.* Princeton: Princeton University Press, 2010.

Vickers, Daniel. *Young Men and the Sea: Yankee Seafarers in the Age of Sail.* With Vince Walsh. New Haven: Yale University Press, 2005.

Walters, Ronald G. *American Reformers, 1815–1860.* Edited by Eric Foner. Rev. ed. New York: Hill and Wang, 1997.

Watkins, William H. *The White Architects of Black Education: Ideology and Power in America, 1865–1954.* New York: Teachers College Press, 2001.

Weaver, Ellen Armstrong. "Memories of the Old Palace." *Friend* 89 (May 1920): 105.

Welter, Barbara. "The Cult of True Womanhood: 1820–1860." *American Quarterly* 18, no. 2, part 1 (Summer 1966): 151–74.

West, Elliott. *Growing Up with the Country: Childhood on the Far Western Frontier.* Edited by Ray Allen Billington. Histories of the American Frontier series. Albuquerque: University of New Mexico Press, 1989.

Westad, Odd Arne. *Decisive Encounters: The Chinese Civil War, 1946–1950.* Stanford: Stanford University Press, 2003.

Wexler, Laura. *Tender Violence: Domestic Visions in an Age of U.S. Imperialism.* Chapel Hill: University of North Carolina Press, 2000.

White, Richard. *The Middle Ground: Indians, Empires, and Republics in the Great Lakes Region, 1650–1815.* Cambridge: Cambridge University Press, 1991.

Whitehead, John S. "Hawaii: The First and Last Far West?" *Western Historical Quarterly* 23, no. 2 (May 1992): 153–77.

———. "Noncontiguous Wests: Alaska and Hawai'i." In *Many Wests: Place, Culture, and Regional Identity,* edited by David M. Wrobel and Michael C. Steiner, 315–41. Lawrence: University Press of Kansas, 1997.

Whitney, Henry M. *The Hawaiian Guide Book for Travelers: Containing a Brief Description of the Hawaiian Islands, Their Harbors, Agricultural Resources, Plantations, Scenery, Volcanoes, Climate, Population and Commerce.* Honolulu: Henry M. Whitney, 1875.

Wight, Elizabeth Leslie. *The Memoirs of Elizabeth Kinau Wilder.* Honolulu: Paradise of the Pacific Press, 1909.

Wright, Blanche Fisher. *The Real Mother Goose.* New York: Barnes & Noble, 1992. First published in 1916 by Checkerboard Press.

Yokota, Kariann Akemi. *Unbecoming British: How Revolutionary America Became a Postcolonial Nation.* Oxford: Oxford University Press, 2011.

Zakaria, Fareed. *From Wealth to Power: The Unusual Origins of America's World Role.* Princeton: Princeton University Press, 1998.

Zwiep, Mary. *Pilgrim Path: The First Company of Women Missionaries to Hawaii.* Madison: University of Wisconsin Press, 1991.

# INDEX

Castle, William Richards, 38, 84, 184n75, 194n77
Castle & Cooke, 37, 58
Catholics, 82–85
Ceylon, 6, 18–19, 21
Chamberlain, Dexter, 135
Chamberlain, James, 36–38, 101, 104, 112, 114, 127, 135, 165
Chamberlain, Jeremiah "Evarts," 98, 104, *105*, 113–14
Chamberlain, Levi, 17, 28–29
Chamberlain, Levi T., II, 36, 58
Chamberlain, Maria, 36, *111*, 112
Chamberlain, Martha, 36, 102, 109–12, *111*
Chamberlain, Warren, 37, 80, 98, 101–2, 183n52
chants, 11, 46, 83, 171n31
Charles M. Cooke, Ltd., 58
Chiang Kai-shek, 196n42
*Children's Picture Book* (American Tract Society), 141
China, 8–9, 63–64, 96, 100, 106, 137, 159–61, 166, 189n106, 196n42
Chinese immigrant laborers, 14, 118, 121, 156
*Christian Nurture* (Bushnell), 24
Chudacoff, Howard, 54, 177n4
citizenship: John Gulick on, 64; of missionary children, 10, 15, 89, 94, 100–101, 114, 117–18, 126–28, 146, 153, 155, 186n19; of native Hawaiians, 107, 131; of Samuel Chapman Armstrong, 89, 114, 155; of Sanford Dole, 117–18
Civil War. *See* U.S. Civil War
Clark, Ann Eliza, 48, 76, 83, 110, 132, 146
Clark, Ephraim, 20

cleanliness, 48, 74, 197n54
Cleveland, Grover, 122
Coan, Sarah, 129
Coan, Titus, 114, 137
Committee of Public Safety, 85
common-stock system, 18, 23, 27
Conde, Samuel, 114
*The Conquest of Canaan* (Dwight), 13
Conroy-Krutz, Emily, 2–3, 11
Cook, James, 4, 135, 141
Cooke, Amos (father), *35*, 37, 58, 79, 91
Cooke, Amos (son), 39
Cooke, Charles, 58
Cooke, Joseph, 66, 136
Cooke, Juliette, *35*, 79
corporal punishment, 76
Cousins' Society, 136–37
*Critic*, 72

Damon, Samuel Mills, 39–40, 85, *123*
Darwin, Charles, 9, 52, 59–61, 63–64, 94
De La Cour, Emily, 63
deportment, 77, 88, 145, 164, 183n40
discourse of family, 12–14
disease, 8, 39, 56–57, 127, 176n92, 179n53
Dodge, Charlotte Peabody, 181n4
Dole, Charlotte Knapp, 117
Dole, Daniel, 26, 71, 74–76, 117
Dole, Emily, 26–27, 71, 117
Dole, George H., *41*, 134, 146
Dole, James, 170n25
Dole, Sanford Ballard, *41*, *123*; adoption of Elizabeth Puiki Napoleon by, 158–59; adult life of, 152–53, 158–59; appointment of, to Hawaiian Supreme Court, 39, 119; bicultural

Dole, Sanford Ballard (*cont.*)
upbringing of, 152–53, 159, 162;
citizenship of, 117–18; and cultural difference, 196n33; early life
of, 117–23; on English-language
instruction in Hawai'i schools,
132; as first president of Hawaiian
Republic, 44, 85; on Hawaiian
labor situation, 118; and Hawaiian
League, 184n75; and James Dole,
170n25; judged as colonialist, 153;
on legislative authority, 120; Mark
Hopkins's influence on, 117; as
member of Hawaiian legislature,
118; on missionary experience,
117–18; and overthrow of Hawaiian
monarchy, 9, 15, 85, 119–23, 146–
47; and parents' relationship with
monarchy, 175n81; poetry of, 134;
on protecting missionary children's
familial legacy, 39; and religious
and economic missionary ideals,
44; on value of missionary lands,
38; at Williams College, 110, 117–18
domestic economics, 3–4, 17–22
Dwight, Timothy, 12–13

Emancipation Proclamation, 154
Emerson, John, 114, 166
Emerson, Joseph, 37–38, 84
Emerson, Nathaniel, 38, 114, 184n75
Emerson, Oliver, 37, 40, 42, 54, 112
eminent domain, 179n65
English-language instruction in
Hawai'i schools, 131–34
Evarts, Jeremiah, 21

Fass, Paula, 171n37
Fieldston, Sara, 171n37

filial obedience, 78
Forbes, Anderson, 39
Forbes, Joseph, 114
Forbes, Theodore, 114
Forbes, William, 114
Fornander, Abraham, 39
foster children (*nā hānai*), 57–60
French missionaries, 82–83

Gabaccia, Donna, 116, 189n110
gambling, 85, 129
Gandhi, Mohandas, 157–58
gender roles, 51, 73–75, 182n21
genealogical chants, 11, 46, 83, 171n31
Gibson, Arrell Morgan, 140
Gibson, Walter Murray, 84
Gold, Harriet, 6
gold rush, 8, 33, 56, 61, 103, 139, 163
Gopnik, Alison, 66, 166
Graham, Gael, 160
grass houses, 77
Great *Māhele*, 31–32, 38, 119
Green, Jonathan, 154
Green, Mary, 114
Green, Porter, 114
Greven, Philip, 113–14
guano, 58, 180n67
Gulick, Ann Eliza Clark. *See* Clark,
Ann Eliza
Gulick, Charles, 124, 182n31
Gulick, Emily De La Cour, 63
Gulick, Fanny, 60, 103
Gulick, John Thomas, *65*; adoption of
Chinese children by, 159; bicultural
upbringing of, 152, 161–62; and
California gold rush, 103; childhood and adult life of, 15, 51–52,
60–66, 103–4, 153, 159–62; and
China, 9, 63–64; on citizenship,

64; and *habitudinal* evolution, 64; and Japan, 9, 61–64; judged as colonialist, 153; and land snails, 52, 61, 63–64; on language and culture of missionary children, 130; and manual labor at Punahou, 72; on missionary children's rejection of parents' faith, 140; and racism at Punahou, 79, 144; thwarted naturalist career of, 52, 60–61, 63, 66, 104, 134, 162

Gulick, Luther Halsey, 129, 136

Gulick, Orramel, 76, 132, 146

Gulick, Peter, 52, 61, 104, 124, 160, 173n33

*habitudinal* evolution, 64

Haleakala Crater, 55

Haleakala Sugar Company, 58

Hamakua Ditch, 58

Hampton Institute, *91*, *164*; founding of, 9, 153, 155–56; and Mark Hopkins, 108; as model for minority and colonial education, 89, 153–57, 195n24; Mohandas Gandhi on, 157; and Samuel Chapman Armstrong, 9, 15, 89, 108, 153, 155–57

*hānai*, 57–60, 145, 158–59

Hanapepe Falls, *53*

*haole*, 143–45, 166, 194n77

Harris, Paul, 108

Hawaiian Board of Education, 39

Hawaiian Board of Health, 83

Hawaiian Chiefs' Children's School. *See* Royal School

Hawaiian constitution (1840), 25

Hawaiian creation story, 11, 46

Hawaiian Evangelical Association (HEA), 32–35, 39

Hawaiian Homestead Act, 118–19

Hawaiian language: and Hawaiians, 4, 18, 20, 79, 140, 143; importance of, to modern scholarship, 11, 170n30; and missionary children, 70, 103, 113, 128–34, 165

Hawaiian League, 10, 84, 120, 123, 184n75, 194n77

Hawaiian legislature, 39

Hawaiian marriage customs and sexual freedom, 46, 98

Hawaiian Mission Children's Society (HMCS), 136–37, *147*, 170n26

Hawaiian monarchy, overthrow of: and Henry Obookiah, 95; and Lili'uokalani, 4, 10, 122; and missionary children, 2–4, 42–44, 58–60, 70, 92, 119–24, 149; and Punahou School, 70, 85; and Sanford Ballard Dole, 9, 15, 85, 119–22, 146–47. *See also* annexation of Hawai'i

Hawaiian oath of allegiance, 127, 191n10

Hawaiian sovereignty, 23, 31, 42–44, 122

Hawaiian Supreme Court, 39

HEA. *See* Hawaiian Evangelical Association (HEA)

HMCS. *See* Hawaiian Mission Children's Society (HMCS)

Hobbs, Jean, 38

Homestead Act (1862), 118

Ho'ohōkūkalani, 46

Hopkins, Mark, 108, 117

Hopu, Thomas, 95–96

horseback riding, 50–51, 73

household economics, 3–4, 17–22

*How to Be a Man* (Newcomb), 114, 125, 191n3

*How to Be a Woman* (Newcomb), 125

Hunt, Michael, 171n35

MacLennan, Carol, 66

*Māhele. See* Great *Māhele*

*makaʻāinana*, 47, 142

Malo, David, 11, 47–48, 143

marriage customs, Hawaiian, 98

Marshall Islands, 142

Masaoki, Shimmi, 61

Mason, Sarah R., 161

Masters and Servants Act, 134

*meles*, 11, 46, 83, 171n31

Menton, Linda, 92, 166

*A Missionary Catechism* (Yale College), 141

missionary children: adult lives and careers of, 151–67; as agents of imperialism, 12–14, 162–67, 171nn37–38; ambition of, 57, 179n62; American assimilation and acculturation of, 14, 93–124; as Anglo-Hawaiians, 2, 56–57, 60, 179n57; attachment of, to Hawaiian *ʻāina*, 9–12; attitudes of, toward ABCFM, 35–42; attitudes of, toward native Hawaiians, 143–44; bicultural identity of, 14, 91, 142–49, 152, 155, 159, 165–66; business endeavors of, 57–60; of China, 161; as chroniclers of change, 9–12; citizenship of, 10, 15, 89, 94, 100–101, 114, 117–18, 125–28, 146, 153, 155, 186n19; and cleanliness, 74; closeness among, 134–35, 154; coming of age of, 35–42; as commodities, 100–104; cruelty and bullying by, 54, 74–75; and decline of indigenous population, 184n60; and dichotomies of learning, 73–78; distrust of foreigners by, 83; education of, 19–30, 49–50, 93–124, 107, 131–34,

152, 187n49; employment of, as teachers, 38; and English-language instruction in Hawaiʻi schools, 131–34; environmental and ecological explorations by, 50–56, 66–68, 177n4; and familial colonialism, 42–44; and filial obedience, 78, 137–42, *138*; as goodwill ambassadors, 104–10; as Hawaiian government appointees, 38–39; and household economics, 3–4, 17–22; as *kāmaʻāina*, 46–50; language and culture of, 70, 103, 113, 128–30, 165, 191n15; lessening of missionary influence on, 83–85; loneliness of, 46, 75–76; marriage of, to native Hawaiians, 80; moral education and economic independence of, 43, 115, 176n111; as *nā hānai*, 57–60; and overthrow of Hawaiian monarchy, 2–4, 42–44, 58–60, 70, 92, 115–16, 119–24, 149; overview of, 1–16, *3*; parents' expectations of, 151; and parents' rebellion against ABCFM parenting rules, 22–30; peer bonding of, 74; political awakening of, 85–88; pride of, in parents' missionary work, 36; rejection of parents' faith by, 140, 193n64; and returning to Hawaiʻi, 14–15, 38, 60–61, 94, 102, 104–6, 110–13, 115–18, 129, 135–37, 152, 159, 189n96; and reverence for Hawaiian monarchy, 79–80; segregation of, from native children, 47–48, 163; and size of missionary families, 2, 21, 43; as "third culture" children, 112, 188n80. *See also names of specific missionary children*

West, Elliott, 50, 179n62

whaling industry, 7–8, 22, 25, 56, 82, 96–98

Whitehead, John, 147

Whitman, Marcus, 7

Whitman, Narcissa, 7

Whitney, Henry, 51, 98, 102, 115, 175n81

Whitney, Maria, 38, 102

Whitney, Mercy, 96, 98, 102–3

Whitney, Samuel (father), 98

Whitney, Samuel (son), 98

Wilcox, Abner, 24, 71, 103, 128, 175n75

Wilcox, Albert, 24, 37

Wilcox, Charles, 103

Wilcox, Edward, 37–38

Wilcox, George, 38, 47, 50, 55, 58, 81–82, 140, 182n25

Wilcox, Lucy, 37, 128

Wilcox, Sam, 130

Williams College, 10, 15, 61, 88, 92, 107–10, 117–18, 135, 137, 153–56

Willis, Albert, 120–22

women's education and political rights, 74–75, 109–10, 160, 182n20, 182n25. *See also* Mount Holyoke Female Seminary

Yokota, Kariann, 106

Zakaria, Fareed, 120

Lightning Source UK Ltd.
Milton Keynes UK
UKHW012112220520
363695UK00010B/41

9 781496 219497